Praise for
Books That Build Character

"Values do not fly on their wings. They are communicated, effectively, around stories, historical narratives, legends and such. Here is *the* source book of moral tales for educators and parents and grandparents."

—Amitai Etzioni, author of *The Spirit of Community: Rights, Responsibilities, and the Communitarian Agenda*

"This volume is a valuable resource for parents, teachers, and all others concerned with the moral development of children. The guidance it provides is both wise and practical, pointing the way to rich and enduring treasures for the soul."

—James Davison Hunter, author of *Culture Wars*

"*Books That Build Character* is a very valuable and much needed tool for parents and teachers. I can't imagine anyone who wants to encourage character development through literature not starting with this exceptional resource."

—Michael S. Josephson, President, Joseph and Edna Josephson Institute of Ethics and the Character Counts! Coalition

"It is gratifying—indeed, a time for rejoicing—to see character-building books like this one coming onto the market again. Children and grownups are, in large part, what they read, and who could seriously argue that our society today is not in desperate need of a positive offering such as *Books That Build Character?* It is my conviction that these great stories that celebrate virtues and values can be effective in redeeming a generation of America's young people."

—D. James Kennedy, Senior Minister, Coral Ridge Ministries

"If we want to raise good children, we must help them fall in love with what is noble and good. This guide is a gold mine of value-rich literature from which young and old alike can draw moral inspiration. No parent or teacher concerned about America's moral and spiritual crisis should be without this resource."

—Thomas Lickona, author of *Raising Good Children* and *Educating for Character*

"*Books That Build Character* is one of the best friends a parent, teacher, or school librarian can have! It is an excellent, practical guide to good literature with moral values, ranging from the classics to the contemporary, from picture books to novels. Whether choosing a book to read aloud or to give as a gift, this guide is a must."

—Young Jay Mulkey, President, The Character Education Institute

"We are a people of the story, but this generation of Americans has left the storytelling to television. *Books That Build Character* is just the book for those who wish to rediscover with their children our great stories. This is the guide for which concerned parents and teachers have been waiting."

—Kevin Ryan, Director, Center for the Advancement of Ethics and Character, Boston University

"Reading stories of virtue and creating the love of quality literature in our children is a worthy if not critical endeavor, if the values of our American culture are to be transmitted to the next generation. *Books That Build Character* makes that task of finding such stories a pleasant and rewarding one. Every home should have a dog-eared copy on the coffee table."

—Robert W. Sweet, Jr., President, the National Right to Read Foundation

Also by William Kilpatrick

Books That Build Character

A Guide to Teaching Your Child Moral Values Through Stories

WITHDRAWN

WILLIAM KILPATRICK

AND

GREGORY AND SUZANNE M. WOLFE

Foreword by Dr. Robert Coles

A MAKE A DIFFERENCE FOUNDATION BOOK

A TOUCHSTONE BOOK
Published by Simon & Schuster
New York London Toronto Sydney Tokyo Singapore

For Crystal, Heather, and Christopher—W. K.
For Magdalen, Helena, and Charles—G. W. & S.M.W.

TOUCHSTONE
Rockefeller Center
1230 Avenue of the Americas
New York, New York 10020

TOUCHSTONE and colophon are registered
trademarks of Simon & Schuster Inc.

Designed by Deirdre C. Amthor

Manufactured in the United States of America

3   5   7   9   10   8   6   4

ISBN: 0-671-88423-9

"I would ask you to remember this one thing," said Badger. "The stories people tell have a way of taking care of them. If stories come to you, care for them. And learn to give them away where they are needed. Sometimes a person needs a story more than food to stay alive. That is why we put these stories in each other's memory. This is how people care for themselves."
—Barry Lopez, *Crow and Weasel*

Contents

Acknowledgments

The authors would like to thank the following individuals and institutions for friendship, support, and advice: John Crumpler and the Make A Difference Foundation, The Earhart Foundation, Kathleen Rice, Clyde Feil, and the staff of the Wichita Public Library system. Thanks also to our editor Becky Cabaza and our agent Carol Mann.

Foreword

Days into my years as a medical intern (an exhausting, demanding, scary time when young men and women keep learning, night and day, how much they have to learn), I was on the hospital pediatric service, working with children who had leukemia. We had no drugs then that saved such seriously endangered lives, only blood and more blood to offer those boys and girls, so unlucky through the dread action of an inscrutable fate, as they all well understood. In that regard, I recall the first child I had to "transfuse," a verb I kept hearing all the time—a nine-year-old girl who had more than an inkling that she'd never celebrate another birthday. When I had gotten her latest pint of blood suitably going into her right leg (her arms had ceased being useful in that respect: over-used veins), she gave me a smile, even as I visibly relaxed (one more tough job done). I prepared to leave, mouthed some piety I've long forgotten. But she snapped me out of the complacency I'd learned to summon as protection (Lord, the terrible tragedies in that ward, bed after bed of them!) by asking me this, "How many more bottles will you be giving me?" Quickly, I said I didn't know—thinking she was trying to pin me down as to the details of a therapeutic regimen. But she had a much broader, larger perspective, as I quickly discovered. "I mean, before I die."

Of course, I hastened to reassure her—but she had scant patience with my evasive platitudes. When they'd been uttered, she countered with this, "I'll never get to ten. Ten is two digits, Daddy [an engineer] keeps saying. But I hope before this leukemia wins, I can win." Needless to say, I wondered what she had in mind—this resort to a kind of military imagery, so I thought. She clearly was inviting me, indirectly, to pursue the matter, and I did—I asked her which victories she had in mind. She told me right off, "I'd like to be good, so people would say: 'she was a good girl.'" My response, of course, was all to predictable, well intentioned, and yes, sincere: she *was* "good," so I kept noticing. But she begged to disagree, "I'm all right here; I'm even good, here. But before this [illness], I was a 'hellion.'" Who in the world told her that, I wondered aloud, and was told: her mom and her dad, both. On what basis, I wanted to know. She was ready with a list that made me wonder whether she was exaggerating wildly, dramatically, a consequence of her state of mind as she struggled with a (then) fatal illness. After all, I'd heard other such afflicted children hype things up as they remembered what had been, and came to terms with what wouldn't ever be. But the next day her dad and mom confirmed her self-description, and her mom added this, a remark so pointed, and surprising I believe I recall it virtually word for word over three decades later, "She tells us she wants to prove herself a really good person before she dies, and she asks us for help [in becoming so]."

There followed, of course, a discussion among the three of us as to the "meaning" of this, and the best response—not that I knew what to say, to recommend. I was not then a husband or a father, and I had no training yet in child psychiatry and had exactly two weeks' experience in a pediatric rotation. Unfortunately, I had a certain narrowness of vision that came with my situation at the time, and so I kept trying to interpret the girl's self-appointed ambition or purpose as an idiosyncratic response to a quite dreadful disease that was, alas, nearing its culmination. But the mother, having heard me muse and ramble in the above over-all direction, suddenly took issue with me (with herself, actually, as I'd been hearing her: a hitherto quizzical, perplexed posture), and the result was this surprising comment, again not to be forgotten by me, "We live a lifetime trying to find out *how* to live—and this is her last chance to do that for herself." As I well recall, the girl died a month or so later (I was just moving to another service, another ward), but during those few weeks her parents and she read and read, and did a lot of talking about what life means, and the manner in which one ought to live it—an impressive kind of moral scrutiny on their part, under great duress.

Not that children whose lives are far luckier, who have, say, a half-century and more ahead of them, don't have their own wish to explore things ethically, to stop and think about the rights and wrongs, the oughts and naughts of this life, and their reasons. It is the essence of our humanity to do so—and stories give us a wonderfully vivid, engaging, suggestive way to embark on such an inquiry (a search, really) with our children. "Character is not cut in marble," George Eliot reminds us in *Middlemarch,* and she amplifies with another negative, "it is not something solid and unalterable." Rather, she insists, "It is something living and changing"—her way of asking us to forego the satisfactions of categorical complacency, not to mention moral smugness. Put differently, our characters are tested constantly by the people, the occasions that all the time come our way. Each day offers us any number of opportunities for affirmation or, alas, calamity. With our children (and with ourselves), we can, then, do no better than to accept the challenge storytelling presents: an openness to life's complexities, ironies, paradoxes, inconsistencies, with a willingness as well to examine the most important moral questions with energy and subtlety and seriousness.

Stories offer us a chance to affirm our nature, as the creatures of words, of consciousness—and do so with pleasure and purpose, both: the enjoyment of carefully crafted narration, the chance to reflect, to respond by thinking of one's own life, its nature, its assumptions, its aims. We are lucky indeed to have such stories as a great heritage, a moral reservoir of sorts, from which we may constantly draw, and we are lucky, certainly, that three scholars—who happen to be parents and teachers—have chosen to assemble this great gift for us to have and to share, for years and years to come, across the generations—a precious instrument of introspection for innumerable readers.

—Robert Coles, Cambridge, MA

CHAPTER 1

Imagination:
The Heart's Best Guide

WHEN HER TWO-YEAR-OLD sister began to cry over a missing stuffed bear, Crystal, age four, declared, "She wants her Dogger," and proceeded to offer one of her own stuffed animals as a substitute. *Dogger* is a story about a boy who loses his worn, stuffed dog, and about his older sister, Bella, who trades a large and beautiful stuffed bear to get Dogger back for him. Crystal, who had heard the story only the night before, was putting into practice the good example set by Bella.

Crystal is a lucky girl. Her mother reads to her. And her mother is selective in what she reads. As a result, Crystal is beginning to develop a picture in her mind of the way things should be, of how people can act when they're at their best.

This book is intended to introduce the reader to books that help youngsters grow in virtue—books like *Dogger*. There is no shortage of such books. In fact, there are thousands of finely crafted stories for children that make honesty, responsibility, and compassion come alive. But they are not always easy to find. Concepts such as virtue, good example, and character have been out of fashion in our society for quite some time, and their absence is reflected in the available guidebooks to children's literature. Although there are many such guides, they all suffer from a common limitation: that is, their focus is almost solely on readability or, worse, on popularity. What is missing from these guides—what seems to be avoided—is any suggestion that certain books may help to develop character, and that others may not. The distinctive feature of this book, by contrast, is its focus on the moral dimension of reading. We think many parents want books for their children that are not simply a good read but good in the other sense of the word— books that not only capture the imagination, but cultivate the conscience as well.

Such books bestow a double blessing. They provide hours of pure pleasure. They also provide good companions. They introduce your child to friends who are a little older, a little wiser, a little braver. Along with these companions your child gets to ask some tough questions. Is Long John Silver good or bad? Should Beauty keep her promise to Beast? Should Frodo continue on his seemingly doomed mission while there is still a chance to return to the safety of the Shire? These are not easy questions to answer, especially when time is running out or the edge of the cliff is crumbling underfoot, but they are the kind of questions with which we are all confronted sooner or later. And when they come they often come in situations in which we have little time to think or at times when we may be angry, fearful, or just plain exhausted. It's exactly at times like this that the half-forgotten memory of a story can rise to our aid.

A 1985 report by the National Commission on Reading declared that reading aloud is the single most important contribution that parents can make toward their child's success in school. We want to go a little further than that. We believe that reading aloud may also be one of the most important contributions parents can make toward developing good character in their children. Why? For several reasons. First, because stories can create an emotional attachment to goodness, a desire to do the right thing. Second, because stories provide a wealth of good examples—the kind of examples that are often missing from a child's day-to-day environment. Third, because stories familiarize youngsters with the codes of conduct they need to know. Finally, because stories help to make sense out of life, help us to cast our own lives as stories. And unless this sense of meaning is acquired at an early age and reinforced as we grow older, there simply is no moral growth.

Why is a book of this nature so crucial now? After all, the importance of reading has long been known. We know that millions of Americans, young and old, are crippled in their daily activities and in their future prospects by poor reading skills. The problems caused by illiteracy are all too evident. But there is a new factor to contend with. We are now faced with another kind of illiteracy—one that may prove even more costly to our society. The new illiteracy is *moral* illiteracy. In addition to the millions who can't read or can't read well, there are millions more who don't know the difference between right and wrong—or don't care.

Across the country, teachers, parents, and police are encountering more and more youngsters who don't really think that stealing or lying or cheating is wrong. Says a fifth-grade teacher quoted in Thomas Lickona's *Educating for Character:*

> About ten years ago I showed my class some moral dilemma film strips. I found they knew right from wrong, even if they didn't always practice it. Now I find more and more of them don't know. They don't think it's wrong to pick up another person's property without their permission or to go into somebody else's desk. They barge between two adults when they're talking and seem to lack manners in general. You want to ask them, "Didn't your mother ever teach you that?"

There is an important sense in which the two kinds of illiteracy—as well as the solutions to them—are connected. One way to help youngsters to know and care about right and wrong is to acquaint them with good books. When we see others from the inside, as we do in stories, when we live with them, and hurt with them, and hope with them, we learn a new respect for people. This was understood by our ancestors. Stories, histories, and myths played an essential role in character education in the past. The Greeks learned about right and wrong from the example of Ulysses and Penelope, and a host of other characters. The Romans learned about virtue and vice from Plutarch's *Lives.* Jews and Christians learned from Bible stories or stories about the lives of prophets, saints, missionaries, and martyrs. And new research suggests that they were right. In the June 1990 issue of *American Psychologist,* Paul Vitz, a professor at New York University, provides an extensive survey of recent psychological studies, all pointing to "the central importance of stories in developing the moral life." Narrative plots have a powerful influence on us, says Vitz, because we tend to interpret our own lives as stories or narratives. "Indeed," he writes, "it is almost impossible not to think this way."

But why stories? Why not simply explain the difference between right and wrong to your children? Why not supply them with a list of dos and don'ts?

Such explanations are important, of course, but they fail to touch children on the level where it really matters—the level of imagination. Imagination. The word comes from "image"—a mental picture. And these pictures have a way of sticking in our memory and making demands on our conscience long after the explanations have been rubbed thin by the frictions of daily life.

There is just such an image in Lois Lowry's book *Number the Stars,* a story about the Nazi occupation of Denmark. To protect her Jewish friend, a Christian girl tears from her neck a gold chain bearing a Star of David and clenches it in her fist moments before Nazi soldiers arrive. She clenches it so tightly that, by the time the soldiers have left, an impression of the Star of David is imprinted in her palm.

A fourth-grade teacher who had read the book to her class passed on the following story to Lowry. On the day the teacher read that particular chapter, she had brought into the class a chain and a Star of David similar to the one described in the book. As she read the chapter she had the students pass the chain around the class. And while she was reading she noticed that one student after another pressed the star into his or her palm, making an imprint.

And that's the kind of imprint a good story can make on our minds. We need moral propositions and moral principles, but we need images too, because we think more readily in pictures than in propositions. And when a moral principle has the power to move us to action, it is often because it is backed up by a picture or image. As the short story writer Flannery

O'Connor observed, "A story is a way to say something that can't be said any other way. . . . You tell a story because a statement would be inadequate."

Stories present us not only with memorable pictures, but with dramas. Through the power of the imagination we become vicarious participants in the story, sharing the hero's or heroine's choices and challenges. We literally "identify" ourselves with our favorite characters, and thus their actions become our actions. In a story we meet characters who have something to learn; otherwise we would not be interested in them. When we first meet the hero, he has not achieved moral perfection or ultimate wisdom. If the story grips us, though, we root for the hero, suffering with him and cheering him on. This imaginative process of participation and identification gives us hope, because we want to believe that in the stories of our lives we too can make the right choices.

Are stories alone sufficient for the task of raising good children? No, of course not. Parents also need to set a good personal example, to encourage good habits, to explain rules, and to enforce them through appropriate discipline. There is no single "magic bullet" approach when it comes to raising children. But we do feel that a reemphasis on storytelling is long past due because, if anything, the power of stories has been vastly underrated in recent decades. The world of books and stories constitutes an enormous but neglected moral resource—a huge treasure house lying largely unused. According to one study, once out of school, nearly 60 percent of adult Americans never read a single book. And even in school there is likely to be a reading gap. Jim Trelease says he was prompted to write *The Read-Aloud Handbook* when he discovered that in many classrooms he visited, the only books children were familiar with were their textbooks.

Why this neglect of books? Part of the reason, again, is that we seem to have forgotten about the power of imagination. We've forgotten that children are motivated far more by what attracts the imagination than by what appeals to reason. We've forgotten that their behavior is shaped to a large extent by the dramas that play in the theaters of their minds.

The other reason for the neglect is television. "Television," as one critic says, "eats books." Because we've underestimated the power of imagination, that power has slipped more and more into the hands of people whose main interest in children is a commercial one. More and more, the songs, stories, and images that play in the minds of young people are the ones that are put there by the entertainment industry. If you have any doubts about the power of images, take a few minutes to observe the mesmerizing effect that TV and MTV have on youngsters. Better yet, look into the latest research on television and film violence. There is a growing consensus that repeated exposure to violent or sexual scenes does have a profound effect on the attitudes and behavior of young people.

Moreover, television as a medium does little or nothing to extend the imagination. Instead of drawing us inside the story, in the manner of a book, television forces us to remain spectators, outside the action. Increasingly, television serves up meaningless conflicts that are, more often than not, resolved by violence. Precisely because we are outside the action, scenes of violence can't hurt us; they can only provide us with a diminishing number of emotional jolts. The same syndrome affects the depiction of romantic love and sexuality. In the absence of real, believable relationships on the screen, sex becomes the only means by which characters come together.

If you as a parent don't take steps to educate your child's imagination, it's an almost sure bet that his imagination will be seduced by the power of popular culture. You need a way to inoculate his imagination against the electronic viruses he will be exposed to as he grows older. Books are one of the best ways to do this, because they provide a ground for judgment and comparison. They help us develop a "sense" that alerts us when something is morally out of tune.

A mother we know recalls a discussion with her thirteen-year-old son about a popular rock star whose songs encouraged sexual experimentation and rebelliousness. "He's just like the Pied Piper, isn't he, Mom?" remarked the boy. That's the kind of perceptive observation that reading makes possible, and it's an insight that's not likely to occur to a youngster whose only exposure has been to television.

Beyond sharpening perceptions, books enter and occupy and make safer those areas of heart and mind targeted by popular culture. In *Honey for a Child's Heart,* a guide to children's classics, Gladys Hunt writes, "A good book has a profound kind of morality—not a cheap, sentimental sort which thrives on shallow plots and superficial heroes, but the sort of force which inspires the reader's inner life and draws out all that is noble . . . I cannot believe that children exposed to the best of literature will later choose that which is cheap and demeaning."

Hunt may be overstating the case slightly—individuals are always free to turn away from what is noble—but she is right in her belief that good literature increases our resistance to cheapening influences. Children who read have broader sympathies and a larger picture of life. They develop more powerful, healthy, and discerning imaginations.

And imagination is one of the keys to virtue. It's not enough to *know* what's right. It's also necessary to *desire* to do right. Desire, in turn, is directed to a large extent by imagination. In theory, reason should guide our moral choices, but in practice it is imagination much more than reason that calls the shots. Too often our reason obediently submits to what our imagination has already decided. This was well understood by Plato, who had quite a bit to say about educating the imagination. Children, he said, should be brought up in such a way that they will fall in love with virtue and hate vice. How does a child fall in love with virtue? By being exposed to the right kind of stories, music, and art, said Plato. Such an education helps a child develop the right sort of likes and dislikes, and without those dispositions it won't matter how much formal training in ethics a youngster later receives.

This is why books are so important for moral education. They inspire a love of goodness. Who can read about King Midas and his golden touch without desiring to always put people before possessions? Who can read *A Christmas Carol* without desiring like Scrooge to honor Christmas in his heart and keep it there all year? Who can read *To Kill a Mockingbird* without wishing to be a little more like Atticus Finch—a little braver,

kinder, wiser. And who can resist the attractions of Sir Percy
Blakeney, the Scarlet Pimpernel, as he carries off his bold ex-
ploits with coolness, wit, and charm? After reading *The Scarlet
Pimpernel,* one young teenager of our acquaintance was so
caught up by its exuberant spirit that he went about the house
for the next week reciting Sir Percy's catchy poem about the
Pimpernel:

> *We seek him here, we seek him there*
> *Those Frenchies seek him everywhere.*
> *Is he in heaven? Is he in hell?*
> *That damned, elusive Pimpernel.*

Stories, then, because of their hold on the imagination, can
help to create an emotional attachment to goodness. If other
things are in place, that emotional attraction can then grow
into a real commitment to goodness. The dramatic nature of
stories enables us to "rehearse" moral decisions, strengthening
our solidarity with the good. But if the desire to do right is not
developed at an early age our other efforts to teach values to
children won't bear much fruit.

What prevents parents from taking steps in this direction?
Curiously, one of the biggest obstacles is a sense of fate. Curious, because we were long ago supposed to have emerged from
a belief in fate. Nevertheless, it's there. Instead of doing something to break the media's stranglehold on our children, we
take an attitude similar to that of primitive people who, in the
face of famine or plague or flood, could only throw up their
hands and say "The gods are angry" or some such formula. It's
the same with us. Too many adults, when they see the pervasive
influence of popular culture, tend to throw up their hands and
say "What can you do?" Like the parents in the old story, we
watch helplessly as today's pied pipers lead our children off in
all the wrong directions. Although we live in a modern age we
have succumbed to an old myth: the myth of the powerless individual against an all-powerful force.

Not that thinking mythically is a bad thing. Perhaps if we
kept in better touch with the myths and stories of our civiliza-

tion we wouldn't give up so easily. Perhaps we need to refresh our imaginations with stories of individuals who overcame the odds: David defeating Goliath, Horatius holding the Tiber bridge against the foes of Rome, or, perhaps most appropriately for our television-dominated age, Odysseus outwitting Cyclops, the original one-eyed giant.

"How shall a man judge what to do in such times?" asks a character in *The Lord of the Rings*. "As he ever has judged," comes the reply. "Good and evil have not changed. . . . It is man's part to discern them." The more we expose our children to good literature the more they will develop such habits of discernment. Gladys Hunt recounts the following from a phone conversation with her college-age son:

> Am I ever glad we read *That Hideous Strength* together last summer! I found myself in a situation this week in which I felt all the pressures to conform to the group and compromise my values to be part of the inner-ring. Then I remembered that story and the awful mistake it is to play the game that way.

That passage says a lot about literature's power to put the imagination on alert, but there's something else of interest that may have caught your attention. Reading together? A college student? With his family? It seems hard to believe. Hasn't TV made that sort of scenario impossible? Don't we have to resign ourselves to the fact that once adolescence is reached (or sooner) youngsters will retreat into a world of headphones and Nintendo? And won't that be the end of any shared world of ideas?

Not necessarily. In the days before television, reading aloud—from Dickens, from Walter Scott, from treasured poets—was common fare for families. It was also common for favorite books to be passed around among adults and older children. There are many families today who carry on the same practices. And, if anything, their number may now be on the increase, thanks in part to the influence of books like Jim Trelease's *The Read-Aloud Handbook*. Mr. Trelease is not one who thinks reading aloud is only for children. It's great for adolescents and adults, too, says Trelease:

> Secondary students being read to? Certainly. . . . When my daughter returned from England after a summer studying at Cambridge University, she told me the professors read aloud to literature classes all the time. A year later, I met a Kansas teacher returning from her second straight summer at Oxford University, where she'd been read to regularly. I figure that if it's good enough for Oxford and Cambridge, it's good enough for any junior or senior high school in America.

Why does shared reading work? It works because the right book, read in the right way, brings a thrill of excitement and enchantment. No one who has traveled with Frodo through the land of Mordor in Tolkien's *The Lord of the Rings* is likely to complain that the journey is a long one. No one who has stood on the deck of the *Dawn Treader* in the company of Caspian and Reepicheep is likely to regret the experience of listening to C. S. Lewis's *The Chronicles of Narnia*. No child who has trembled in fear with Beauty in the castle of the Beast is ever likely to forget that strange story of love's transforming power.

But how about the adult reader? Isn't reading aloud to children, especially very young children, a bit of a bore? Something done out of a sense of duty? Not at all. Indeed, the adult reader, who can understand all the levels of a story, may have the most fun of all. As Gladys Hunt writes, "They [children] may read the story again years later and find that their experiences in life help them see more. Adults will read the same book and begin to better understand why they loved it as children." Reread some of the better children's books and you may be surprised to discover how adult (in the best sense of the word) they are. You will find it difficult to adopt a condescending attitude toward them. For one thing, the "lesson" may apply as much to you as it does to your child; for another, the writing is often of exceptional quality. Both C. S. Lewis and Isaac Bashevis Singer observed that children are deeply con-

cerned with serious questions, more so than adults may realize; and both men said that they couldn't imagine writing
something for children that they themselves would not want to
read. "I am almost inclined to set it up as a canon," wrote
Lewis, "that a children's story which is only enjoyed by children is a bad children's story." Lewis was of the opinion that no
book is worth reading at age ten that is not equally worth reading at age fifty.

If you're a parent, you've got a battle on your hands—a battle with popular culture over your child's imagination. And like
every battle this one has moments when it seems impossible to
carry on. But it's not all grim, because one of the best ways of
empowering your child's imagination is also one of the most
enjoyable. The books we've listed are stories of virtue and character, but they are many other things as well. Some of them are
hilarious, some mysterious, some adventurous, some heartbreakingly poignant, some a combination of all of these.

You will enjoy sharing them with your children. And you
will find an added benefit. Just as good stories help to create an
emotional bond to goodness, family reading strengthens the
family bond. Shared reading draws families together. It provides mutual delight and builds emotional bridges. It establishes intimacy between parent and child in a way that few
other activities can match. And this is true whether you read
aloud to a younger child, pass along a favorite story to an older
reader, or pick up a book a child has recommended to you. If
we feel an obligation to get to know our children's friends,
then we should also enter their imaginative worlds with enthusiasm and respect.

But how, exactly, do stories do their work? How do they
stimulate the moral imagination? How do they catch us up in
their net and make us feel a part of some larger enterprise?
And how do they do all this without falling into the pit of
preachiness?

Read on!

CHAPTER 2

Example and Empathy

HOW DO STORIES help to encourage character? William Bennett gave a good reply to that question in a speech delivered when he was secretary of education:

> Do we want our children to know what honesty means? Then we might teach them about Abe Lincoln walking three miles to return six cents and, conversely, about Aesop's shepherd boy who cried wolf.
>
> Do we want our children to know what courage means? Then we might teach them about Joan of Arc, Horatius at the bridge, Harriet Tubman and the Underground Railroad.
>
> Do we want them to know about kindness and compassion, and their opposites? Then they should read *A Christmas Carol* and *The Diary of Anne Frank* and, later on, *King Lear.* . . .

Bennett points to two things good stories provide: codes of conduct (honesty, courage, kindness) and good example (Abraham Lincoln, Harriet Tubman, Joan of Arc). Stories acquaint us with the ideals by which people in our society hope to live, and they give examples of people trying to live by those standards.

Let's talk about good example first. It's the most obvious way stories and histories exert an influence over us. And that influence stems from our built-in need to identify and imitate.

Just look at the way your child identifies with a particular baseball or basketball hero. Look at the hours of practice he is willing to put in in order to more closely approximate his model. Or look at the influence that characters in films have on your child's behavior. He sees a Tarzan movie one day, and the next day he is stringing up rope swings in the backyard. He watches "Teenage Mutant Ninja Turtles" and suddenly his favorite word is "dude."

It is not a question of *whether* your child will find someone to identify with, the only question is with *whom*. The problem, of course, is that youngsters all too often make the wrong sorts of identifications. Bruno Bettelheim observed that for a child the question "Who do I want to be like?" is more important than "Do I want to be good?" There is no guarantee your child will want to emulate only good models. Crooks or con men can be glamorous or can be portrayed in an appealing Bonnie-and-Clyde fashion by the media. In some neighborhoods the most attractive and adventuresome figures are gang members. A lot depends on the available supply of models.

Obviously, there is something drastically unbalanced in the mix currently available to youngsters. When people like Snoop Doggy Dogg and Madonna are heroes to millions, it's time to worry. More than that, it's time to do something.

Fortunately, you can greatly improve the odds for your child. Books are one of the best—if not *the* best way—to increase the available supply of good examples. It would be nice if sufficient good examples could be found among family, friends, and neighbors, but life rarely works that way. None of us is perfect, and we need all the help we can get when it comes to showing youngsters the difference between right and wrong. Good stories help to compensate for our own deficiencies and for those of the community. This fact, understood by all other societies, is especially relevant to our own. In this age of broken neighborhoods and broken families, where adults are too busy, too self-absorbed, or too exhausted to supply strong personal example, the stock of good examples available in books becomes all the more important.

And the kind of identification that takes place through reading is potentially stronger than identification with an athlete or entertainer seen on television because, to some extent, the reader gets pulled into the story. He is not allowed to be simply an observer or a fan. It is a much more intimate relationship. The story gives him a chance to live along with the characters, to keep company with them, and, in doing so, to experience what they experience and learn what they learn. Fiction gives us more than good examples to admire from the sidelines; at its best it gives us an experience of the struggle to attain goodness. It allows us to share the courage of Henry Fleming (in *The Red Badge of Courage*) as he faces up to his duty as a soldier, to apologize with Almanzo (in *Farmer Boy*) for his hot temper, to experience the generosity of Jo (in *Little Women*) when she sells her hair to provide needed money for her parents, to sweat it out with the Scarlet Pimpernel as he smuggles refugees through the French sentry posts.

Of course, not all of the characters we meet will be fictional. Biography shows us that real people as well as fictional ones can overcome difficulties and set their own course in life. Part of the encouragement that comes from reading biography is to learn how many times great people fail before they succeed. Francis of Assisi, Clara Barton, Louis Braille, Frederick Douglass, and Winston Churchill all suffered setbacks that would have put an end to the careers of less determined people. One thing that may account for the determination of real-life heroes is that they themselves tend to be avid readers of biography. Douglass was inspired by Pitt and Fox, Churchill by Marlborough, Martin Luther King, Jr., by Douglass and Gandhi. Many of those individuals whom we think of as "self-made" would be quick to remind us how much they owe to the example of the men and women who preceded them.

We're not suggesting that children read only stories about "good" people. We can learn from bad examples as well as good ones—which is why we have included biographies of Hitler and Stalin in our book list. Moreover, the good people sometimes behave quite badly. Achilles was vengeful, Peter was cowardly, Lancelot and Guinevere committed adultery, Silas

Marner was miserly. But in these stories there is no doubt about how these people should have acted. Young readers don't need to have heroes of undiluted virtue as long as they are the kind of persons who want to get back on course once they get off it.

In addition to good examples, stories supply codes of conduct. It's a mistake to think children already know these codes, and an even bigger mistake to assume they will discover them on their own. Contrary to some faddish theories that arose in the seventies, children do not have an infallible inner guide. Children have to be socialized in order to behave properly, and they need to be taught right from wrong—not asked to go figure. Fortunately, we don't have to do all the telling ourselves. We can let stories do some of it for us. In Bennett's words they provide "a stock of examples illustrating what we believe to be right and wrong, good and bad." And they are able to convey these lessons in a more engaging form than we can usually muster.

Consider this paragraph from *The Little House on the Prairie:*

> Laura and Mary were up next morning earlier than the sun. They ate their breakfast of cornmeal mush with prairie-hen gravy, and hurried to help Ma wash the dishes.

Helping Ma wash the dishes: children helping their parents is a fairly elementary lesson in responsibility but not a bad one to learn. And not a hard one to swallow, as it is presented here. Notice that not much is made of this helpful behavior. It's passed over quickly and taken for granted. But we all benefit a great deal from the fact that such lessons are reinforced in literature as a matter of course.

It is often remarked that good literature does not moralize, but that is not to say that it does not teach us. In fact, it does. Often the lessons are quite simple ones. In *Pinocchio,* for instance, much is made of obedience to one's parent, of keeping promises, of telling the truth even when it hurts. Because the lessons are so simple, however, there is a tendency to take them for granted. Teachers assume that parents will attend to the basics, and parents assume that children will learn them in school. We also tend to forget how much repetition is required before basic moral principles sink in. One of the benefits of encouraging a child to read good books is that it saves his parents from doing all the reminding.

Adults also need to be reminded. The basic lessons are not only for children; the same simple truths are the stock of great novels as well. For example, Book Four of *War and Peace* contains a touching scene in which Nicholas Rostov, after losing a huge sum at gambling, must face his father, from whom he has borrowed only the week before. Nicholas, who has promised to borrow no more, is filled with grief over this breach of honor, yet when the time comes he manages to compound his error by affecting a casual attitude:

> "It can't be helped! It happens to everyone!" said the son with a bold, free, and easy tone while in his soul he regarded himself as a worthless scoundrel whose whole life could not atone for his crime. He longed to kiss his father's hand and kneel to beg his forgiveness, but said in a careless and even rude voice, that it happens to everyone!
>
> The old count cast down his eyes on hearing his son's words and began bustling, searching for something.
>
> "Yes, yes," he muttered, "it will be difficult, I fear, difficult to raise . . . happens to everybody. Yes, who has not done it?" And with a furtive glance at his son's face the count went out of the room. . . . Nicholas had been prepared for resistance, but had not at all expected this.
>
> "Papa! Pa-pa!" he called after him, sobbing, "forgive me!" And seizing his father's hand he pressed it to his lips and burst into tears.

The moral lessons brought forward in this scene are not terribly advanced. Nicholas Rostov is an intelligent young man of good education, but he can't master the simple task of refraining from throwing away the family fortune in a card game or the simple duty of offering an immediate apology.

But if right and wrong of this sort are so plain, why does Tolstoy trouble us with such scenes? The answer is that it is precisely these "simple" things that most of us have difficulty with. We know these obligations—self-control, respect for parents—but manage to forget them quite easily and need constantly to have our memory refreshed. "In matters of morality," observed Samuel Johnson, "we need not so much to be instructed as to be reminded."

Reread some of the great classics of literature and you will be surprised to find how often the plot revolves around simple moral failings on the one hand, and simple kindnesses on the other. More often than not the protagonists are faced not with thorny ethical dilemmas (of the type that many of today's educators love to throw at students) but rather with temptations of gambling, anger, lust, lying, and thievery. In other words, the "usual suspects." The great authors understood that people are brought low by common problems more often than by extraordinary ones. Likewise, the best of children's literature is concerned not with the latest ethical quandaries but with the perennial problems of growing up.

All this talk about right and wrong in stories is bound to raise some red flags, and perhaps some hackles, too. After all, one of the worst criticisms that can be leveled against a story is the charge of didacticism—that the story tries to teach or preach. Many writers and critics insist that there should be a wall of separation between literature and morality. They argue that the moral in the story always kills the story.

Well, then, what about didacticism? Can a story teach the moral norms without being moralistic? Can it avoid sounding like a sermon? The answer in both instances is "Yes, it can," but before making that case, let us issue some disclaimers.

We don't think fiction, whether for adults or children, ought to hit us over the head with a blunt moral. We don't think writers should write primarily out of a moral intent. A storyteller is, preeminently, a person who has a story to tell. Those who are primarily concerned about morals and only secondarily about art would probably be more effective as policemen or judges or professors of ethics. Some of the best children's stories are an interesting blend of morality and amorality because they were not consciously created with any lesson in mind:

they grew out of a picture in the author's mind, or they were written to please a son or daughter or young friend, or they were written to please the child in the author. If Robert Louis Stevenson had a moral in mind when he wrote *Treasure Island* he might have taken care to make Long John Silver a less engaging character. What is the lesson of *Alice's Adventures in Wonderland,* except to stay away from rabbit holes? The author tells us it has "no moral." Likewise, we would be hard pressed to find any clear moral in the old fairy tales before they were tidied up by later writers; many of them, as literary critic Humphrey Carpenter points out, "occupy a moral no-man's land." Moreover, the imagination works in mysterious ways. Many writers say that their stories take on a life and shape of their own. Given these considerations it's not surprising that books written with the conscious intent of improving the young reader are not, in the main, either well written or effective. Anyone looking for a MORAL in bold letters will be disappointed in much of children's literature.

On the other hand, we also want to avoid the other extreme of suggesting, as is now fashionable, that good writers never have a moral in the back of their heads. We think it evident that many writers for children do. Aesop's fables and *Pilgrim's Progress* are clear examples of moral tales that are also part of the canon of classic stories. But so, in a somewhat different vein, are *Robinson Crusoe* and *Gulliver's Travels.* And the fairy tales of Hans Christian Andersen, unlike those of the Brothers Grimm, always have a clear moral structure. The same is true of Oscar Wilde's stories for children: "The Selfish Giant," for example, is a conscious parable on the theme of charity. Leo Tolstoy, who is generally considered to be among the greatest of novelists, wrote fables for children that are obviously instructional in intent (see *The Lion and the Puppy,* page 98, in our book list), yet powerful and moving.

Contemporary writers for children tend to disavow moral intent. Katherine Paterson, for example, was once annoyed by a reporter who asked, "What is your philosophy of writing for children? Isn't there some moral you want to get across to them?" She replied, "I'm trying to write for my readers the best story, the truest story of which I am capable." This is a good antidote for those with simplistic notions about stories and morals. Yet, at the same time her answer suggests an overriding sense of responsibility to her audience, as well as an obligation to be truthful. Her answer is shot through with the language of morality. Likewise, if we look into any one of her many fine stories, we are not left with an impression of moral neutrality. In practice most good writers for children, while they are concerned with being truthful, are also concerned with the impact their books will have on their readers, just as most good parents, whatever their views on censorship, tend to buy their children books by A. A. Milne and Mark Twain rather than books by the Marquis de Sade. The children's writer, after all, has a responsibility to children as well as to art.

We cannot mention Twain in this context without also mentioning his famous preface to *The Adventures of Huckleberry Finn*. In it he cautioned that "persons attempting to find a moral" in his story would be "banished." Twain, as usual, was joking. In fact there are many morals to be drawn from *Huckleberry Finn*. But Twain gets away with his joke because his morals are never preachy. When they are present they flow naturally from the story. We never feel that our arm is being twisted. Instead we are caught up in the life, adventures, and qualms of conscience of a very real boy.

It is this true-to-life element that prevents moral fiction from becoming didactic. The didactic writer has a bunch of precepts to impart, and he invents a narrative to string them together. He is not particularly interested in the plot or the characters, only in the message. It is quite the opposite with true moral fiction. In fact, the codes of conduct inherent in such stories may not even be spelled out. Learning them is more a matter of learning by immersion into the culture of the book at hand—the same way we learn the rules of our own culture. Thus C. S. Lewis remarks of Mr. Badger in *The Wind in the Willows* ("that extraordinary amalgam of high rank, coarse manners, gruffness, shyness, and goodness") that "The child who has once met Mr. Badger has ever afterwards in its bones a knowledge of humanity and of English social history which it could not get in any other way."

Something similar could be said of the child who has read

the fantasies of George MacDonald, a nineteenth-century Scottish writer: he will have acquired an almost organic knowledge of the decency that humans ought to show one another. MacDonald has the ability to portray the beauty of well-ordered relationships and the ugliness of disrupting them. In a MacDonald story, selfish behavior appears to be boorish and dull, whereas selflessness is full of risk and excitement. There is a scene in MacDonald's *The Princess and Curdie* where a boy must place his hands in a magical fire if he is to be able to battle evil. At first he feels pain, but it eventually disappears. He then discovers that he has been given a gift: he can touch other people's hands and discover what they are like inside. Some people's hands feel like snakes, some like donkeys or hogs, and others like lions. This capacity to gauge the moral qualities of those he meets enables him to achieve his mission. According to the poet W. H. Auden, MacDonald was one of those rare writers able "to create an atmosphere of goodness about which there is nothing phony or moralistic."

C. S. Lewis achieves much the same effect. Gladys Hunt remarks of one scene in Lewis's *The Magician's Nephew,* "Suddenly anything other than obedience and loyalty seems incredibly stupid. We have never read this story without feeling a profound longing to keep our promises and to do what is right—not because we have heard a sermon but because of the actions and decisions of the characters in the story."

For those who still object to morals in their stories there is one other point worth considering. Literature doesn't really work well without an ethical scale in the background. The absence of values is not only bad for us, it's bad for fiction as well. As the English writer Dorothy Sayers observed, "The dogma is the drama." Unless codes of conduct are taken seriously by both writer and reader, the violation of these codes can produce no dramatic tension. In short, if murder becomes unimportant, so do murder mysteries (Miss Sayers's specialty).

One of the reasons drama is in trouble today is that many codes no longer have the force they once did. The problem is plainly evident in Hollywood, where filmmakers must contend with ever higher levels of audience tolerance for misbehavior (a tolerance the filmmakers themselves helped to create). For example, once infidelity becomes common and acceptable, it is difficult to build a drama around the theme of adultery. As a result directors find it necessary to compound adultery plots with other tension-arousing elements. In *Fatal Attraction* they add a homicidal maniac to the mix; in *Indecent Proposal* a million-dollar incentive is thrown in. By contrast, the mere hint of adultery gave Shakespeare all the dramatic material he needed to write *Othello*.

Values don't have to be lit up in neon, but they do have to be there, and they have to carry a certain force, otherwise we're no longer talking about art but about sensationalism or titillation or, more likely, boredom. Imagine, if you will, *The Hobbit* without its backdrop of the struggle between good and evil; or imagine *Huckleberry Finn* minus the moral questions of slavery and equality. What we would have in both cases would not be great books, but well-written and mildly interesting travel stories.

Even Vladimir Nabokov, who is often cited as a foe of moralism, admits the point. "I never meant to deny the moral impact of art which is certainly present in every genuine work of art," wrote Nabokov, and he often defended his controversial *Lolita* on moral grounds, saying it had "high moral content."

For obvious reasons we've left *Lolita* off our list, but we have been on the lookout for high moral content, and we've discovered there are many fine children's books that succeed in teaching important moral lessons without a trace of didacticism. There is an old maxim that says a book should both delight and instruct, and that has been our criterion for selection. We believe that children deserve better moral guidance than they have been receiving, but we also believe they deserve books that will capture their imagination.

This is not to say that there is no problem of didacticism in contemporary children's literature. In fact there is a serious problem. But it's not where you would expect to find it. More about that in the next chapter.

CHAPTER 3

Transport:
Seeing with Myriad Eyes

IN *THE INNOCENTS ABROAD* Mark Twain writes, "Travel is fatal to prejudice, bigotry and narrow-mindedness . . . broad, wholesome, charitable views cannot be acquired by vegetating in one's little corner of earth."

It's the same with books. Like travel they broaden the mind. They give us a bigger picture of the world and its inhabitants. While sitting safely at home we get to meet people in different lands and different centuries. We can have the sensation of experiencing life at sea with the crew of the *Pequod* or the dangers of battle along with The Shining Company, or we can share the fervor of love felt by Romeo and Juliet. Most important, we get to meet people of different types. One result is that we become better judges of character. By meeting certain character types in stories we are better prepared for the day when we will meet that type in person. A young reader who has met Mr. Toad in *The Wind in the Willows* is less likely to be taken in by that peculiar blend of recklessness and charisma when he encounters it in a real person. An adolescent girl who has read Jane Austen is better prepared for the fact that dashing and handsome young men often turn out to be liars and fakes. A reader who has encountered Madame Defarge in *A Tale of Two Cities* will have grasped the unpleasant but important knowledge that some people in this world are thoroughly ruthless. A young person who reads widely gets more than the pleasure of plot and setting; he or she gets an introductory course in character studies.

But acquaintance with a wide variety of "types," important as it is, is only the beginning. With some of the characters we meet in stories, we form a much deeper relationship than acquaintance. We enter imaginatively into their lives. We form a bond of empathy and even identity. And psychologists tell us that no other factor is more crucial to moral development than empathy. The ability to see and feel things as others see and feel them is the key that unlocks our prison house of self-absorption.

Even so it's not an easy thing to do. Children see things from their own perspective, and it takes quite a bit of doing to get them to see things from the point of view of their mothers, fathers, sisters, brothers, and friends. Even as we grow older it's difficult to get inside the minds of others. For one thing we have our own preoccupations; for another, people don't always let us in.

Reading affords us the opportunity to do what we often can't do in life, to become thoroughly involved in the inner lives of others. The sustained involvement with a character in a story enlarges our sympathies and gives us those "broad, wholesome, charitable views" that are the reward both of travel and of reading. In *Reading for the Love of It*, the Canadian author Michele Landsberg provides a description of her own experience as a young reader:

> I was *inside* those children who stepped back through the magic arch into ancient Egypt, shivering their shiver of apprehension and excitement. And nobody knew (except perhaps my librarian) that while I plodded dutifully to school . . . I was secretly living a hundred other lives.

This secret sharing is not simply the sharing of adventures, but also of ideas, emotions, loyalties, and principles. It's a shared testing of strength and resolve. For the reader it can be an ex-

perience of self-discovery of the kind that occurs only in intimate conversation. Why? Because reading certain books *is* a
form of intimate conversation.

You can see that book traveling not only gives us perspective
on others but also on ourselves. C. S. Lewis wrote:

> But in reading great literature I become a thousand men
> and yet remain myself. Like the night sky in the Greek
> poem, I see with myriad eyes, but it is still I who see.
> Here, as in worship, in love, in moral action, and in
> knowing, I transcend myself; and am never more myself
> than when I do.

At one and the same time reading carries us out to others and
becomes the mirror by which we discover ourselves more fully,
exactly because we have escaped self-concern.

Parents should be aware, however, that while reading is a
potentially enlarging experience, it can also have an opposite
effect. Many books for children seem to be designed to introduce them to the world of mass marketing rather than to the
wider world. Of the twenty best-selling paperback children's
books of 1990, almost all were "product" books: nine spin-offs
of Teenage Mutant Ninja Turtles, four Baby-Sitters Club
books, and two books about the New Kids on the Block.

Such books do have their defenders. One authority even recommends "junky" and "trashy" literature for children as the
best route to developing an avid love of reading. Reading has
so many benefits, it is argued, that we should be encouraged by
any sign of a reading interest—even if it's only on cereal boxes
and in comic books. "As long as they're reading something" is
the phrase we use to express this faith in reading.

Of course, there is something to this view. And there is
something to the related idea that, once started on the reading
road, children will almost automatically move on to better
books, that they will soon enough graduate from trash to Tolstoy. Sometimes they do. Moreover, comic books, horror stories, mysteries, romances, fantasy, and other types of
"drugstore" literature often have a sound moral structure. By
and large the child who reads is better off than the child who

only watches television, even if much of that child's reading consists of comics, thrillers, and serials.

But the idea can be carried too far. If—as all the adventure stories suggest—life is full of traps and pitfalls, why shouldn't books be also? One of the traps of mass-market stories is that they encourage youngsters to become fixated at the level of what might be termed "mall culture"—that is, a level of concern that doesn't go beyond changing fashions in clothes, lifestyles, and language.

How do you deal with such fixations? An attitude of "I appreciate the fact that you're reading, but I think you're underestimating yourself" may help to push a child more quickly through this phase. Of course, we tend to think that children who have been exposed to very good literature early on will be more immune to the attractions of "mall" literature.

Another way of handling the problem is to suggest a book in the same genre, only something richer and deeper and truer to life. If your child is hooked on the Baby-Sitters Club at a particular stage in her life it might be fairly futile to try and substitute *Little Women,* but *The Saturdays* might be just the ticket. The doctrine of the all-wise inner child says that such nudging is not necessary, that your child will move on to better stuff when she is ready. But don't count on it. Children can choose only from the alternatives that are available, and unless you provide some assistance they may never know what some of those alternatives are.

Sooner or later your child will come across a genre that encourages especially narrow self-preoccupation. As we all know, the early teen years are a time of introspection and rumination, and there is an entire literature devoted to ensuring that no emotional scab remains unpicked. This is the genre known as the realistic problem novel for young adults—although the readers of these stories are actually in the age range of nine through fourteen. The problem novel may range from stories about acne and unpopularity to stories about divorce, AIDS, and anorexia. The intent of such books is mainly therapeutic: to help a child with a similar problem learn self-acceptance, to let him know that there are other children just like him, with problems and concerns just like his.

Some of these stories, it is true, are thoughtful, well-crafted treatments of the difficulties that confront today's young people. But there are some serious drawbacks to this problem approach. One is the problem of what might be called a trendy didacticism. As Judith Saltman observes in her introduction to *The Riverside Anthology of Children's Literature,* many of the writers in this genre "see books as cures to be prescribed for a given sociological, political, or emotional problem." The problem with so much of this literature, which wants to give children "proper" attitudes about divorce, sex, war, and gender, is the problem that inevitably arises when writers are more interested in messages than in writing: "Some of this determinedly progressive fiction for youth has an eerily Victorian ring to it," writes Michele Landsberg. "Didacticism clangs on every page like an iron bell, heavy, clumsy, reverberant with good intentions."

A second drawback to books in the problem novel genre is that they often don't allow for much moral growth. In these books self-acceptance rather than moral growth is the badge of maturity. For example, the characters in stories like Judy Blume's *Blubber* and *Then Again Maybe I Won't* aren't particularly nice kids. They bully and intimidate other children and make fun of their parents, but there is no suggestion they should mend their ways. The reader is supposed to accept them as they are and, presumably, if the reader shares some of the same faults, he can accept those, too. Children in these stories ruminate about their problem situations, but there is no real soul searching.

For a contrast, look at the children in Mildred D. Taylor's *Roll of Thunder, Hear My Cry,* a Newbery Medal novel about an African-American family living in the South in the 1930s. Stacey Logan knows he shouldn't be at the Wallace store; he has promised his mother that he won't go near that place of gambling and violence. But his score with T. J. has to be settled. When Mr. Morrison, a family friend, finds the boys fighting, Stacey is sure that he is in deep trouble. But Mr. Morrison says he won't tell Stacey's mother. The story is told by Stacey's sister Cassie.

Stacey stared long and hard at Mr. Morrison.

"How come, Mr. Morrison?" he asked. "How come you ain't gonna tell Mama?"

Mr. Morrison slowed Jack as we turned into the road leading home. "'Cause I'm leaving it up to you to tell her."

. . . Stacey nodded thoughtfully and wound the handkerchief tighter around his wounded hand. His face was not scarred, so if he could just figure out a way to explain the bruises on his hand to Mama without lying he was in the clear, for Mr. Morrison had not said that he *had* to tell her. But for some reason I could not understand he said, "All right, Mr. Morrison, I'll tell her."

It is clear that Stacey experiences a real moral struggle, as his response indicates. This soul struggling, this sense that we all have an obligation to work on improving our characters, was very strongly felt in our culture in the era depicted in Taylor's novel. But it seems now to be on the wane. Young people today tend to find fault with systems and institutions but not with themselves. A colleague of ours once asked his college philosophy class to write an essay about a personal struggle over right and wrong, good and evil, but found that most of his students were unable to complete the assignment. The reason? "We haven't done anything wrong," they told him. And apparently they meant this quite sincerely. This attitude probably had more to do with psychology texts they had read in college than with books they read as children, but the problem novel, with its heavy overlay of psychology, doesn't do much to counter such attitudes.

Perhaps the main trouble with literature intended as therapy is that there is no self-forgetfulness, no room to stand back and get a larger view. As a result it is questionable whether such stories work even on the therapeutic level. Stepping back into ancient Greece may be a healthier step than stepping across the street to meet a boy or girl just like oneself. As the psychologist Bruno Bettelheim has pointed out, fantasy and fairy tales are more useful than realistic stories when it comes to working on inner problems. Why? Because fantasy provides necessary dis-

tance. For example, a child whose parents are going through a
divorce doesn't necessarily want to read a realistic novel about
some other child with divorcing parents. Such difficulties are
sometimes better handled by turning to myth or fantasy. A
mother of a ten-year-old boy tells this story about his struggle
with cancer: "At first he was very upbeat, but after several
painful treatments his optimism faded. We were afraid that he
was ready to give up. We were really afraid for his life. Then he
came upon the story of the labors of Hercules in a book of
myths, and he read it and re-read it, and it seemed to give him
back his spirit." The story about Hercules allowed the boy to
transcend his fears and to cast his personal struggle on a
mythic level. He was probably fortunate that some well-mean-
ing adult didn't hand him a book about a boy with cancer.
That sort of thing often serves only to increase the depression.

We sometimes forget that the first gift of a story is transport.
The story takes us somewhere. More important, it takes us out
of ourselves. To enter a story we must leave ourselves behind,
and this, it may be argued, is precisely what is needed to get a
proper perspective on ourselves. The willingness to let go of
self-concern is a requisite for both moral health and mental
health. Here's a sample of literary transport:

> I take up my pen and go back to the time when my father
> kept the "Admiral Benbow" Inn, and the brown old sea-
> man, with the sabre cut, first took up his lodging under
> our roof.
>
> I remember him as if it were yesterday. . . .

With these words Robert Louis Stevenson draws us head-
long into the world of *Treasure Island*. He does it so swiftly
and surely we have no time to bid farewell to our concerns of
the moment. They simply vanish. And the Admiral Benbow
Inn becomes more solid than the room we sit in. Were we preoccupied with bills to be paid or assignments to be done? That
can be ignored for now. A strong arm with a long reach has
pulled us into the midst of more pressing matters.

Many people in the business of writing and recommending
children's books, many of them with the best of intentions,

seem set on removing this element of transport. Let's hope they don't succeed. The danger facing children's literature does not come from the ogres and villains that haunt the pages of fairy tales and adventure stories; the danger lies, rather, in the continued proliferation of normless books that cater to anxiety and self-absorption, and have nothing to teach about life except, perhaps, that whatever happens is okay. The danger is not that such books lead to a life of crime, but to a life of boredom, selfishness, and limited horizons.

Fortunately, there is no shortage of stories of another sort: books that challenge, thrill, and excite, and awaken young readers to the potential drama of life, especially to the drama of a life lived in obedience to the highest ideals. Such books have something better to offer than therapeutic reassurance. Like true friends they encourage us to be our best selves.

CHAPTER 4

Worlds of Meaning

"WE TURN TO fiction for some slight hint about the story in life we live," observed Robert Penn Warren. Media theorist Neil Postman elaborates on this idea:

> Human beings require stories to give meaning to the facts of existence . . . ever since we can remember, all of us have been telling ourselves stories about ourselves, composing life-giving autobiographies of which we are the heroes and heroines. If our stories are coherent and plausible and have continuity, they will help us to understand why we are here, and what we need to pay attention to and what we may ignore.

Stories, in short, help to make sense out of our lives. There is a wonderful example of this in the film version of *Captains Courageous*, Rudyard Kipling's tale of life aboard the Gloucester fishing schooners. The story concerns a spoiled rich boy who, on a transatlantic voyage, falls overboard in the vicinity of the Grand Banks, is rescued by a fisherman named Manuel, then taken aboard the *We're Here* and put to work alongside the men. Except that he won't work. The boy, Harvey Cheyne, is self-centered, lazy, and manipulative. He doesn't understand concepts such as loyalty and hard work because he has no framework within which they make any sense. His transformation into a better and infinitely more likable boy comes about largely through the influence of Manuel, who not only possesses admirable qualities of character but is also a fine storyteller. Manuel tells stories about his father, about the sea, about the songs he sings. In one memorable scene he relates his life to those of the Twelve Apostles, who were also fishermen. Their story is the larger one within which his own life story makes sense.

A plot. A purpose. A sense that our struggles and sufferings have meaning. The supreme gift of stories is their reassurance that these can be found. By giving us a larger vision a story may help us find meaning in experiences that might otherwise seem chaotic or pointless. Because there are many more things that don't make sense to them, children need this reassurance every bit as much as adults. If you've ever wondered why a child wants to hear the same story over and over, night after night, here is part of the reason.

Of course, the stories we read don't have to be the same stories we live. We've already suggested why that isn't necessarily a good idea. The important thing about good literature, whether set in the twentieth century or the second, is that it opens our eyes to the significance of our own dramas and helps us to find continuities and connections we might otherwise miss.

Stories also help make sense of morality. How well do motives for virtuous behavior hold up without the sense that there is something like a plot to our lives? Not well at all. If life is "a tale told by an idiot, full of sound and fury, signifying nothing," then it doesn't really matter how one behaves. But to feel that one has been given a role to play in a meaningful story, and that one has the chance of acting one's part well—that is a considerable source of motivation.

The perfect cinematic example is the film *It's a Wonderful Life*. A man on the point of suicide finds renewed hope when he discovers (courtesy of an angelic revelation) that the story of his life makes a great deal more sense than he imagined. The fact that year after year this fifty-year-old classic consistently polls as one of the best-loved films suggests that its theme strikes close to home. A very different film, *Casablanca*, conveys, though in more subtle ways, a similar theme. The cynical and self-concerned Rick Blaine manages to transcend his bitterness because he has caught sight of a larger vision. When, near the story's conclusion, he says that "the problems of three little people don't amount to a hill o' beans in this crazy world," he means precisely that it is *not* a crazy world.

One of the duties adults have toward children is to teach them that the world is not a crazy place. A child needs the security of knowing that he lives in an ordered world. As Michele Landsberg points out, the attractiveness of order is part of the appeal of such classic stories as *Madeline* (twelve girls in two straight lines) and *The Story About Ping* (the duck who wanders away from the ordered existence of his family). The need for order may also account for the ambivalence children feel about *Alice's Adventures in Wonderland*. Far from being the favorite children's book of all time, as some suppose, *Alice's Adventures in Wonderland* is a book that commonly upsets young children. Humphrey Carpenter, in an essay on *Alice's Adventures in Wonderland,* writes that "many adults retain vague memories of being somehow frightened by the *Alice* books in childhood to the extent of positively disliking them." Why? Partly because *Alice's Adventures* comes closer to upsetting the idea of a natural moral ordering than any other book written for children. Nothing happens in a normal way in *Alice's Adventures in Wonderland*. Alice grows abnormally small (almost to the point of annihilation) and then abnormally large, babies change suddenly into pigs, and all the rules are utterly relative—subject to change without notice. Along with undermining notions of normality, *Alice's Adventures in Wonderland* attacks the sense of meaning itself. The universe that Lewis Carroll creates is a meaningless universe. All rules are arbitrary, and life is a Mad Tea-Party in which we are all condemned to the endless repetition of pointless activities. *Alice's Adventures in Wonderland,* which can be a delight to an adult or an older child with a secure sense of the way things connect, can be a shock to a younger child who is trying to find those connections.

What kind of stories are we recommending? Any and all kinds as long as they are animated by a sense of moral order.

What does that mean? In the case of fairy tales, it means that evil is punished, virtue is rewarded, things are set straight, effort pays off, and riddles are solved. In novels, of course, whether realistic or fantastic, the moral order is not always upheld so decisively and permanently. An outstanding writer crafts a novel in such a way as to draw the reader into the process of discriminating between appearance and reality, since the wrong choices are often dressed up to look like the right ones. Even tragedies assert the reality of a moral order in the face of human failure to live up to that order.

Ironically, one of the most satisfying of all story genres is the mystery or the detective story. W. H. Auden explains why in his perceptive essay "The Guilty Vicarage." Murder mysteries satisfy, writes Auden, because they are about order. First you have an ordered and peaceful community. Then you have the crime that disrupts order. And finally, through the intervention of the detective, the restoration of order.

Perhaps this is the reason that the reading of mystery stories is reported to rank among the favorite pastimes of presidents and other world leaders. Perhaps they, especially, need reassurance that there is a structure and order to events. There's no doubt, of course, that mystery stories are also read for escape. But it's an escape from which we can come back with a better perspective on our daily lives. Like the Lord, books work in mysterious ways, and by a strange paradox stories about murder are often the most soothing thing to read. In *Reading for the Love of It,* Michele Landsberg tells how, after the death of her mother in a terrible accident, the only consolation she could find was in reading Swedish detective stories.

If adults need reassurance that life makes sense, so do children and young adults. The number of youngsters who are directly affected by acts of senseless violence is still small, but more and more young people are aware of the possibility of sudden and senseless tragedy. They need plenty of help in understanding that, despite the surrounding chaos, there is still purpose, plot, and meaning. The mystery story can be a real help in this regard because it shows us that although life is mysterious, it is not meaningless. It's a lucky teenager who discovers that the pleasure of reading Agatha Christie or Patricia

Wentworth is not just the pleasure of suspense but also the pleasure of justice and harmony triumphant. Advanced readers will also respond to the stories of Ellis Peters—both to her medieval mystery series featuring Brother Cadfael, a twelfth-century monk, as the detective, and to her contemporary stories featuring Inspector Adam Felse. Peters's stories invariably have a strong moral backbone and are full of incident, colorful characters, love interests, and shrewd observations about human nature. There's no shying away from ugliness in her novels, but there's no despair, either. The overall theme is always one of hope: good brought out of evil, love out of hate. With Brother Cadfael the reader gets to look at life's problems *sub specie aeternitatis*—from the aspect of eternity. For today's youngsters, bombarded with daily reports of the latest explosions of sound and fury, it's a much needed perspective.

The worst kind of sound and fury, however, is not the kind that emanates from the streets but the kind that comes from inside one's own house. Much of life's meaning is found in family life. When we are born we are introduced into a family story and to the characters who are already part of it. Just as a novel requires a theme or a narrative thread, so does a life, and home is the place where we first pick up that thread. But the family itself needs a story. If there is no family story to pass on, if the family is not tied into some larger tradition, history, or religious story, youngsters are not likely to gain much perspective on their lives. As a character in an Isaac Bashevis Singer tale puts it, "If stories weren't told or books weren't written, man would live like the beasts, only for the day."

Unfortunately, because of high rates of illegitimacy and divorce, more and more youngsters are subjected to family situations that lack sense and order. As a result, more youngsters are living only for the day—for whatever immediate sensation they can find. Yet they still have what seems to be a built-in longing for a stable home life. As Michele Landsberg observes:

The enduring popularity of family stories written as far back as the 1930s, such as the imperishable *The Moffats* by Eleanor Estes, or the 1950s, such as *Henry Huggins* by Beverly Cleary, show us how much children still want to live, imaginatively, in a world where family love is the un-questioned basis of existence.

Can books be of help in offsetting difficult family situa-tions? We think so. Books can provide a picture of what family life can be like at its best and, for that matter, what romance and courtship can be like. Not all writers would agree with this. Some insist that if families are falling apart, books should obediently reflect the trend. Consequently, their depictions of family life come with generous helpings of chaos and cynicism mixed in. But we think there is a danger in trying to accommo-date fiction to every new social malady, the danger being that, after a while, no one remembers what a stable family looks like. It's not possible to break the cycle of broken or unformed marriages unless you have a picture in mind of what the alter-native is. Children, as the author Jane Yolen observes, need a "star map" for the future. In real life, she says, "Endings are as often unhappy as happy . . . babies starve and there is no res-urrecting them. . . . Families are torn asunder and there is no mending them." But a certain kind of fiction, she maintains, tells us something else: "It tells us of the world *as it should be*. It holds certain values to be important. It makes issues clear. . . . [It] becomes a rehearsal for the reader for life as it *should* be lived."

The foregoing is not a criticism of realism in stories. Rather, it is a criticism of an approach that wants to give children only the slice of reality they already have. The thinking behind it goes something like this: "Your parents are divorced? Here, read this book about divorcing parents. It will make you feel better."

But too many children already know about the more disas-trous facts of life. They know about broken marriages and do-mestic quarrels and absent fathers. What they need is not a further cataloging—that only leads to confusion or cynicism—but a way of making sense of these facts, of ordering them and judging them. And they need a vehicle for finding out what they don't know about life but ought to know.

That means giving them a broader world than they currently possess. Ever since *The Catcher in the Rye,* books for teens and preteens have tended to reflect back to them their own limited adolescent or preadolescent world. But in trying to depict the world through the eyes of a teenage protagonist, many authors have succeeded only in conveying the impression that there is nothing more profound in life than the teenage view of things. Young readers deserve to know that there is a grown-up world worth aspiring to, that it is not all phony, and that some things are worth waiting for.

This is not an easy thing for a writer to do. It is far easier to be cynical about the facts of life than it is to invest them with the significance they deserve. But it can be done. Consider two passages from Tolstoy. The first is from the wedding of Kitty and Levin in *Anna Karenina*. It describes Levin's feelings as the full impact of the ancient ceremony comes down on him:

> Levin felt more and more that all his ideas of marriage, all his dreams of how he would order his life, were mere childishness, and that it was something he had not understood hitherto, and now understood less than ever, though it was being performed upon him. The lump in his throat rose higher and higher, tears that would not be checked came into his eyes.

The second is Tolstoy's introduction of Princess Lise in *War and Peace*:

> Everyone brightened at the sight of this pretty young woman, so soon to become a mother, so full of life and health and carrying her burden so lightly. Old men and dull dispirited young ones who looked at her, after being in her company and talking to her a little while, felt as if they too were becoming, like her, full of life and health.

The noted book critic Clifton Fadiman has said that Tolstoy had a "genius for the normal," and these passages are examples of that genius at work. They convey an enormous appreciation for the mysteries and blessings of ordinary life. Of course, *Anna Karenina* and *War and Peace* are not for youngsters (although some of Tolstoy's stories are); the point is that

today's young people (and many adults) are sorely in need of a
picture of life that conveys both depth and normality—or, better, the depth and satisfaction that a morally ordered life can
offer (with the qualification that even the most normal life has
its share of conflict and contradiction). The things that tradi-
tionally were thought to give adult life meaning—love,
courtship, marriage, children—have suffered a tremendous
trivialization in recent years, largely as a result of television.
The consumer of mass entertainment learns that these things
are material for jokes and gags without learning much more
about them. The fact that some notable exceptions to this
rule—*The Waltons, The Little House on the Prairie*—played on
TV so well over a long period suggests a certain hunger on the
part of youngsters for depictions of these ordinary blessings.

Along with "reality," children also need a diet of normality—not Dick and Jane "normality," but stories in which children take part in a larger cycle of life. A number of recent
children's books offer this experience. In *Waiting for Hannah,*
a mother recounts for her daughter the preparations the family made for her arrival, including the planting of a morning
glory vine, which blossoms on the day Hannah is born. *Yonder,* another picture book, follows the life of a nineteenth-century farmer and his bride as they marry, have children, and
eventually see their children marry and start their own families. To mark each important family event, prayers are said and
trees are planted. *In My Mother's House,* a collection of verse
sung by the Tewa children of Tesuque Pueblo near Sante Fe,
celebrates the ordered domestic life of these Native Americans.
"In my Mother's house," begins one poem, "there is a fire-
place: . . . The fire is always there, . . . / To keep me warm."

Although it plays little part in the lives of television families,
religion plays a significant role in the lives of real families. This
is reflected in *Hello Amigos!,* a picture book about a Mexican-
American family's celebration of a birthday. Frankie, whose
birthday is the cause of the celebration, tells how, after the
party, "Papa and I walk to our church. He helps me light a candle, and I count my blessings." In *The Happy Funeral* a Chinese-American girl comes to terms with her grandfather's
death by participating in family rituals and remembrances. For

middle readers, *All-of-a-Kind Family* depicts the daily life of a
Jewish family in the Lower East Side of New York City at the
turn of the century.

"Normality" as we are using it here does not mean an alle-
giance to the status quo or to suburban living, but a recognition of norms that guide and also limit our behavior, a sense of
moral fixity in the midst of flux. The Depression years in Mississippi are the setting for *Roll of Thunder, Hear My Cry*, a
story about the Logan family's efforts to teach goodness to
their children in the teeth of racism and poverty. In one heart-
to-heart talk Mrs. Logan tells her daughter Cassie, "Baby, we
have no choice of what color we're born, or who our parents
are, or whether we're rich or poor. What we do have is some
choice over what we make of our lives once we're here . . . I
pray to God you'll make the best of yours."

It is interesting that some of the strongest presentations of
ordinary domestic blessings can be found in fantasy stories.
Mrs. Frisby and the Rats of NIMH is one example. Tolkien's
The Lord of the Rings is another. Despite whatever adventures
or misadventures come, there is always time for cakes and teas
and fireside chats. Or, at least, time to think of them. In fact,
there is a strong suggestion throughout these books that this is
what all the trials and perils are for: so that hearth life and
home life can be protected, so that in the end the adventurers
can return to just such a life. So too in the *Odyssey*. After all, it
is Odysseus's keen desire to get home that drives the plot. More
than a simple adventure story, this prototype of all adventure
stories is also about the restoration of family life. It anticipates
by twenty-five hundred years Samuel Johnson's observation
that "the end of all endeavor is to be happy at home."

Odysseus was a navigator trying to find his way home. It
took him a very long time to do it—more than twenty years.
Today's navigators are luckier. They have a framework of lon-
gitude and latitude, and a prime meridian from which to take
their bearings. Children, likewise, need a prime meridian—a
fixed standard—to reach their destinations in life. The voyage
from childhood to responsible adulthood is long, difficult, and
stormy. Good stories provide compass, chart, and bearings for
the journey.

CHAPTER 5

Selecting and Sharing Good Books: Some Guidelines

Because of space limitations, there are many good books that couldn't be included in our guide. For those who want to go beyond the list here are some suggestions for choosing books that build character.

THINK BACK TO stories that had a positive impact on you when you were growing up. There's a good chance the same story will have a similar effect on your child.

Choose books that are in keeping with your own values. Don't choose a book simply on the basis of its reputation. Reading the book yourself is the only sure way of knowing if it reflects your outlook on life.

Try to distinguish between issues and virtues. Many contemporary children's books focus on trendy issues rather than character development. You should be looking for books that reinforce courage, responsibility, and perseverance rather than books that offer prepackaged opinions on divorce, euthanasia, and the like. You want your child to acquire strengths of character before he acquires a lot of secondhand opinions. It's one thing to have an opinion on an issue such as immigration, and quite another to develop a habit of helping those you have an opportunity to help. Having enlightened opinions is no substitute for having character.

Of course, there are good books for children that do deal with contemporary issues, but the issues are integrated with the characters, setting, and plot. Good books are people centered, not problem centered. The characters are real. We are gladdened by their victories and saddened by their sufferings. They are not there just to teach a lesson. The author has an interesting story to tell, not a message to convey. In short, you don't feel he or she has designs on your child.

Context is crucial. Character-building books are not simply about good people doing good things. Moral books may deal with immoral behavior. The question is not whether unethical behavior is present but how it is presented. The hero or heroine of a story may well give way to temptation, but a good book will show the real costs of such a choice. In the Arthurian legend, for example, the adultery of Launcelot and Guinevere leads to awful consequences both for themselves and for many others. So does Arthur's own earlier indiscretion. It's not a matter of preaching at the reader but of showing him how certain behaviors work themselves out over the course of time.

Of course, the story can't do all the work. The reader has to sort things out and draw conclusions. This is easy enough with a simple story such as *Peter Rabbit* but not so easy when it comes to plots requiring more mature judgments. So parents need to ask some hard questions. Are the consequences of an undesirable action clear to any reader? Or only to a more sophisticated reader? Will your child be able to make the proper distinctions? In the last analysis it's a judgment call. Perhaps the most important question is this: How well do you know your child?

Context is also crucial in making judgments about rough language. Many contemporary authors use "street" language to give an authentic flavor to their stories. You need to weigh the redeeming elements of the story against the coarsening effect of overexposure to vulgar language. Is the language truly necessary to the story? Or is it there just for shock value or to demonstrate the author's hipness? A few vulgar expressions here and there may add a certain realism to a story, but too many may simply have a desensitizing effect.

Allow some room for growth. Although you want to be

careful about books that are way over your child's level, it's legitimate to challenge her with books that are somewhat above her level. After all, one of the reasons we read is to extend ourselves. Children also need to involve themselves in life more deeply as they grow. A good story will often force the reader to struggle with the protagonist through trials and difficult decisions. Like Jacob wrestling with the angel, the story won't let you go without extracting some commitment. So look for stories that open up new possibilities and stretch the imagination. At the same time be wary of stories that focus exclusively on narrow teen or preteen preoccupations, or those that offer nothing more than the therapeutic reassurance that everything is okay.

How do you determine which books will help your youngster grow? A simple rule of thumb is to look for books in which the main character grows. As your child becomes involved with the protagonist, he vicariously shares in that character's development.

But don't always look for steady growth in stories. In fact, the prelude to growth is often some sort of fall. A fall from grace. A falling short of the mark. Well-known examples are Peter's denial to the servant girl, Boromir's defection to the wrong side in *The Lord of the Rings,* Pip's ingratitude in *Great Expectations,* Jim Nightshade's bargain with the evil Mr. Dark in *Something Wicked This Way Comes.* Some sort of revelation (not necessarily religious) may be required, however, before the protagonist realizes how far he has fallen. Although the norms are there for everyone to see, sometimes a dramatic incident is needed for us to see them. Consequently, the revelation often comes in the form of an accident, an illness, or some other misfortune. It can be the experience of losing one's nerve in a crisis—as happens in *Lord Jim.* It can be an experience of hitting rock bottom—the experience of the prodigal son. Ironically, the revelation might come in the form of an actual physical fall: Ivan Ilyich falls off a stepladder; Louisa falls off the "Cobb" in Jane Austen's *Persuasion;* the spoiled boy in *Captains Courageous* falls off an ocean liner.

As a result of his troubles the protagonist learns something important. It can be a revelation of self-discovery as, for exam-

ple, when Pip's illness leads him to see himself for the crass social climber he has become. Or it can be a revelation of another's character as, for example, when a young lady in a Jane
Austen novel discovers the essentially worthless nature of an
attractive and dashing young man.

How about the reader? One of the great possibilities of the
story form is that he may also experience a recognition. The
hard knock that the protagonist receives may startle him into
awareness too. It's common knowledge that in life as well as in
stories, it often takes such hard knocks to wake us up. Our life
goes on in its accustomed patterns, we become blind to what is
really important, and suddenly something strikes us with the
force of a revelation, and we are compelled to see. Perhaps a
family man is arrested for drunk driving, or perhaps a young
woman develops cancer, or perhaps a son or daughter is discovered to be using drugs. When things like this happen we
may find ourselves wondering, as Ivan Ilyich does, whether we
have spent our lives attending to the wrong things, and
whether we have not missed the real thing altogether. A good
story can provide some of this jolt while saving us the trouble
of having to experience a real catastrophe. And it may better
prepare us for those times when real tragedy does strike.

The same holds true for younger readers. Just as a child
learns from real experiences, he can also learn from vicarious
ones—and far more safely. Through books he can experience
revelations that might not come to him until much later in the
normal course of events: revelations of fear, of failure, of love,
of understanding. What's more, reading provides a sort of
mental rehearsal for the time when he encounters these experiences firsthand.

Here are some practical suggestions for sharing books with
children:

• Try to set aside some time each day for storytelling.

• Recommended reading levels are only a rough guide. Parents need to develop a feel for what will work with their own
children. Since there are so many good books available there's
no reason to try to force a particular book on a child. This is
doubly true for classics. They can be introduced too early or in
the wrong way, spoiling a child's taste for them later on. Bev-

erly Cleary, author of the Ramona series, relates, "When I was a child, a relative gave me *Ivanhoe* to grow into. I was so disappointed that I still have not grown into it."

• Keep in mind that children can understand and enjoy listening to stories that are above their actual reading level.

• For very small children the main thing is to hear stories that are rhythmic and repetitive. It's the sound of the language that counts the most at this stage.

• Be aware that myths, fairy tales, and folktales come in many versions—versions that range from the sublime to the abysmal. For example, you wouldn't think that a fine story like "Rumpelstiltskin" could be rolled out flat as a pancake, but it has been done. Another factor in choosing a version of a book is the quality of the illustrations. While illustrations are not all important, they do make a difference; look for editions with illustrations that do justice to the text rather than trivialize it.

• When reading aloud choose stories that you, yourself, like. Reading should be enjoyable for everyone involved.

• Practice when possible. Good stories deserve a good reading. Read the story yourself before reading it to your children. That way you'll have a better idea of its plot and rhythm and bumpy spots.

• Be expressive. Learn when to slow down, when to speed up, when to pause. Create suspense by lowering your voice, create a dramatic effect by raising it. You might try changing your voice to fit each character. Don't be concerned that you lack the vocalization skills of a professional actor; children constitute a forgiving and enthusiastic audience.

• It is important to set the right mood when reading aloud. Allow time for your children to settle down. If you're reading from a picture book you might spend some time talking about the book's cover. Ask your children what they think the story will be about. If it's a chapter in a novel, you might want to follow Jim Trelease's advice and ask, "Let's see—where did we leave off yesterday?" or "What's happened so far?"

• Don't be tempted to explain the "moral" of the story. Let the book speak for itself. Family reading time should not be confused with a class in textual interpretation. On the other hand, it's fine if a story leads to conversation. Occasionally it might be appropriate to ask a question or two about a character's actions or motivations. But don't overdo it. It's better if questions come spontaneously from your child.

• Read-aloud time should be balanced with silent reading time. Even prereaders should have time alone with picture books. Try instituting a practice of silent reading time for the whole family. Instead of gathering around the television at night make the bookcase the focus of attention.

Middle to older readers can continue to participate in read-alouds and should even be encouraged on occasion to take on the role of reader to their younger siblings, but most of their reading will be done independently. This is the age for them to make their own discoveries and, therefore, adults should avoid pushing books at them. If you've made a practice of reading aloud from exciting and imaginative books when your children were younger, if you've helped them develop the habit of regular trips to the library, and if your house is well stocked with books of all kinds, you've already given them the preparation they need to make good choices. At this stage it's a mistake to inundate children with piles of books they "ought" to read. "Here's one you might enjoy" or "I came across another interesting science fiction book" is a much better way to spark an interest. From time to time you might also make a gift of a book about a subject that you know is of special interest to a child. But perhaps the best advertisement for a book is your own obvious delight in it. If your older child sees that you are absorbed and entertained by a particular novel, it's a good bet that he or she will want to find out more about it.

The list that follows focuses on stories with a moral theme. This is not to suggest that this is the only kind of book children should read. There are all types of books and all kinds of reasons to read them: for suspense, for humor, for the beauty of the language, for the pleasure of wordplay and nonsense rhymes. There is no discernible moral in *Good Night Moon, To Think That I Saw It on Mulberry Street, The Jumblies,* or *The Cremation of Sam McGee,* but it would be a shame to deprive your child of the pleasure they bring.

Book List

A Word About the Book List

IN ORDER TO ASSEMBLE the book list that follows, we have read hundreds of books—an exhilarating journey across the literary landscape. Along the way we were reunited with many old and dear friends from our own childhoods. We also found ourselves exploring new, previously uncharted territories. A large number of these books have been "test driven" on our own children—our best and toughest critics!

Though any selection is bound to be somewhat subjective, we believe that we have identified many of the classic children's books informed by the moral imagination. Our list constitutes a reading plan that can enrich your child's heart and mind from kindergarten to college.

We have encountered an astonishing richness and diversity in children's literature and we hope that our list reflects this variety: books written hundreds of years ago and books written yesterday; books from East and West; books about boys and girls, dragons and fairy godmothers, saints and sinners.

A large number of these titles are well known, including classics once common in the classroom. Unfortunately, fewer and fewer of the "Great Books" are read, at home or in school.

We hope that in our summaries we have found fresh ways of interpreting the relevance of these classics. Too many of us know these books only from movie versions; we hope you and your children will go back to them with a sense of discovery and delight.

Though our focus in this list is on the moral imagination, that does not mean that all of these books are "uplifting." A central part of our moral life concerns our recognition of the reality of evil and its allure. Some of the stories we have chosen (primarily for older readers) recount tragic events: they do not always have happy endings, if by happy we mean that death, betrayal, loss, and suffering are always averted. On the other hand, all of the books on this list put such experiences in a context of meaning. We have taken care to note which books may present an emotional challenge to a child.

Whenever possible, we have selected the editions of a book that have the most beautiful and suggestive illustrations. In the case of fairy tales and myths, the selection has been done with particular care; many classic stories have been marred by illustrations that are saccharine and trivial. When it comes to classic novels, such as *Robinson Crusoe* and *At the Back of the North Wind,* we have also selected beautifully illustrated versions. But if your budget will not stretch to these gift editions, do not worry. Try the library or find an inexpensive paperback edition. The text is the most important thing, so almost any edition will do. However, you should watch out for abridged editions, which can sometimes butcher a story. We have tried to indicate which books are best suited to abridgment.

We have tried to keep our bibliographical references short and sweet. Remember that many of these books are available in a variety of editions: pick the edition that's best for you.

The categories we have used are far from airtight. There are times when categories overlap—myths and fairy tales, for example. Use the categories as rough guides to the genre of a story.

In presenting fiction, we have stuck with three basic categories, rather than imposing narrow, specialized distinctions. "Historical" novels are thus set anytime before World War II, while "Contemporary" fiction takes place after the war.

Even though history books tell us about the past in narrative form, we have not included a separate "History" section. Rather, we have chosen to focus on historical novels and biographies because they center on one or two major characters who are faced with moral choices. Children learn more about history when it is told in this personal form.

Reading levels, like the categories, are only rough approximations. Again, we have chosen to stick with three basic levels rather than attempt to break up the list into smaller divisions. In each of our reading levels there are gradations. The only way to ensure that you are matching your child with the right book is to glance through it yourself.

The three levels we use are: Younger Readers (4 to 8), Middle Readers (8 to 12), and Older Readers (12 and up). Remember that books that may be too difficult for children to read themselves can be read aloud to them with great success. A few of the books we have included for older readers are verbally dense and challenging, but in these instances, we have placed a warning in the summary.

We have deliberately weighted our selection in favor of books that are currently in print and thus readily available in bookstores. The titles we have included that are out of print should be available in most public libraries. Books go in and out of print quickly, even books that have been published within the last five years. If you are coming up empty, ask your librarian about interlibrary loans.

At the end of our book list we have appended a brief list of films available on videocassette. Nothing can be substituted for books, nor can a child develop the habit of reading if he or she does not start early. But there are plenty of times when watching a film is just the right type of entertainment—for moms and dads, as well as kids! As with reading, watching a film together, as a family, is a wonderful way to grow together. The films we have listed are meant to give only an indication of the better-quality material available in the video stores.

A few other points to keep in mind: The books are listed in alphabetical order by title, with the exception of the biography section. In that section books are listed alphabetically according to the name of the subject. Dates in parentheses indicate when the books were originally published. Picture books usually do not have page numbers; they are mostly between 30 and 40 pages long.

The following symbols are placed after the titles of award-winning books: (N) is a Newbery Medal winner; (NH) is a Newbery Honor book; (C) indicates a Caldecott Medal winner; and (CH) is for a Caldecott Honor book. These are the most prestigious awards for children's literature in America.

Picture Books

The world of the [very] young . . . [is] a place where good and evil are clearly stamped. It's a place where the better part of human nature triumphs over tragedies, and where innocence rides high.

—Rosemary Wells

Younger Readers

The Black Falcon
Boccaccio. Retold by William Wise.
Illustrated by Gillian Barlow.
Philomel, 1990

FROM BOCCACCIO'S MASTERPIECE, the *Decameron,* comes this moving story about an impoverished knight's passion for a beautiful woman and his determination to give her the only treasure he possesses—his black peregrine falcon. Federigo has long loved Lady Orsini but, because she is married, he vows never to show the least sign of his passion. Then her husband dies and her son falls gravely ill. Desperate to find a cure, she determines to beg Federigo for his falcon—the only thing that will raise the boy's spirits. Now Federigo is forced to choose between his loyal companion and the woman he loves. Sumptuously illustrated in bold watercolors, *The Black Falcon* evokes the very essence of the fourteenth century, a time when honor and selfless love were the hallmarks of chivalry.

The Boy Who Held Back the Sea
Lenny Hort. Illustrated by Thomas Locker.
Dial Books for Young Readers, 1987

AS SOON AS we are introduced to Peter, we know he is a typical child—he has been sent to his room for misbehavior! Then the door opens, and instead of the expected punishment, Peter's grandmother comes into the room and offers to tell him a story. Long ago, she tells him, there was a little boy called Jan and he was always getting into trouble. One Sunday, he runs off into the woods instead of going to church. On his way home after a day of mischief, he spots a small leak in the dike. The hole is not very large but even Jan knows that it will not be long before the force of the sea makes it wider, and then the whole town will be washed away. Jan's attempt to warn a passerby comes to nothing—after all, Jan is a naughty boy and not to be trusted. Jan's only recourse is to lie down in the ditch and put his finger in the hole. After a whole night of lying face-down in a muddy ditch, Jan is finally discovered and the town is saved. After telling her story, Peter's grandmother does not admonish him. Instead, she lovingly invites him down to dinner. Peter bows his head and resolves to do better . . . like Jan. *The Boy Who Held Back the Sea* is preeminently a story of *hope*. It is never too late, it tells children, to have a change of heart and do something loving for others. But its wise message is also for adults. Never assume, it tells us, that just because a child has a history of bad behavior, he or she is beyond reform. It is an inspiring story of childhood courage and contrition, and the illustrations alone are almost worth the price of the book! Each page is sumptuously illustrated by the renowned Thomas Locker, whose beautiful oil paintings evoke the art of the Dutch masters, reminding us of a time when life was simpler and the boundary between right and wrong was more clearly defined than it is today.

Brave Irene
William Steig
Farrar, Straus and Giroux, 1993

WHEN IRENE SEES that her mother is too sick to deliver
the dress she has made for the duchess, she volunteers to go to
the palace herself. But when she ventures into the howling
wind, Irene realizes that this may not be such an easy task after
all. And when the dress is torn from her grasp by the wind and
she flounders in a deep snowdrift, Irene is tempted to give up.
The only thing that keeps her going is the thought of her
mother's and the duchess's disappointment if she fails. Whim-
sically written in the tradition of the fairy tale, *Brave Irene* is
the story of a little girl's love for her mother and how this gives
her the courage to persevere despite almost insurmountable
odds.

Clancy's Coat
Eve Bunting. Illustrated by Lorinda Bryan Cauley.
Warne, 1984, 48 pages

THE MENDING OF a coat becomes the means by which
two Irish neighbors learn how to forgive. Ever since Tippitt's
cow, Bridget, got into Clancy's garden and made a mess of
things, the two friends haven't spoken a word to each other.
But Clancy's coat needs turning, and he won't trust anyone but
Tippitt the tailor to do the job. So he grudgingly brings it over.
The mending of the coat seems to take forever, because the two
men engage in a flow of witty and inventive dialogue. Sharing
conversation, good tobacco, and food, they slowly regain their
friendship. Clancy's visits are supposedly to check on the
progress being made on his coat. The coat never does get
mended, but the friendship is renewed. In the meantime each
man learns to forgive and to realize that a moment's anger cannot destroy true friendship.

The Clown of God
Tomie de Paola
Harcourt Brace Jovanovich, 1978

ONE OF THE most insistent questions in a child's (or an adult's) life is what to do with the talents he or she has been given. What am I good at? What will I be when I grow up? A child's belief that he or she has something to offer is the basis of hope and of future achievement. The alternative is despair, which can lead to withdrawal or even violence. *The Clown of God* is an ancient story, first told in the Renaissance, which assures a child that everyone has been given a gift that can bring happiness to others. The orphan boy Giovanni survives by juggling in front of Signor Baptista's vegetable stand, for which he is paid with a bowl of soup. Later, he sees a troupe of traveling players and joins them. As Giovanni matures into manhood, he develops a wonderful act: the grand finale involves juggling a large number of rainbow-colored balls, the last one being golden, "the Sun in the Heavens." One day he meets two Franciscan friars who tell him that "everything sings the glory of God . . . even your juggling." Giovanni doesn't pay much attention to the friars. He goes on to play for princes and their courts. But there comes a time when, as an old man, his act is so well known that no one wants him anymore. He stumbles into a Franciscan church, where he sees the townspeople bearing gifts to the Christ Child at Christmas. When the church is deserted he juggles for the Mother and Child—the only gift he can give. When he throws up the "Sun in the Heavens" he falls down, dead. When the friars find him, one of them points to the statue of the Christ Child, who is holding the golden ball and smiling.

Dogger
Shirley Hughes
Mulberry, 1993 (1977)

AS PARENTS, WE have all rejoiced when we witnessed one of our children performing an unselfish act, whether it was pushing a little sister on a swing or helping a baby brother climb the stairs. It reassures us that we are succeeding in the demanding task of teaching our children to develop into compassionate and caring individuals, more concerned with the needs of others than of themselves. *Dogger* is a story of just such an act of selfless love. When Dave loses his favorite friend—a stuffed toy called Dogger—he is heartbroken. Where can it be? Dave's family turns the house upside down in its search . . . but to no avail. The next day, Dave is horrified to discover Dogger sitting on a stall at the school fair. But before Dave can get Dogger back, a little girl buys him and refuses to give him up. Then Bella, Dave's older sister, does a remarkable thing; she offers the teddy bear she has just won in a raffle in exchange for Dogger. Childhood is full of these small, but significant, acts of heroism. We actually know of a six-year-old girl who, having just had *Dogger* read to her by her mother, immediately went and wrapped one of her Mickey Mouse toys in left-over Christmas paper, then presented it to her four-year-old brother. When her mother asked her why she had done this, she replied: "I had two Mickeys and he didn't. So I gave him one of mine, just like Bella."

Elfwyn's Saga
David Wisniewski
Lothrop, 1990

IN MANY OF the best children's stories, it is a child who saves the day. The child's innocence and lack of guile enable him or her to see evil for what it is; the adults are too caught up in their own cares and desires to perceive the dangers that lurk nearby. *Elfwyn's Saga* is just such a story, a breathtakingly beautiful picture book illustrated with photographic reproductions of paper cutouts. Drawing on ancient Icelandic tales, David Wisniewski tells an original story of Anlaf Haraldson and his people, who claim a rich valley for their dwelling place.

Gorm the Grim, who wants the valley for himself, pronounces a curse on Anlaf, and the result is that Anlaf's daughter, Elfwyn, is born blind. Young Elfwyn, however, is beloved of the Hidden Folk, good spirits who can intervene in human affairs. One day Gorm delivers a gift that is supposed to bring reconciliation—a huge crystal. But when Anlaf and his people gaze into the crystal, they see visions that make them discontented with their lot in life. Elfwyn's mother, for example, sees herself as a younger, more beautiful woman. Only the blind Elfwyn is protected from the evil of the crystal. She destroys it, and in doing so, she gains her sight, and Gorm is blinded. Children need to be reminded that they possess special qualities that they should never lose—such as an innocence that is precious, that must somehow survive the complex process of growing up. Books like this help to instill this belief in their hearts.

The Emperor and the Kite
Jane Yolen. Illustrated by Ed Young.
World, 1967

THE EMPEROR OF China has four sons and four daughters, but the youngest of the daughters is so tiny that no one pays her any attention at all. Djeow Seow, whose name means "the smallest one," cannot compete with her powerful prince brothers or her radiant princess sisters. So she consoles herself by flying a kite. She does this with such intensity that her kite is described as "a flower in the sky" and "a prayer in the wind." But only a passing monk recognizes the beauty of Djeow Seow's kite; he composes a haiku poem for her: "My kite sails upward, / Mounting to the high heavens. / My soul goes on wings." The peace of the kingdom is shattered when evil men kidnap the emperor and rule in his stead. All Djeow Seow's brothers and sisters give up hope and do nothing. But she uses her kite to take food to the high tower where her father is kept. Thanks to a hint from the monk, she figures out a way to rescue her father. In gratitude, the emperor gives her his love, and she is allowed to rule beside him. Jane Yolen's fairy tale is a wonderful affirmation of a small child's loyalty and love. One of the oldest morals in all traditions is that large size, strength, or beauty do not necessarily make for goodness. As a child grows up, confronting older siblings and tired, harried parents, he or she needs to hear this moral. The Caldecott prize winner Ed Young brings his knowledge of Chinese culture to bear on the book's illustrations.

Forest of Dreams
Rosemary Wells. Illustrated by Susan Jeffers.
Dial Books for Young Readers, 1988

FOREST OF DREAMS is a little girl's hymn of thanksgiving for God's marvelous handiwork—nature and her own five senses. In winter she says, "God gave me eyes. . . . To watch the winter sun last every evening one more minute," and we see her frolicking in the snow among the animals of the field. In spring she says, "God lets me . . . smell the sunlight burrow softly underground." Illustrated with beautiful paintings by Susan Jeffers, this delightful book is filled with a child's unalloyed joy in nature. We know a young mother who, having given birth to her baby during the long Canadian winter, took her infant daughter out into the garden on a warm day in May. She was astonished when the baby burrowed her nose deep into the young grass to smell it. Although only three months old, that tiny girl, like the little girl in *Forest of Dreams,* knew a miracle when she smelled it.

The Gold Coin
Alma Flor Ada
Atheneum, 1991, 32 pages

THERE ARE TIMES when we learn something important without seeking that knowledge. There are times, indeed, when we run away from the truth, only to end up stumbling right into it. This original tale, set in Central America, will introduce children to just such an irony. Juan has been a thief for many years: he is pale, stooped, and shriveled because he steals at night. One night he peers into the home of an old woman, Doña Josefa, and sees her looking at a gold coin. He immediately assumes she is hiding a fortune in gold. When he ransacks her house the next morning, after she has gone out, he finds nothing. The rest of the story tells of his attempt to track her down. Each time he tries to catch up with her, he discovers that he is too late. He is told that Doña Josefa is a "healer" who has gone on to help the next sick person. In order to get transportation, Juan is forced to work in the fields to enable the farmers to finish their jobs and bring him closer to Doña Josefa. Children will recognize that the honest work Juan is forced to do begins to change him. The illustrations show Juan's face and figure becoming more natural and healthy. But he pursues Doña Josefa doggedly, and finally demands all her gold. "Have you come for the gold coin?" she replies. "I have been trying hard to give it to someone who might need it." But, she says, no one will accept it; people are grateful for her skills as a nurse. When she gives him the coin—the last thing he expects—he is stunned. Then she is called away to deliver a baby. But Juan knows, at last, what to do with that coin.

The Griffin and the Minor Canon
Frank Stockton. Illustrated by Maurice Sendak.
HarperCollins, 1986 (1963), 56 pages

THIS CHARMING TALE of the mythical beast who befriends a minor canon teaches, among other things, that it is not always wise to judge by appearances. When the last griffin on earth hears of a stone griffin carved over the door of a church, he is filled with curiosity. His arrival in the town causes great alarm; who's to say that this fearsome-looking beast won't gobble up all the children for breakfast? Only the minor canon is brave enough, and wise enough, to know that a beast that looks so terrifying on the outside might be as gentle as a lamb on the inside. Masterfully illustrated by the renowned Maurice Sendak, this beautiful story reassures us that it is gentleness of heart, not appearance, that ultimately counts.

The Happy Funeral
Eve Bunting. Illustrated by Vo-Dinh Mai.
HarperCollins, 1982, 40 pages

OVERCOME WITH GRIEF at the death of her beloved grandfather, Laura cannot understand what her mother means when she tells her that he will have a "happy funeral." What's happy about it? she thinks as she sees her grandmother and parents crying. But when she looks at her grandfather's face, she suddenly understands that "when someone . . . has lived a good life, he is happy to go. . . . [Mom] never said it was happy for us to have him go." Laura's understanding of the goodness of her grandfather's life gives her permission to grieve. Set in a Chinese-American community, well known for its reverence for the elderly, *The Happy Funeral* does not evade the reality of death; rather, it shows how to accept it with wisdom and courage. Any child who has suffered bereavement cannot fail to be comforted by such an honest and compassionate approach.

Harald and the Giant Knight
and *Harald and the Great Stag*
Donald Carrick
Clarion, 1988 (both books)

MEDIEVAL ENGLAND WAS a time of great contrasts: the rich were very powerful and the poor very poor indeed. Harald is a peasant boy whose parents farm a baron's lands. At every turn their simple lives are disrupted by the whims of their feudal lord. In *Harald and the Giant Knight,* the baron takes over Harald's farm to use as a jousting ring. Up till now Harald has regarded the knights with respect and admiration; now he sees them in a new light. No longer do they appear to be men dedicated to honor and chivalry; instead, they turn out to be nothing more than robbers, intent on their own selfish gratification. In *Harald and the Great Stag* the baron hunts down a mighty symbol of the forest for mere sport. In both books Harald's inventive wit secretly undermines the baron's destructive plans. In a culture where violence and greed are glorified so extensively by the media, these stories remind us that authentic nobility resides in virtues such as honor and compassion rather than in force of arms or our own selfish desires.

The High Rise Glorious Skittle Skat Roarious Sky Pie Angel Food Cake
Nancy Willard. Illustrated by Richard Jesse Watson. Harcourt Brace Jovanovich, 1990

THE TITLE OF this book is a fairly good indicator of the exuberance to follow. From the marvelous opening sentence—"Let me tell you about my angels"—to its concluding twist, this is a wild and enchanting parable. A young girl is asked by her mother to bake a mysterious cake for the mother's birthday. The cake was invented by the girl's great-grandmother, who kept the recipe secret, because it "is irresistible to man and beast, woman and bird. I fear it may fall into the wrong hands." But the girl searches in her great-grandmother's diaries and around the house, and finds the recipe. As the sun rises on her mother's birthday, and the girl fears her attempt to bake the cake has been a disaster, she is visited by three rather unconventional angels. In the end, she learns something about the bonds of love that link the generations, and the true nature of giving. Richard Jesse Watson's vibrantly colored illustrations provide the perfect visual counterpart to this inventive tale. Nancy Willard begins her story with a quotation from G. K. Chesterton that sets the tone for what is to come: "Angels fly because they take themselves lightly."

Ida and the Wool Smugglers
Sue Ann Alderson. Illustrated by Ann Blades.
Macmillan, 1988

LONG AGO IN Canada, there lived a little girl called Ida. She was not young enough to sleep in the baby's cradle like her little sister, nor yet old enough to accompany her big brother on the annual sheep run. All she was good for, it seemed, was to carry her mother's freshly baked bread to a neighbor who had just had a baby. "Will Mrs. Springman let me hold the baby?" Ida asks her mother hopefully. There must be something she is big enough to do! But her mother shakes her head. "Probably not," she says. "The Springmans' baby is too small to be passed around to small children." Ida's hopes are dashed again! Just as she is about to set off on her errand, Ida's mother warns her of the sheep smugglers and instructs her to run for help if she spots them. How Ida saves her favorite sheep and her two lambs from the smugglers, and how she gets to hold Mrs. Springman's baby after all, complete this satisfying story about a small child's yearning for meaningful responsibility. As all mothers will attest, their children's happiest moments are often spent helping their parents around the house. We have watched a father take his children and a crowd of their friends out into the yard to build a sandbox. Far from getting in his way, they helped him by passing him nails and steadying the pieces of lumber so he could measure them. A year later, their mother reports that playing in the sandbox is still the children's favorite game. It stands to reason; after all, they helped build it!

In My Mother's House (CH)
Ann Nolan Clark. Illustrated by Velino Herrara.
Viking, 1991 (1941), 56 pages

AWARDED THE CALDECOTT Honor Prize for its outstanding illustrations, In My Mother's House is a collection of verse sung by the Tewa children of Tesuque Pueblo near Santa

Fe. "In my Mother's house," begins one poem, "There is a fire-place: . . . The fire is always there, . . . / To keep me warm." Filled with pictures and text that evoke not only the age-old traditions of the Tewa Indians but also the gratitude of a young child who knows himself to be loved and cared for, *In My Mother's House* gives us a privileged insight into a hard-working and closely knit community of Native Americans. The village and the fields, one child sings, "make a strong chain, / To hold me close to home, / Where I live, / In my mother's house."

Just Like Max
Karen Ackerman. Illustrated by George Schmidt.
Knopf, 1990, 32 pages

SEVEN-YEAR-OLD Aaron lives in a large brownstone house in New York City. Although an only child, Aaron is never lonely; his grandparents live on the second floor, Aunt Mala lives above him on the third, and, best of all, great-uncle Max lives at the top of the house, on the fourth floor. Uncle Max is special; he is a tailor, and his tiny room is covered with patterns and great colorful bolts of cloth. Aaron loves watching his grandfather at work but, above all, he loves to listen to Uncle Max's stories. Then one day Uncle Max falls sick, and when he returns from the hospital, he has lost the use of his hands. Now Aaron must continue the legacy that Max has bequeathed to him. Years later, another little boy comes into the fourth-floor room: " 'What's that, Uncle Aaron?' he asks, pointing to the page in the typewriter. . . . 'It's about a boy whose uncle was a tailor and a story-teller,' I say softly . . . and begin to read." *Just Like Max* is more than the heart-warming story of an old man's love for a small boy; it is a reminder of the legacy we can leave to our children by the example of our own lives.

King Nimrod's Tower
Leon Garfield. Illustrated by Michael Bragg.
Lothrop, 1982

BASED ON THE biblical story of the Tower of Babel, *King Nimrod's Tower* relates the consequences of King Nimrod's overweening pride from an unusual perspective—that of a young boy and his irrepressible puppy! In the end, it is the boy and his dog who unwittingly save the people of Babylon from utter destruction. Unwilling to hurt an innocent boy and his dog by destroying the tower, God throws confusion into the workmen by making them speak in different tongues. At that very moment, the boy commands the dog to sit, and then adds as an afterthought, "because I only want to be your friend." Instead of resorting to force like King Nimrod, the boy chose the way of love and humility. By bridging the gap between himself and the dog through friendship, he had unwittingly built a bridge to heaven. God Himself says, "Because My Kingdom of Heaven is better reached . . . by a bridge than by a tower."

The King's Fountain
Lloyd Alexander. Illustrated by Ezra Jack Keats.
E. P. Dutton, 1971

THIS VOLUME IS the product of a collaboration between two of our finest creators of books for children. According to the note at the back of this book, as Alexander and Keats talked in Keats's studio one day, they discussed "the need for the individual to act when life demands action." "I wanted to explore ideas of personal responsibility and of people discovering in themselves resources they never expected," says Alexander. The product is *The King's Fountain*. A poor man discovers that the king plans to build a fountain that takes all of the city's water. He seeks help from a scholar, a merchant, and a blacksmith. None of them can help. The scholar is too caught up in his lofty thoughts. The merchant, despite his way with words, is afraid to confront the king. The blacksmith threatens to smash the castle to pieces—an ill-advised plan that would only bring him a term in the king's dungeon. Distraught, the poor man returns to his home. His young daughter suggests that he go to the king himself. He overcomes his fear and marches off to the castle. When he makes his petition, the king threatens to have him killed. But the poor man states his case once more. The king changes his mind, because he recognizes that the poor man has not attempted to use fancy language or force to get his way. Keats's rich, atmospheric acrylic paintings provide a perfect complement to Alexander's simple tale. In the note at the back of the book, Keats and Alexander quote these words from the Jewish thinker Hillel: "If I am not for myself, who will be for me? And if I am only for myself, what am I? And if not now, when?"

The Little Brute Family
Russell Hoban. Illustrated by Lillian Hoban.
Macmillan, 1966

NO ONE IN the Brute family seems to particularly enjoy life. At dinnertime nobody says please or thank you; nobody says, "How delightful!" (Admittedly, the stew of sticks and stones doesn't exactly encourage this!) The little house resounds all day long with growls, grumbles, and snarls. Then one day, Baby Brute finds a good feeling lost in the forest and decides to take it home with him. What happens when the good feeling flies out of his pocket and how the Brute family eventually comes to live in peace and harmony complete this satisfying story. As in all books for very young children, *The Little Brute Family*'s central theme is a wonderfully simple one—namely, that good behavior is contagious and that true happiness depends upon the way we treat others. Humorously written and accompanied with delightfully droll illustrations, *The Little Brute Family* is guaranteed to civilize the brute in any child!

The Little House (C)
Virginia Lee Burton
Houghton Mifflin, 1969 (1942), 40 pages

WE REMEMBER THAT our daughters couldn't get enough of this story when they were very young. They seemed to love the idea of a little house caring about the family that lived inside its walls, and when the little house was swallowed up by the growth of a huge city around it, they invariably shed tears of sympathy. Long considered a classic of children's fiction, *The Little House* reassures the very young child that permanence and stability are possible, despite a world filled with the pain of separated families and widespread homelessness.

The Man Who Kept His Heart in a Bucket
Sonia Levitin. Illustrated by Jerry Pinkney.
Dial Books for Young Readers, 1991

JACK'S HEART HAS been broken once, and he is determined that it will never happen again. Consequently, he keeps his heart in a bucket! A metalworker by trade, he carries his heart around wherever he goes. But for all its safety, his heart is sadly lacking in feeling. When the baker gives him a piece of blackberry pie to taste, he asks him, "What do you feel when you eat my blackberry pie?" "Full" is the prosaic reply. And when a poor peasant woman offers to let Jack hold her baby, he replies, "I cannot hold little things that squirm and cry." Then one day, Jack forgetfully dips his bucket into the river and—lo and behold!—a beautiful maiden springs out of the river. How the maiden sets Jack a riddle that teaches him how to appreciate blackberry pie, babies, music, and a host of other things completes this delightfully wise tale. The heart cannot be hoarded, the story reminds us. It must be given away if we are to enjoy life's many blessings. In a culture dominated by a psychology of the self, this is liberating indeed!

Marcella's Guardian Angel
Evaline Ness
Holiday House, 1979

MARCELLA'S SCHOOLMATES THINK she has gone
crazy! She keeps slapping the back of her neck and craning her
head around to look behind her. What they don't know is that
Marcella has a guardian angel—a pesky little creature that has
the uncomfortable habit of telling Marcella precisely what she
has done wrong. "RUDE!" she yells when Marcella pushes to
the front of the line at the drinking fountain; "STINGY!"
when Marcella refuses to share; "LIAR!" "SLOB!" No wonder Marcella wants to send her packing—it's not easy having a
conscience! How Marcella plays the "flip-flop" game in order
to get rid of her guardian angel and, more important, how she
comes to reform her selfish ways complete this humorous original story. "Wait a minute," says Marcella at the end of the
story. " 'You said "Angel" is your nickname. What's your *real*
name?' '*Marcella*,' said Angel."

Ophelia's Shadow Theatre
Michael Ende. Illustrated by Friedrich Hechelmann.
Overlook, 1989

THE GERMAN WRITER Michael Ende has become well
known in America for his books *The Neverending Story* and
Momo, both of which have been made into motion pictures. In
Ophelia's Shadow Theatre, Ende has created a tale with the
power and poignancy of myth, a work that demands comparison with *The Golden Key* by George MacDonald. (See page
220.) It is a story about the power of the imagination to plumb
the depths of human experience, and to deepen our compassion and understanding. Ophelia is an old woman who works
as a prompter in a provincial theater; over the years she learns
all the world's great comedies and tragedies by heart. But then
the theater, a casualty of the television age, closes down. In her
loneliness she discovers a shadow named Shady, who is unat-

tached to anyone. Ophelia allows him to become attached to
her. Soon other shadows come to her—Dark Dismay, All
Alone, Nevermore, Sad-and-Sorry. When the shadows begin to
quarrel, Ophelia decides to teach them all the plays she knows.
Then she takes her shadow theater on the road, to great ac-
claim. Until one day a shadow named Death comes to her. But
her greatest performance is yet to come.

Owl Moon (**C**)
Jane Yolen. Illustrated by John Schoenherr.
Philomel, 1987

THIS MARVELOUS BOOK, winner of the Caldecott Medal
for its outstanding atmospheric illustrations, conveys such a
sense of harmony between parent and child that, on publication, it instantly became a classic. A young girl and her father
go deep into the snowy woods in search of owls. Silently, hand
in hand, under a full moon they listen to the sounds of the
night and call to the birds. Suddenly they hear an answering
call and a shadow comes swooping out of the woods toward
them. They stare transfixed, and afterward, as they trudge
home through the snow, they are happy because they have
been vouchsafed an experience of the mystery of nature.
"When you go owling you don't need words or warm or anything but hope."

Miss Rumphius
Barbara Cooney
Viking, 1988

WINNER OF The American Book Award, *Miss Rumphius*
is the story of one woman's determination to "do something to
make the world more beautiful." After traveling around the
world in search of beautiful faraway places, Miss Rumphius
returns home to her little house by the sea. There she tends her
garden and is almost, but not quite, perfectly happy. She can-

not forget her grandfather's words that she should try to leave the world a more beautiful place than she found it. Then she hits upon an idea; in the spring she will walk around the countryside scattering hundreds of lupine seeds. When they grow, she will have shared her love of flowers with countless others. By the time her life is almost over, Miss Rumphius has come to be known as the Lupine Lady and is a great favorite with the local children. She tells them stories of all the places she has visited but, most important, she passes on to them her grandfather's wise words of advice. *Miss Rumphius* is not only about the love of nature, it is about the cultivation of the young so that seeds of virtue will spring up and flourish. Only then, Miss Rumphius tells her great-grandniece, will we have made the world "more beautiful." We also recommend *Hattie and the Wild Waves,* by the same author.

The Runaway Bunny
Margaret Wise Brown. Illustrated by Clement Hurd.
HarperCollins, 1977 (1942), 40 pages

WE KNOW OF no other author for children who can create such an atmosphere of loving security as Margaret Wise Brown. In *The Runaway Bunny* she perfectly captures the need of the very young child to assert his independence and at the same time to know that he is cherished and safe. When a little bunny tells his mother that he will run away, she replies that she will always be near him, for she loves him so. "If you become a bird and fly away from me," she says, "I will be a tree that you can come home to." This is a marvelous book that warmly asserts the value of motherly love within the protective confines of home.

The Story About Ping
Marjorie Flack and Kurt Wiese
Viking, 1961 (1933), 32 pages

IN ONE OF our favorite childhood stories, we can still re-member the picture of Ping the little duck waddling up the gangplank of a boat on the Yangtze River in China. Sur-rounded by his large family, Ping is blissfully happy until the day he is inadvertently left behind on the shore of the river. Lonely for his mother, father, two sisters, three brothers, eigh-teen uncles and aunts, and forty-two cousins (we told you it was a *large* family!), he swims into the middle of the river in search of them. How Ping is found by a small boy, comes close to being eaten for dinner, is rescued by the same boy, and is eventually reunited with his family completes this charming tale. Any child who has experienced the terror of being lost in a crowded shopping mall or in a park cannot fail to sympathize with Ping. Along with Ping and with Dorothy in *The Wonder-ful Wizard of Oz,* all children instinctively know that "there is no place like home."

The Story of Ferdinand
Munro Leaf
Puffin, 1977 (1936), 68 pages

ALL THE WORLD knows that Ferdinand the bull is as placid as a lamb and wishes for nothing better than to smell the flowers under the corkwood tree. All but the bullfighters, that is. When Ferdinand is stung by a bee, the men mistake his an-gry snortings of pained surprise for fierce valor. This charming and wise tale teaches that we should not always judge others by our own, sometimes flawed, standards.

Through Grandpa's Eyes
Patricia MacLachlan
Illustrated by Deborah Kogan Ray.
Harper Trophy, 1983

THIS HEARTWARMING STORY is about the gift of sight that a grandfather gives his little grandson. But it is no ordinary gift . . . for Grandpa is blind. "Where's Nana?" John asks one morning. "Close your eyes, John, and look through my eyes," his grandfather replies, and straightaway John hears pots banging and smells food cooking. His grandmother is in the kitchen fixing breakfast. By looking through Grandpa's eyes, John comes to realize that the world is a much more interesting place than he had once thought: he hears more, smells more, feels more. *Through Grandpa's Eyes* is a story in the tradition of older, wiser cultures than our own. Like the Native American, African, and Asian cultures, it not only illustrates treatment of the elderly with great respect, but also shows that we can learn much from their wisdom if we have the patience and humility to see the world "through [their] eyes."

Thy Friend, Obadiah
Brinton Turkle
Puffin, 1982, 38 pages

SET ON NINETEENTH-CENTURY Nantucket Island, this story is as simple and wise as the Quaker community in which little Obadiah lives. Surrounded by a loving family with four brothers and sisters, Obadiah does not consider himself in need of another friend. The only trouble is that a sea gull seems to have adopted him. When he comes out of the candle maker's, the gull is there. It even follows Obadiah to the meetinghouse on Sunday, and at night keeps vigil on a chimney pot by his bedroom window. "Thee has a friend, Obadiah," his father teases him, but Obadiah is embarrassed by all this attention and refuses to reciprocate the friendship. Then one day the sea gull disappears and, unaccountably, Obadiah misses its loyal presence. When he finds it starving some time later, its beak ensnared by a fishing hook and line, Obadiah repents of his hardness of heart and sets it free. "Mother," he says as he is being tucked into bed that night. "Since I helped him, I'm *his* friend too." His mother smiles; Obadiah has learned a lesson of friendship.

Tico and the Golden Wings
Leo Lionni
Dragonfly, 1975 (1964)

A FRIEND OF ours remembers this as one of his favorite books in his childhood, and well he may. Lionni's parable about the hopes and dreams of childhood is hauntingly illustrated. As a young bird, Tico has no wings; his friends bring him food and take care of him. He wishes for golden wings, and to his great surprise he gets his wish. But Tico's friends resent his golden wings and shun him. Despite his loneliness, Tico notices the distress of a poor basket maker and offers to help him by giving him one of his golden feathers. Underneath the plucked golden feather is a silky black one, just like the feathers of his friends. Tico goes on to help others in distress, until he has given away all his golden feathers. Though he is now like his friends in outward appearance, and once more accepted by them, Tico knows that he is different, a unique individual. Tico learns that the gifts we are given are valuable only if we share them with others. Our friend, a nonconformist if there ever was one, felt that this book enabled him to cherish his individual identity, while at the same time reminding him to be generous to others.

Tim and Ginger
Edward Ardizzone
Walck, 1965

TIM AND HIS best friend, Ginger, love to play on the beaches at the ocean. Tim also loves to listen to the old boatmen talking about their experiences at sea, but Ginger has little patience for this. "Poof," he says. "I . . . know all about the silly old sea." One day Ginger announces he is going shrimping; when Tim begs him to be careful he gives his characteristic response. "I'm not afraid of your silly old tides." But when Ginger doesn't return and the tide starts to come in, Tim begins to worry. Plucking up his courage he borrows a little rowboat and sets out to find his friend. Beautifully illustrated by the renowned Edward Ardizzone, *Tim and Ginger* is more than a simple story about friendship and courage; it is also a tale that reminds us that pride invariably comes before a fall.

The Tunnel
Anthony Browne
Knopf, 1989

THE TUNNEL IS a contemporary fairy tale; like most fairy tales, it depicts a world in which love and courage can triumph over fear and discord. On the surface, Jack and his sister, Rose, are as different as night and day; Jack lives in the rough-and-tumble world of sports and friends, whereas Rose is a timid and solitary child who lives in an interior world peopled by imaginary characters. They are always fighting. One day, exasperated by their constant bickering, their mother banishes them from the house until lunchtime. Jack immediately begins to look for something to explore and decides to investigate a dark tunnel set in a wall in a junkyard. "Don't go in there," pleads Rose. "There might be witches . . . or goblins." "That's kid's stuff," retorts her brother contemptuously and confidently enters the hole. But Rose knows that, like Alice following the White Rabbit, Jack has entered the realm of the imagination, where terrible things can happen to the unwary. Despite her fear, she resolves to save him. This emotionally charged and dramatically illustrated story tells of the often unsung heroisms of childhood, when courage can overcome fear, and of sibling rivalry resolved through a mutual gift of unselfish love.

Wagon Wheels
Barbara Brenner. Illustrated by Bill Bolognese.
HarperCollins, 1984, 64 pages

BASED ON A true story, *Wagon Wheels* recounts the extra-ordinary courage of one African-American pioneer family and their search for freedom in the West. When Ed Muldie and his three young sons arrive in Nicodemus, Kansas, they believe that they have finally arrived at their destination. But before they can build a house, the winter is upon them and, as one of their neighbors warns, "Winter in Kansas is *mean*." With the help of the Osage Indians, the settlement manages to survive the winter but, come spring, Mr. Muldie is determined to move the family to more sheltered terrain. He sets off alone, leaving his sons behind. Then, one day, he sends word for them to join him and gives them directions. With nothing but a rifle to protect them, the boys embark on their journey of one hundred fifty miles. *Wagon Wheels* is the inspiring story of three boys' courage, and how their trust in their father enables them to make such an arduous and dangerous journey on their own.

Waiting for Hannah
Marisabina Russo
Greenwillow, 1989, 32 pages

ONE DAY LITTLE Hannah asks the question that most young children ask their mothers sooner or later. Pointing to a pregnant lady in a grocery store, she says, "Mama, did you look like that when you were going to have me?" What ensues is the loving recounting of the joyful anticipation felt by Hannah's parents while awaiting her birth. Paralleling the growth of Hannah inside her mother is a morning glory vine that has been planted in her parents' window box. On the day that Hannah is born the morning glory blossoms. "It was a beautiful pink flower," her mother recalls in wonder. This warm, simple tale of the miracle of life reassures the very young child that she has been beloved and cared for by her parents from the very beginning.

The Warrior and the Wiseman
David Wisniewski
Lothrop, 1989

"LONG AGO IN Japan, an emperor had twin sons. They were alike in every feature and gesture, yet very different in nature and temperament." Although both sons are beloved of their father, Tozaemon is a warrior, fierce and brave, whereas Toeman is mild of temperament but wise. In order to decide which son is to rule after him, the emperor sets them a task; they must bring him the five elements—earth, wind, fire, air, and water—commanded by the five eternal Demons. Whoever does so first, the emperor decides, will be worthy to succeed him. Each brother carries out his quest according to his own particular nature, and with very different results. Tozaemon brings home all five elements, whereas Toeman can manage only one. The emperor is about to confirm Tozaemon as emperor when he becomes aware of a vast army gathered at the gates of his palace in revenge for Tozaemon's destructive method of acquiring the elements. Now only the gentle but quick-witted Toeman can save them. If the story is noteworthy, the unusual illustrations to *The Warrior and the Wiseman* are even more so. Cut out of art paper with an X-Acto blade (over eight hundred pieces of paper were used!), the illustrations, with their painstaking intricacy, are a reminder that in this world beauty and harmony are achieved more through moral precision than through the use of brute strength.

When I Was Young in the Mountains (**CH**)
Cynthia Rylant. Illustrated by Diane Goode.
Puffin, 1982

"WHEN I WAS young in the mountains" is the refrain that runs through this childhood recollection, weaving together scenes of family worship, mealtimes, quiet evenings on the porch, childhood play, and much more. Narrated in a tone filled with gratitude for a happy childhood and dedicated to the author's grandparents, *When I Was Young in the Mountains* is a hymn of thanksgiving for the simple joys of family life.

Where the Wild Things Are (**C**)
Maurice Sendak
Harper Trophy, 1963

LONG CONSIDERED A masterpiece of children's fiction, Maurice Sendak's *Where the Wild Things Are* is much more than a celebration of the glorious anarchy of the imagination. It is a story of how a young boy comes to understand the loneliness his mother feels when he rebels against her firm, though loving, discipline. Banished to his room for bad behavior, Max decides to "run away" to the imaginary kingdom of the "wild things." Here he proves himself more than a match for their wildness, and is promptly made "king of all the wild things." Gleefully, he presides over the "wild rumpus" that ensues—a comic equivalent to the havoc he has caused in his home. But once the festivities are over and the monsters are asleep, Max begins to realize that ruling over the wild things is not such an easy task after all, and he begins to feel homesick. When he returns home, he finds that his mother has brought his supper to his room and that "it [is] still hot." Max's relieved smile tells us that parental discipline at a child's misbehavior does not cancel out love and that the sense of estrangement that sometimes follows is only temporary. This story is as much an affirmation of the enduring bonds between parent and child as it is about the wonderful breadth of the imagination.

Wilfred Gordon McDonald Partridge
Mem Fox. Illustrated by Julie Vivas.
Kane/Miller, 1985

WILFRED GORDON MCDONALD Partridge is incongruously small to have such a big name. But, as we are soon to discover, his young heart is big enough to do justice to it. Living next door to a home for the elderly, Wilfred soon makes friends with all the inhabitants; "Mrs. Jordan who played the organ . . . Mr. Tippett who was crazy about cricket," and, best of all, "Miss Nancy Alison Delacourt Cooper because she had four names just as he did." Then one day, Wilfred learns that Miss Cooper has lost her memory. "What's a memory?" he asks his father. "Something you remember" is the reply. Dissatisfied with this answer, Wilfred asks all the old people in turn and gets a different answer each time. A memory is "something warm," says Mrs. Gordon; "something from long ago," says Mr. Hosking; "something that makes you cry," "something that makes you laugh," "something as precious as gold." He is determined to give his friend her memory back— and the results are extraordinary. This warm, humorous story about the friendship between a very young boy and a ninety-six-year-old woman reminds us that our memories are the storehouses of all that we are. As the great Saint Augustine said in his *Confessions,* "The power of the memory is great, O Lord. It is awe-inspiring in its profound and incalculable complexity. Yet it is my mind: it is my self."

Yonder
Tony Johnston. Illustrated by Lloyd Bloom.
Dial Books for Young Readers, 1991, 32 pages

THERE IS NO overt moral to this story. Rather, its value lies in its simple evocation of the glories of family life and of nature. "Yonder," it begins, and our eye is immediately drawn to a lush sweep of land in the background and, in the foreground, to a single figure riding a black horse. This is a farmer who is soon to be married. He brings his wife to live on the land and they plant a tree to signal the beginning of their new life together. They have many children, and, for each one, a young tree is planted. The trees and the children grow together and, in time, the children's children are playing in their sturdy branches. Life is precious, the story tells us through its simple text and vibrant oil color illustrations. Let us cherish and respect it.

The Young Artist
Thomas Locker
Dial Books for Young Readers, 1989

THIS IS A special book because it deals directly with the central moral issue of art. Is the artist obliged to be honest in his depiction of the world around him? Is art merely a pleasing decoration, or should it tell the truth, regardless of those who are offended by such honesty? An old and accomplished painter takes on a phenomenally talented young man named Adrian as his apprentice. When Adrian is asked to paint a portrait of the king's chef, he experiences for the first time the dilemma about truth in art. The success of this portrait leads the king to commission Adrian to paint his entire court on a huge canvas. All the members of the court, with one exception, demand that Adrian paint them without their blemishes: the stooped duchess wants to be depicted standing erect, and the fat finance minister expects to be shown as a trim and handsome man. Adrian is plunged into despair. His attempts at this flattering portrait are false and unconvincing. Only the young princess refuses to make any demands on Adrian, and her innocence draws him out of his depression. When the king and court storm into Adrian's studio to demand what he is doing, they see dozens of portraits of the princess. The king, despite the outrage of his court, recognizes the beauty of these works and rewards Adrian. Locker's luminous oil paintings, in the tradition of the Dutch masters, make the tale completely convincing. If you have a budding artist in your home, this is the book for him or her.

Fables and Fairy Tales

Fairy tales, then, are not responsible for producing in children fear, or any of the shapes of fear; fairy tales do not give the child the idea of the evil or the ugly; that is in the child already, because it is in the world already. Fairy tales do not give a child his first idea of bogey. What fairy tales give the child is his first clear idea of the possible defeat of bogey. The baby has known the dragon intimately ever since he had an imagination. What the fairy tale provides for him is a St. George to kill the dragon.

—G. K. Chesterton

Younger Readers

Beauty: A Retelling of Beauty & the Beast
Robin McKinley
Green Tiger, 1989, 45 pages

MOST CHILDREN TODAY are familiar only with the Belle of the celebrated Walt Disney production, in which she agrees to be a perpetual prisoner in the Beast's castle. But in the original story the stakes are infinitely higher—Beauty knows that she is going to certain death when she agrees to take her father's place. It is precisely this act of sacrificial love that ultimately leads to the restoration of the Beast's humanity. Through Beauty's unselfish example, he comes to realize that true beauty resides in the power to love rather than in external appearances. Beauty tells the Beast, "I would rather have goodness under an ugly form than evil hidden under the form of beauty. I remember having seen many brutes in the form of men." Sumptuously illustrated by a variety of renowned nineteenth-century illustrators, this retelling breathes life back into an ancient and wise tale.

The Book of Virtues: A Treasury of Great Moral Stories
Edited, with commentary, by William Bennett
Simon & Schuster, 1993, 831 pages

WHATEVER ONE MAY think of Bill Bennett's neoconservative politics, his collection of moral stories, *The Book of*

Virtues, ought to be welcomed by all Americans. There is nothing ideological or partisan about this humane and balanced anthology. *The Book of Virtues* contains fables and fairy tales, and much more—including fiction, poetry, songs, speeches, biblical stories, and oaths. The book is divided into ten virtues: Self-Discipline, Compassion, Responsibility, Friendship, Work, Courage, Perseverance, Honesty, Loyalty, and Faith. From Greek myths to Chinese Taoism, from the Founding Fathers to the heroes of the Underground Railroad and the civil rights movement, from Aesop to William Faulkner—this huge treasury is a library unto itself. Bennett's brief introductions to each section and his notes are succinct and to the point. The selections are geared primarily to younger and middle readers.

Dawn
Molly Bang
Mulberry, 1983

MOLLY BANG'S ADAPTATION of the Japanese folktale "The Crane Wife" is a bittersweet fable about love and self-sacrifice. One day a shipbuilder sees a Canada goose in a swamp. The goose has been shot. He nurses it back to health and it flies away. Not long after, a tall, beautiful woman arrives and asks the shipbuilder if he needs someone to make sails. He hires her, then falls in love with her. They marry and she bears a child. When he builds a boat for his little family, his wife makes a special set of sails that are strong and yet light; he calls them Wings of Steel. When a man commissions a racing schooner from the shipbuilder, he demands sails made like the Wings of Steel. At first his wife refuses, saying that they are only for the family, but the shipbuilder is eager to build the boat and persuades her to agree. She forbids him to enter the room where she weaves the sails, but just before they are finished he bursts into the room. He finds a large Canada goose that has plucked the last of her breast feathers to complete the sails. Then a flock of other geese come and take her away. The Wings of Steel, of course, represent the self-sacrifice that the woman makes for her family, something that cannot be turned into a commodity. The shipbuilder, who rescued the goose-woman, has betrayed his own act of kindness by becoming obsessed with the building of the boat. Though bittersweet, the story ends on a note of hope: Dawn, the daughter, promises to go off in the sailboat and find her mother; Dawn will return in the spring, with the other geese.

Dear Mili
Wilhelm Grimm. Illustrated by Maurice Sendak.
Farrar, Straus and Giroux, 1988

THE TITLE OF this charming fairy tale comes from a recently discovered letter written to a little girl by Wilhelm Grimm in 1816. In it he writes, "Dear Mili . . . you say, 'Tell me a story.' [My heart] replies: 'Yes, dear Mili, just listen.' " And he goes on to recount the adventures of a little girl called Mili, who is sent into a forest by her mother to hide her from the soldiers who are threatening the village. Mili wanders on alone and eventually becomes lost; a white bird leads her to the hut of a saintly old man, who receives her graciously and cares for her. Mili stays with him three days and, at the end of that time, the old man gives her a rose to take to her mother, saying, "When this rose blooms, you will be with me again." Mili carries the flower to her mother and discovers that not three days but thirty years have elapsed. That night the rose blooms, and both Mili and her mother die and go to heaven, where the old man, Saint Joseph, is waiting to welcome them. Despite the enchantment of the fairy tale mode, Dear Mili is actually a profoundly psychological story. It addresses a child's deepest fear—namely, the fear of separation from a parent, either by growing up or by death. By reversing Mili's experience of time—usually, a child feels that three days is the same as thirty years, but the time passes swiftly and happily for Mili—the story reassures the young child that love is able to withstand change and uncertainty. In the end, Mili and her mother are united forever and the family is completed by a father figure. We will never know if the real Mili lived at a time of social unrest (the Napoleonic wars were going on at this time), nor if she lacked a father figure in her life. What we do know is that many children nowadays suffer from the same uncertainties and fears as suggested in this story. No doubt this is why the renowned illustrator Maurice Sendak, who specializes in the pictorial interpretation of children's deepest anxieties, chose to grace such a story with his tender and exquisite illustrations.

The Emperor's New Clothes
Hans Christian Andersen
Retold by Virginia Lee Burton.
Houghton Mifflin, 1949, 44 pages

CHILDREN ARE ENDLESSLY delighted with this fairy tale, because it is a child who points out that the emperor is stark naked. The child gets to laugh at the naughtiness of the naked emperor, and to know that he or she is on the side of truth. But this tale is more than a satire on the emperor's vanity: it is really about the way his courtiers and the inhabitants of the city accept an outrageous lie instead of confronting the truth. The two swindlers who pretend to be making a magnificent new suit for the emperor tell the courtiers that if they cannot see the clothes it is because they are stupid or unworthy for their office. Even the "faithful old Minister" decides to echo the lie rather than risk losing his position. The moral is clear: telling the truth often has a cost. It is the innocence of the child, who has nothing to protect, that allows him to see through the deception. Andersen ends the tale without a trace of sentimentality: instead of running back to his palace in shame, the emperor continues with the procession. Virginia Lee Burton's illustrations for this story have entertained children for over forty years.

Fables
Aesop. Illustrated by Arthur Rackham.
Avenel, 1992 (1912), 224 pages

AESOP'S FABLES have a timeless appeal for the very young.
With the droll use of animal characters and a specific moral at
the end, each story presents the child with an ordered universe,
a world made secure by the inevitability of the lesson drawn at
the end. Recent data in the field of child psychology have revealed that young children develop better when they have
some concrete principle to hold on to than when they are presented with the still popular "discover for yourself" mode of
moral inquiry. This is not new to parents; they have always
known that the best way to teach their children has been
through the medium of story and good example.

The Hare and the Tortoise
Caroline Castle. Illustrated by Peter Weevers.
Dial Books for Young Readers, 1985

THIS RETELLING OF Aesop's well-known fable is particularly fresh and creative. The Hare is depicted as a sweat-suited
fitness freak who is obsessed with himself: an image-conscious
rabbit. The Tortoise, on the other hand, is a retiring scholar,
living in a book-lined room and writing a huge tome entitled
Great Tortoises of the World—at the rate of two pages a day.
Even if he is a bit stuffy, the Tortoise seems more at peace with
himself; he does not feel it necessary to prove his prowess. This
story just might help your child remember that in a fast-mov-
ing, self-conscious society like ours, it is all too easy to start
"running in circles," as the Tortoise chides the Hare.

It Could Always Be Worse (**CH**)
Margot Zemach
Farrar, Straus and Giroux, 1992 (1976)

HERE IS A rollicking tale that proves that in the moral life some things are relative. In the great tradition of Yiddish folk-tales, Margot Zemach introduces us to a man who lives in a small house with his wife, his mother, and his six children. In the cramped quarters the noise, the bickering, and the wailing of children are just too much for the man to take. So he goes to the village rabbi and asks for advice. The rabbi asks if he has any geese or chickens, and then advises him to take them inside his house. When the man returns to the rabbi in greater dismay, the rabbi insists that he take the goat and the cow in too. Children will find Zemach's illustrations of the human-and-animal riot in the house delightful. Finally, the canny rabbi tells the man to put the animals out. The house now seems a heaven of peace and harmony. A child's desires are often just this side of infinite—children are all too apt to complain that they are being given a raw deal. Zemach's tale is a funny, gentle reminder that we should not take our blessings for granted, that the generosity of our emotions can help us to cope with the daily grind of life.

The King of the Golden River
John Ruskin. Illustrated by Richard Doyle.
Dover, 1974 (1841), 68 pages

FIRST PUBLISHED IN 1841, this fairy tale was written by one of the Victorian era's most serious thinkers, the art historian and social thinker John Ruskin. But here Ruskin has subordinated his intellectual earnestness to a story marked by quirky humor and cleverly administered poetic justice. The result is an all-but-forgotten classic. Young Gluck lives with his two older brothers in Treasure Valley, a lush and fruitful place where the Golden River runs. But despite this bounteous place, Gluck's brothers, Hans and Schwartz, are so selfish that they are nicknamed the "Black Brothers." One stormy evening, when his brothers are away, Gluck hears a knocking at the door. He discovers a funny little bearded man, soaking wet, and in need of a meal. He overcomes his fear of his brothers and lets the man in. When the brothers return they are furious, but the old man warns them that he will visit again that night. A devastating storm arrives that night that ruins Treasure Valley. The next morning the brothers find a business card on the kitchen table; it reads, "South West Wind, Esquire." Driven from their valley, the older brothers become goldsmiths who cheat their customers. But Gluck encounters the King of the Golden River, who tells him of a quest that will turn the river into real gold. Of course, the Black Brothers learn of this and attempt the quest themselves. They get their just deserts, while Gluck, through his unselfish willingness to share what he has, succeeds. Richard Doyle's original illustrations grace this edition.

The Lion and the Puppy
Leo Tolstoy. Illustrated by Claus Sievert.
Henry Holt, 1988, 61 pages

COUNT LEO TOLSTOY lived on a large and beautiful estate in the rolling Russian countryside south of Moscow; it was called Yasnaya Polyana, or Whispering Glades. But even as a young man he was concerned with the education of the desperately poor peasant children who lived nearby. And so he opened up a school on his property where children could come and go as they pleased, learning to draw, read, write, and play games. But soon Tolstoy discovered that there was no readily available edition of outstanding folktales and fables to read to the children. And so he wrote his own. What sets the tales in *The Lion and the Puppy* apart from the textbooks of Tolstoy's day is their lack of preachy and moralistic lessons. Most of them, however, are filled with moral wisdom. Among the best are the title story, about friendship, and "The King and the Shirt," a parable about happiness. These brief stories are funny, sad, wise, and utterly timeless—miniature classics from the hand that penned *War and Peace*.

The Little Match Girl
Hans Christian Andersen
Illustrated by Rachel Isadora.
G. P. Putnam and Sons, 1987, 31 pages

IN OUR TIME of increasing homelessness, despite the fact that we live in one of the most affluent cultures the world has ever known, Hans Christian Andersen's story "The Little Match Girl" is a poignant wake-up call to the plight of the less fortunate—many of them street children. The spurt of the matches lighting up the blackness of a cold winter's night casts light on the tragedy of poverty in a way that news reports and statistics can never do. It is with an ache in our hearts that we watch the little match girl expend, one by one, the matches that are her only source of income in order to keep herself from freezing to death. It is with shame mingled with grief that we learn that she has been taken up into a world where man's deadly indifference cannot harm her again. Any child who has been introduced to the desperation of the little match girl will never be tempted to label the poor as "a social problem." Instead, the child will know that true charity consists in buying that one box of matches, or giving a dollar to the "crazy" man on the corner, or filling the pink Salvation Army bag stuck into the mailbox of his warm, comfortable home. For all we know, our simple act of generosity may be the only thing that stands between a homeless person and starvation.

The North Wind and the Sun
Jean de La Fontaine. Illustrated by Brian Wildsmith.
Watts, 1964

LA FONTAINE, LIKE his master Aesop, crafted fables in which our everyday experiences are crystallized into memorable tales. In this fable, the North Wind and the Sun see a man wearing a new cloak; they agree to take turns trying to get the cloak off his back. The North Wind blows hats off people's heads, sends animals scurrying for shelter, and even sinks the ships in the harbor. But the man retains his cloak. Then the Sun comes out, bringing out the flowers and the birds, and inducing people to come out and gossip. Finally, the Sun's heat is too much and the man removes his cloak to go for a swim. "So the Sun was able to achieve by warmth and gentleness what the North Wind in all his strength and fury could not do." Brian Wildsmith's colorful, stylized illustrations complement the text.

The Pied Piper of Hamelin
Retold by Sara and Stephen Corrin
Illustrated by Errol Le Cain.
Harcourt Brace Jovanovich, 1989

THE SLEEPY TOWN of Hamelin is in an uproar! There are rats everywhere—in the baker's flour, under the beds, in every cupboard and kitchen—and the situation is only getting worse. Then a mysterious stranger strolls into town and offers to rid the people of their problem. Our world is very much like the town of Hamelin, ruled more often than not by materialism and a quick-fix mentality. Once the rats are gone, and life returns to normal, the people begin to have second thoughts and resolve to cheat the Piper out of his rightful due. The Piper's terrible revenge—he leads the children through a crack in the mountain to a magical kingdom, and they are never seen again—teaches us that our children cannot flourish in a world that values silver and gold above human life. Perhaps that is why the children of Hamelin follow the Piper so joyfully and why the little crippled boy is broken-hearted at being left behind. Ironically, in recent generations the Piper has come to symbolize an evil, seductive person—quite the opposite of the story's intention. A strongly positive story, *The Pied Piper of Hamelin* reinforces a child's need to feel valued whatever the cost.

The Selfish Giant
Oscar Wilde. Illustrated by Lisbeth Zwerger.
Picture Book Studio, 1984 (1888)

OSCAR WILDE IS legendary as a cynical wit. But he also had a streak of moral and spiritual idealism in him that never died. After all, he himself said, "What is a cynic? A man who knows the price of everything, and the value of nothing." *The Selfish Giant* is one of the most perfect parables ever written to remind us what is valuable in life. When a giant returns after seven years of visiting his friend, an ogre, he discovers children playing in his garden. He immediately puts up a NO TRESPASSING sign. But the results of his selfishness are soon felt: when spring comes to the country, his property remains locked in the sterility of winter. Then one day he thinks spring has come: when he looks out his window he sees children sneaking into his garden. Everywhere they go the trees burst into bloom. Finally his cold heart is warmed. But when he goes out to the garden the children all run away. All but one little boy, who is too small to climb a tree. The giant breaks down the garden wall and welcomes the children into his garden, but the little boy does not come back. Years later he sees the boy again, but his hands and feet have wounds in them. The giant is outraged and wants to punish those who have hurt the child, but the boy says that they are the "wounds of Love." "You let me play once in your garden, today you shall come with me to my garden, which is Paradise." Wilde's use of Christian imagery at the end of the story is appropriate, and far from sentimental. For the giant is really Adam, whose sin is to want the garden all to himself. But the child who reads this story has the assurance that the giant's redemption is achieved.

The Sleeping Beauty
Mercer Mayer
Macmillan, 1984

A FAIRY TALE like that of Sleeping Beauty has been told so many times that the poor versions outnumber the outstanding ones. So often the story seems to be about nothing more than competing magical powers—an excuse for the uttering of spells and for battles with dragons. Mercer Mayer's version, however, is not only a rich and subtle treat for the eye, but also a believable tale of human vanity, envy, courage, and hope. In Mayer's retelling, the story begins when the king's household manager secretly sells a gold goblet and replaces it with a lead goblet that is painted gold. This false goblet offends the Blue Fairy, who pronounces the famous curse on the royal family. Mayer's embellishments include a darker than usual portrait of Sleeping Beauty's father, the king, who suffers from jealousy. When the young prince must pursue his quest for Sleeping Beauty, he does not encounter huge dragons but subtle temptations. The point is not that Mayer is making the story depressing or negative; rather, the psychological integrity of this version is deeply satisfying to us. The resolution of the story requires forgiveness, and it is Sleeping Beauty who forgives the Blue Fairy at the end. Mayer has set the story in the ancient Celtic culture, with its complex, interwoven artistic designs, suggesting the twists and turns of the heart. This is easily the best retelling of the Sleeping Beauty story we have seen.

The Ugly Duckling
Hans Christian Andersen. Retold by Marianna Mayer. Illustrated by Thomas Locker. Macmillan, 1987

WE ARE SO familiar with Hans Christian Andersen's story of the ugly duckling that it has become part of common speech. He or she is "an ugly duckling," we say of a clumsy youth whose arms and legs seem too gangly for his body or of a girl who wears braces on her teeth. "But they'll grow out of it," we add confidently. Without that last statement, the label "ugly duckling" would seem a cruel one indeed. But to admit that it takes time for a child to grow into his or her true identity is far from cruel. All children instinctively know that, before true maturity can be achieved, they must undergo some kind of rite of passage. That is why most fairy tales deal with the theme of transformation through suffering. Cinderella casts off her rags to become a beautiful princess, but only after she has patiently endured the taunts of her ugly sisters; Hansel and Gretel must

suffer hunger and imprisonment before they can kill the
wicked witch in order to make their fortune; and the ugly
duckling must endure loneliness and rejection before he can
grow up to be a beautiful white swan. That is why the great
child psychologist Bruno Bettelheim has called fairy tales
"wishes in disguise." Retold by Marianna Mayer and illustrated by the incomparable artist Thomas Locker, *The Ugly
Duckling* reassures the young child that his wish to grow up
strong and independent will one day come to pass.

Middle Readers

The Cat Who Went to Heaven (**N**)
Elizabeth Coatsworth. Illustrated by Lynd Ward.
Aladdin, 1985 (1958), 64 pages

THE BOOKS THAT are hardest to summarize are often the
best: they seem to contain worlds of meaning; they cannot be
reduced to single themes or issues. This Newbery Medal winner is just such a book. A poor Japanese artist struggles to feed
himself and his housekeeper. One day the housekeeper brings
home a cat; the artist is outraged, because there is so little to
eat. Soon the cat, named Good Fortune by the housekeeper,
amazes the artist by her virtuous behavior: she eats little, and
somehow knows how to encourage him and bring warmth to
his art. Then the artist receives a major commission from the
monks at the temple: they want him to paint the death of the
Buddha. The artist works furiously, but his work always begins
with contemplation. In order to paint the Buddha, he recalls
ancient stories of the Buddha's compassion and mercy. The
Buddha he paints must have the "look of one who has been
gently brought up and unquestioningly obeyed . . . one who
has suffered greatly and sacrificed himself . . . one who has
found peace and given it to others." The painting must have all
the animals that came to pay homage to the dying Buddha. As

the artist draws each animal, he remembers stories of the Buddha in which they play a role. But he is pained by the traditional story that the cat refused to pay homage and was shut out of Paradise. In the end he includes the cat, because Good Fortune has shown such love, but the chief priest rejects the painting—until a new miracle occurs and a cat is allowed to enter heaven.

The Cuckoo Clock
Mary Stolz. Illustrated by Pamela Johnson.
Godine, 1987, 86 pages

THIS IS A story that begins with the spell-weaving incantation "Once upon a time. . . . " Immediately we are drawn into the world of old Ula the clockmaker and his apprentice Erich the Foundling, where anything is believable, provided we look with the eyes of love and not of pride. Ula's last wish before dying is to fashion a clock the like of which has never before been seen in the Black Forest. This is a labor of love, and when the clock is completed, the cuckoo comes magically to life and sings enchanting melodies inside the clock. But only the simple souls of Ula and Erich can hear the cuckoo, because "being very old and very young, Ula and Erich had no difficulty in accepting a miracle." *The Cuckoo Clock* is a tale of wonder and of faith, reminding us that if we wish to witness the miraculous, we must look with the eyes of innocence and love. That is, we must become "as little children."

Gudgekin the Thistle Girl and Other Tales
John Gardner. Illustrated by Michael Sporn.
Knopf, 1976, 59 pages

BRUNO BETTELHEIM ONCE wrote that "the fairy-tale helps in [the] process [of maturation] because it only beckons; it never suggests, demands or tells." Nowhere is this more true than in John Gardner's whimsical and original tales. In the title story, Gudgekin's wicked stepmother forces her to labor long and hard collecting the thistles that constitute their only livelihood. But Gudgekin never complains; filled with compassion for the sorrows of others, she sheds barely a tear for herself. In reward for Gudgekin's kindness, the Queen of Fairies allows her to travel to Fairy-land, where the Prince promptly falls in love with her. How the Prince tricks Gudgekin into marriage and how her stepmother repents of her wicked ways complete this charming tale. But we caution you not to look for such a clear-cut outcome to the other stories in the collection. In the dryly witty "The Griffin and the Wise Old Philosopher," for example, the solution to the problem of the Griffin is to ignore it altogether! As a reviewer in *The New York Times Book Review* noted, "everything [in the stories] is sacred and nothing is sacred. The form of the fairy-tale is honored, but wild deviations are taken within it . . . with consequences that are hilarious and wonderful." Sometimes a fairy tale's meaning does not have to be explicit to be meaningful.

The Light Princess
George MacDonald. Illustrated by Maurice Sendak.
Farrar, Straus and Giroux, 1977 (1864), 120 pages

GEORGE MACDONALD, ONE of the most imaginative writers of the nineteenth century, cared deeply about the way children saw the world. Widely admired as the inventor of modern fantasy literature, MacDonald found a way to take the preachiness out of children's literature without sacrificing a concern for morality. His style, which C. S. Lewis called "mythopoeic," dramatizes moral conflicts through the use of symbols and metaphors. *The Light Princess* is one of his funniest and most boisterous tales. A foolish and frivolous king becomes impatient for an heir. When his queen finally bears him a daughter, they discover something horrifying about her: she has no gravity, the result of an evil witch's curse. Unless she is tied down or kept indoors, she floats. The princess is full of laughter: she finds her royal parents and the court hilarious. Her humor shows them to be silly, vain people, obsessed by trivialities. But then MacDonald gives the story a neat twist: we begin to find the princess's levity a bit tiresome, and just at that moment a young prince enters the kingdom and falls in love with her. At first, she is too flippant to take him seriously, but when she discovers the delight of holding on to him and diving into a lake—a simulation of gravity—she is intrigued. When the prince has to sacrifice himself to save the princess, she realizes that she loves him, and gains her gravity. Maurice Sendak pays a personal tribute to MacDonald in his arresting illustrations for this edition.

The Little Prince
Antoine de Saint-Exupéry
Harcourt Brace Jovanovich, 1982 (1943, 1958), 96 pages

IN THE DEDICATION of this delightful story, the author declares that it is not intended for grown-ups. Instead, *The Little Prince* is a tale for the child in all of us. No sentimentalist, Antoine de Saint-Exupéry had witnessed the worst that human nature had to offer; he had fought as a pilot in two wars and was eventually to lose his life in a flight over occupied southern France in 1944. Despite this, he managed to preserve a child-like faith in the essential grandeur of the human heart and the power of the imagination. With his infectious curiosity and exuberance for life, the Little Prince confounds the grown-up world of fact and superficial judgment. As the Little Prince himself says: "The eyes are blind. One must look with the heart." Banned by the Nazi Vichy government in France in 1942, *The Little Prince* has been delighting children and adults alike since its translation into English in 1944.

Pinocchio
Carlo Collodi
Schocken, 1985 (1883), 206 pages

WHEREAS MOST AMERICAN children are familiar with
the story of Pinocchio through the classic Walt Disney production, Italian children have been raised on the original story for
generations. In the older version, Pinocchio's promise to the
Blue Fairy to be a "good boy" is explored in much more depth
than in the movie. Not only is Pinocchio expected to attend
school with the other "real" boys, but he must also learn to
obey his father, tell the truth, and keep his promises. His failure to do so suggests that there is much more at stake in Pinocchio's moral life than the film would have us suppose; he is
chased by assassins, he witnesses Candlewick's tragic death as
a beaten and mistreated donkey, and he is swallowed by a truly
fearsome whale. But throughout all his failures and repen-
tances, the loving and forgiving natures of his father and the
Blue Fairy serve to provide a bedrock of security that eventually effects Pinocchio's moral transformation. When he finally
becomes a real boy, we feel that he has well and truly earned it.
Written in an age that did not believe that children should be
swaddled in a blanket of sentimentality, the original *Pinocchio*
is ultimately the more satisfying story.

The Shadowmaker
Ron Hansen. Illustrated by Margot Tomes.
HarperCollins, 1987, 66 pages

"ONCE UPON A TIME, in a place you've never been, there
was a town where nearly everyone was completely happy."
These opening words, which may sound somewhat suspicious
(who ever heard of a town where everyone was happy?), lead
into a fast-paced tale, full of whimsical humor, about our personal vanities and pretensions. Into this happy town comes an
extremely short man riding on a red wagon. He sets up shop,
putting a sign outside his door that reads, SHADOWMAKER. Soon

his business is booming. The mayor buys a shadow of a grand king, chubby boys select skinny shadows, little children get huge monster shadows. A clever orphan girl named Drizzle becomes interested in the Shadowmaker, though she cannot afford a shadow of her own. She finds it hard to love her grumpy brother, Soot, but she does love him and wants him to succeed in his repair business. When Drizzle discovers the Shadowmaker's secret formula for making shadows, she sets off a chain of magical events that threatens to wreak havoc on the town. The townspeople meanwhile have become very uncomfortable with their shadows, which are in need of repair and refurbishing. Drizzle comes up with the ideal solution to rid the town of the Shadowmaker and assure her brother's success.

Myths, Legends, and Folktales

The growth of the imagination demands windows—windows through which we can look out at the world and windows through which we can look into ourselves. The old stories were windows in just this way.

—Katherine Paterson

Younger Readers

Always Room for One More (**C**)
Sorche Nic Leodhas
Illustrated by Nonny Hogrogian.
Henry Holt, 1965

"THERE WAS A wee house in the heather . . . / And in it there lived all together / Lachie MacLachlan / And his good wife / And his bairns to the number of ten." So begins this spirited retelling of a Scottish folktale about the joy of hospitality and a generous heart. Passed on for generations in song, Sorche Leodhas's grandfather sang it to her when she was a child. Lachie MacLachlan is such an exuberant fellow that he calls out to travelers to stay under his roof: "There's room galore. / Och, come awa' in! There's room for one more, / Always room for one more." Well, all sorts of people, from sailors to shepherds to bagpipe players, squeeze into Lachie's wee house, dancing jigs and reels, until—you guessed it—the house explodes and everyone lands on their rear ends. But within moments, Lachie's guests are building him a bigger and better house, where there will always be room for one more. Nonny Hogrogian's sketches, with a purple wash of color reminiscent of Scottish heather, helped this book win the Caldecott Medal.

Anansi Finds a Fool
Verna Aardema. Illustrated by Bryna Waldman.
Dial Books for Young Readers, 1992

IT IS FITTING that Bryna Waldman, the illustrator of this wise African tale, dedicates the book to "Nicole and Chato, who have taught me a great deal." For *Anansi Finds a Fool* is a cautionary tale and, as such, is designed to teach. When Aso's lazy husband announces that he is going into the fishing business, she is skeptical. Anansi has never done an honest day's work in his life! And when he explains that he is going to find a fool for a partner to do all the work for him, she is more skeptical still. Where, in all their village, could there be a greater fool than her husband? It is Bonsu, her husband's best friend, who resolves to teach Anansi a lesson. By convincing him that work has to be shared—"Let me set the trap," Bonsu says. "If I get my leg bitten off, you can die for me."—Bonsu succeeds in making Anansi work for the first time in his life. "Hold it man! . . ." Anansi replies. "I'll set the trap myself. If the crocodile gets me, YOU can die for ME!" Although humorously told, *Anansi Finds a Fool* contains an important message; there is no such thing as something for nothing, and if we are to benefit from God's bounty, we must not shirk from the sometimes irksome stewardship that it entails. To do so would be foolish indeed!

Dream Peddler
Gail E. Haley
E. P. Dutton, 1993, 32 pages

HIS NEIGHBORS THINK John Chapman is off his head! Why else would he go from house to house lugging a huge load of books around on his back? Because he loves stories, that's why. And he is determined to share them with the rest of the world. He is a peddler of "words, wisdom, ideas and dreams," and these things, he believes, cannot "be bought for any price." Still, when he looks around his humble cottage and at the rags his children are forced to wear, he can't help wondering whether books are worth the poverty he has brought upon his family. Then on three consecutive nights, he dreams that he is to go to London Bridge, where he will receive joyful news. What this news is and how it changes John Chapman's life forever makes for a satisfying conclusion. *Dream Peddler* reminds us that little in this life can match the riches that books contain. No matter what our age, economic status, or nationality, books enable us to leave the confines of our own small world and enter the wider world of the imagination.

John Henry: An American Legend
Ezra Jack Keats
Pantheon, 1965

THE LEGEND OF John Henry has deep roots in our cultural memory. Scholars might sort out all its different sources and symbols, but the most enduring meanings of this tall tale concern the dignity of hard work and the preciousness of human life. Born with a hammer in his hand, John Henry is endowed with a superhuman strength—and a desire to use that strength constructively through hard work. He moves from the cotton fields to riverboats and on to work on the railroad. Where the railway line has been stopped by a mountain, he finds his destiny. John Henry proves his strength by beating the inhuman tunneling machine. This legend, set at the dawn of the modern industrial age, reminds us that tools—whether hammers or more complex machines—are valuable only when they express the human spirit. John Henry's massive strength undoubtedly symbolizes the enormous amount of labor that African-Americans—as slaves and freemen—put into the building of this nation. The hammer-wielding legendary man dies of an enlarged heart, a heart that has grown in its willingness to get the job done.

Johnny Appleseed
Reeve Lindbergh. Illustrated by Kathy Jakobsen.
Little, Brown, 1990

THE STORY OF Johnny Appleseed is one of America's oldest and most cherished tales, having been told for nearly two hundred years. This enchanting book not only brings the story to life, but reminds us that it was a *true* story. John Chapman, born in Massachusetts in 1774, spent his adult life walking between his home and the western frontier in Indiana, planting apple trees, and maintaining apple orchards and nurseries. Apples were food that could be eaten at any time of the year, and thus apple trees were extremely helpful to the pioneers moving westward. Because the pioneers could not afford to take apple saplings in their overcrowded wagons, Chapman's nurseries were tremendously useful. A Christian missionary, Chapman always carried a Bible and preached the Good News when he traveled. He was known and liked by the Indian tribes of the Northeast. Reeve Lindbergh tells the story in a lively poetic form. Johnny's motto, we learn, is:

To grow a country or a tree
Takes just a planter who
Will seed and tend till in the end
The earth's best dreams come true.

Kathy Jakobsen's paintings, done in a primitive, folk style, are reminiscent of the needlework found in early American samplers.

Jump On Over!
Joel Chandler Harris. Illustrated by Barry Moser.
Harcourt Brace Jovanovich, 1989, 39 pages

SASSY AND STREETWISE, Brer Rabbit has been entertaining us by his side-splitting antics for over a century. But this magnificently rendered and illustrated edition reveals a rare side to this unlikely hero—Brer Rabbit the family man. On account of Old Man Hungriness, Brer Rabbit has more on his mind than just tormenting Brer Fox and his cronies; he must feed his missus and seven little Rabs. Make no mistake, there is plenty of fun and games in these stories—what Joel Chandler Harris story could be without them?—but like all enduring works of fiction the Brer Rabbit stories contain a deeper theme. Harris intended Brer Rabbit's tribulations to be a reflection of the times in which he lived, a time when African-Americans had only their wits to fall back on, not the law.

Ma'ii and Cousin Horned Toad
Shonto Begay
Scholastic, 1992

A TRADITIONAL NAVAJO STORY, *Ma'ii and Cousin Horned Toad* is in the ancient tradition of the cautionary tale. When Ma'ii, the Native American version of Wile E. Coyote, finds that he is hungry, he determines to seek out his cousin the Horned Toad. Too lazy to work himself, Ma'ii knows that his cousin will be happy to give him a square meal; after all, the Horned Toad farms a cornfield that produces plenty of food. Besides, Ma'ii knows that his cousin would never turn away someone in need. But after eating an enormous meal that the kindly toad has served him, Ma'ii is still dissatisfied. If all this belonged to me, he thinks, looking at the burgeoning cornfield, I would have plenty of food and I could easily trick all my other cousins into working for me. Ma'ii hatches a cunning plot to steal the cornfield from his cousin, but gets more than he bargained for! The author's playful retelling of his own favorite childhood tale, accompanied by his richly imaginative paintings, teaches an important lesson that can benefit any culture. Namely, that slothfulness and greed never pay off. Only honest hard work and, more important, kindness to those truly in need make for authentic success. At the end of the story, Shonto Begay tells us that whenever a Navajo comes across a horned toad, he puts it to his heart and greets it, saying, "Hello, my grandfather!" For, in the author's own words, "We believe [the horned toad] gives us strength of heart and mind."

The Man Who Loved Books
Jean Fritz. Illustrated by Trina Schart Hyman.
G. P. Putnam and Sons, 1981

SAINT COLUMBA HAD one great weakness . . . books! In an age when books were a great rarity, Columba made it his life mission to copy as many books as possible so that others would be able to share his joy. But when he causes a bloody battle in which three thousand and one men are killed—and all for the sake of a book—he realizes that he has let his passion run away with him. In penance, he vows to leave his beloved Ireland and never more to set eyes on it. How Columba returns to Ireland blindfolded so as not to break his vow, and how he makes peace between the king and the bards brings his story to a satisfying close. Based on an ancient legend and retold by the celebrated historian Jean Fritz, with subtle watercolors by

Trina Schart Hyman, *The Man Who Loved Books* reminds us
that although the things of this world are precious, we must
take care not to make them into idols.

Mufaro's Beautiful Daughter: An African Tale
John Steptoe
Lothrop, 1987, 32 pages

BASED ON AN ancient African folktale, and sumptuously illustrated in jewel-tone colors, *Mufaro's Beautiful Daughter*
cautions against judging by superficial appearances. Mufaro
(native for "happy man") has two daughters—Manyara
("ashamed"), and Nyasha ("mercy"). Both are equally beautiful, but only Nyasha possesses a loving heart; Manyara is vain
and selfish. Then, one day, they meet two strangers in the forest—a small boy who begs for food and an old woman. Confronted by representatives of the most vulnerable members of
society, the sisters respond according to their true natures.
Mufaro's Beautiful Daughter is a story that comes to us from a
culture known for its tenderness for the young and respect for
the old. As such, it represents a refreshing perspective on the
true nature of human beauty—the beauty of an unselfish
heart.

The Painter and the Wild Swans
Claude Clément. Illustrated by Frédérick Clément.
Dial Books for Young Readers, 1986

IN JAPAN, THERE was once a great painter who was so
skilled at his art that he was sought after far and wide. Then
one day while painting, he sees a flock of wild swans sweep
across the sky. Overcome by their great beauty, and filled with
despair at ever being able to capture them in paint, Teiji gives
up his art and goes in search of the swans. His quest leads him
to the home of a humble fisherman, where he offers the fisher-

man all his worldly possessions in exchange for his boat so he can cross the lake to the island of the swans. There, Teiji's devotion to beauty is rewarded by a miraculous vision of the swans. *The Painter and the Wild Swans* is an Asian version of the biblical story "The Pearl of Great Price." Only when we are prepared to give up our worldly possessions, the story reminds us, will we finally possess the beauty of truth. Illustrated with paintings of exquisite loveliness, and accompanied by the text written in Japanese script along the margins, *The Painter and the Wild Swans* is, in one reviewer's words, "unforgettable."

St. George and the Dragon (C)
Margaret Hodges. Illustrated by Trina Schart Hyman.
Little, Brown, 1984, 32 pages

MARGARET HODGES'S RETELLING of *Saint George and the Dragon,* accompanied by Trina Schart Hyman's exquisitely rendered illustrations, does more than justice to this ancient story of good against evil. Saint George is portrayed as a chivalrous knight, a moral warrior who has dedicated his life to fighting evil and protecting the innocent. When he hears of a terrible dragon ravaging the peaceful countryside he is determined to do battle with it. But like the moral life itself, Saint George's ultimate victory does not come easily. For three days he courageously battles the dragon, and is sorely wounded in the process, and each night the prayers of the king's daughter, Una, miraculously heal his body so he can rise up and fight another day. At last, on the third day, he succeeds in killing the dragon. This inspiring story reminds us that we must have courage and perseverance if we are to overcome the dragons of greed, hate, anger, and pride that lay waste to all that is good and noble in us. Every child's instinctive love of adventure testifies to the truth of this.

St. Jerome and the Lion
Margaret Hodges. Illustrated by Barry Moser.
Orchard, 1991

WHEN WE THINK of saints and animals, it is probably
Saint Francis of Assisi that comes most readily to mind. Saint
Jerome, on the other hand, is most commonly known today
for being the first translator of the Bible into Latin. But if we
look closely at medieval depictions of Saint Jerome we will see
not only a Bible in his hands but a large lion lying docilely at
his feet. Now the combined talents of Margaret Hodges and
Barry Moser, the renowned illustrator of children's books,
have brought the ancient legend of Saint Jerome and the lion
back to life. When a fierce roaring is heard outside Jerome's
monastery in Bethlehem, the monks are terrified. But Jerome is
not afraid. Filled with compassion for all God's creatures, he
"[goes] to meet [the lion] as one goes to greet a guest," and sees
that one of its paws is filled with sharp thorns. He tenderly removes them and sets the lion free. But instead of returning to
the wilderness, the lion follows Jerome into his study and lies
down by his feet as if to say, "You have healed me. Now I am
your friend." *St. Jerome and the Lion* is an enchanting tale that
brings new meaning to the modern concept of "animal rights."
But Saint Jerome was no activist. All he knew was that the lion,
like himself, was a cherished member of God's creation and
was to be treated accordingly—"like a guest."

The Stonecutter
Pam Newton
G. P. Putnam and Sons, 1990

THIS FOLKTALE FROM India offers a delightful variation
on the old be-careful-what-you-wish-for theme. A stonecutter
works hard every day on the mountainside, taking stone to
build houses and mend walls. But when he comes to a great
palace, he sees for the first time how the wealthy live. The next

day he prays to the mountain spirit and is suddenly transformed into a wealthy merchant. But he soon finds reasons to want more, and so he is transformed into a king. But even a king is subject to the hot sun, and so he becomes the sun. But the sun can be blocked by the clouds. . . . You can see where this story is headed! Like all good wishing stories, it ends where it began, with the stonecutter once again practicing his trade, glad to understand the dignity and solidity of his work, and purged of his greed for power and wealth.

The Tale of the Mandarin Ducks
Katherine Paterson
Illustrated by Leo and Diane Dillon.
E. P. Dutton, 1990

IF WE WERE to examine the majority of movies and television programs today, and ask the question "How do we resolve problems of injustice?" the answer, more often than not, would be "violence." Even the good guys today seem to routinely engage in retaliation, perpetuating a vicious circle of violence that is shaping the imaginations of our children. Katherine Paterson's Japanese folktale is an example of a different, and more humane, way of seeing the world. A wicked lord sees the dazzling plumage of a mandarin duck, and has it captured to be added to his collection of beautiful objects. His servant, a former samurai named Shozo, objects. But the lord despises Shozo, because he has lost an eye in battle and is not pleasing to look at. The duck pines for its mate and loses its radiant plumage, so the lord relegates it to an obscure part of his house. When a serving girl, Yasuko, lets the duck go and is blamed for it, Shozo stands with her. "To his honest mind, desiring to unlatch the cage and actually lifting the latch were one and the same." Reduced to a mere toilet scrubber, Shozo comes to love Yasuko. But their love is discovered and the evil lord condemns them to death. As they are led off to be drowned, they are rescued by two imperial messengers, in dazzling garb, that is mysteriously similar in design to that of the mandarin ducks. Shozo and Yasuko raise a family and grow old together, secure in their knowledge that "trouble can always be borne when it is shared." Paterson, aided by the prize-winning illustrators Leo and Diane Dillon, reminds us that patience and humility can triumph over mere violence, bringing peace into the world instead of conflict.

The Unicorn and the Lake
Marianna Mayer. Illustrated by Michael Hague.
Dial Books for Young Readers, 1982

THE LEGEND OF the mythical unicorn has captured man's imagination since early times. Snow white and with a silver horn upon its head, the unicorn has been seen as a powerful symbol of goodness, and its disappearance from the earth as a sign of man's evil. In this original story based on ancient legend, the unicorn is forced to flee hunters' arrows. But his departure from the lowlands brings a time of great forgetfulness to the earth; the animals find that they can no longer understand one another, and the lake begins to dry up. Only the evil serpent rejoices as he preys on the helpless creatures of the forest, made weak by lack of water. Now the unicorn must come down from the mountains and do battle with the serpent if the world is to survive. How the unicorn spares the serpent and how the serpent feels shame for the first time in his life, "knowing that one of his own kind would never have spared his life," complete this haunting tale of good against evil. Beautifully illustrated by the accomplished Michael Hague, *The Unicorn and the Lake* reminds us that it is goodness mingled with compassion and mercy that will ultimately triumph over evil—not superior force alone.

Middle Readers

The Adventures of Robin Hood
Roger Lancelyn Green. Illustrated by Arthur Hall.
Puffin, 1956, 256 pages

ROBIN HOOD may have been the first action adventure hero, but his story endures because it is based on a moral dilemma. In the absence of legitimate authority, when there is no justice how does a just man react? Robin Hood is a romantic figure because he combines the freedom and craftiness of an "outlaw" with a belief in the true king's justice and order. He is able to deflate the pretensions of the high and mighty and assert the goodness of the common man. Yet he is always vulnerable to betrayal. Robin's redistribution of wealth is only a matter of returning stolen property to the poor. Roger Lancelyn Green is a master storyteller, who has taken many classic works and retold them for children today. In this volume he uses all the different Robin Hood legends to create a coherent novel. Green's Robin is wise as well as adventurous, a lover as well as a fighter. Reading this book will help to insulate your child's imagination from the trivializing effects of popular culture. When a child knows the book, he or she can accept the movie or cartoon as a lighthearted and lightweight version of something more profound and enduring.

Canterbury Tales
Geoffrey Chaucer. Retold by Barbara Cohen.
Illustrated by Trina Schart Hyman.
Lothrop, 1988, 84 pages

THE CHARACTERS DESCRIBED in Geoffrey Chaucer's *Canterbury Tales* may have been on a pilgrimage, but their holiday spirit and colorful personalities turn the event into a rowdy carnival. The pilgrims enliven their journey with a storytelling contest, each attempting to outdo the other. The tales range from the noble deeds of chivalrous knights to the crudest sort of farce. Chaucer's pilgrims represent the whole of humanity, from the lowest class to the highest, and from models of virtue, such as the Knight, to scoundrels and petty criminals, like the Pardoner. Chaucer's brilliance lies in the way each tale reveals something about the teller. Chaucer does not directly comment on his characters' morality; we are invited to interpret the meaning of the tale and draw our own conclusions. Barbara Cohen's faithful retelling of four of the best-known tales is a perfect introduction to Chaucer for young readers who are fascinated by the richness and vigor of medieval England. The Nun's Priest's Tale, of the rooster Chauntecleer and the wily fox, is a fable about the dangers of flattery. The Wife of Bath is well known as a merry widow, but her tale of a man eventually submitting to a woman's will is more than a scandalous joke. Rather, her comic undermining of male pride is an example of feminism at its best. The Franklin's tale of a courtly love triangle is a wise affirmation of married love, while the Pardoner's Tale is a cautionary tale of greed, murder, and retribution. Trina Schart Hyman's illustrations vividly capture the humanity of these pilgrims.

The Children's Homer
Padraic Colum. Illustrated by Willy Pogany.
Collier, 1982 (1918), 248 pages

WE CAN THINK of no better way to explain the origins of Western culture to children than to give them a collection of Greek myths. These thrilling stories tell us more about the ancient Greeks than any history lesson could possibly do, because they awaken the imagination and allow us to see the Greeks through their own eyes. We share Odysseus's longing for his homeland, we sympathize with Telemachus's feeling of helplessness as he watches the suitors of his mother devour his father's wealth, and we admire Penelope's extraordinary loyalty to her absent husband. These marvelous stories teach us that it is not wealth or force of arms that makes a civilization great, but its belief in virtues such as loyalty, courtesy, and piety to the gods. One look at our own culture, with its drugs, pornography, and immense nuclear arsenals, will tell us how much we have strayed from these ideals. Exquisitely illustrated in pen and ink by the renowned Willy Pogany, this collection of Greek myths is an eloquent reminder to us of a time when people were willing to die rather than betray what they believed in.

Crow and Weasel
Barry Lopez. Illustrated by Tom Pohrt.
Farrar, Straus and Giroux, 1990, 63 pages

THIS BOOK-LENGTH FABLE cannot be summarized or reduced to lessons or themes. It is one of those mythic tales that seems to be about the meaning of life itself, so deep are its images and wisdom. Written by the award-winning nature writer Barry Lopez, *Crow and Weasel* is a challenging read, a fable for older children (and adults). Set in a mythical American past, when animals and men spoke the same language, the story concerns two young men, members of a Plains tribe. They set out on a journey, traveling far to the north, where they encounter Eskimos, grizzly bears, and other wonders. Lopez uses the journey to represent the moral and spiritual journey that every person must undertake in this life. Early on, they meet Mouse, who tells them what his people think is important: "To be a good hunter, to be a good family man, to be truthful instead of clever with people, to live in a community where there is much wisdom." Crow replies, "But it takes your life to learn to do these things." In their adventures, Crow and Weasel find that arrogance and selfishness inevitably land them in deadly danger. Only by "giving thanks" can they gain the right frame of mind to survive the dangers of the wilderness. One of the strengths of this story is the way the friendship between Crow and Weasel is portrayed. They do not always get along, but they care for each other, and laugh together. They also challenge each other to transcend their faults. Their friendship is a source of moral growth and the basis of their courage. At the end, Weasel says, "It is good to be alive. To have friends, to have a family, to have children, to live in a particular place. These relationships are sacred." As in any good journey of discovery, the ultimate destination is one's own home.

Cupid and Psyche: A Love Story
Edna Barth. Illustrated by Ati Forberg.
Clarion, 1976, 64 pages

BASED ON THE ancient Greek myth, *Cupid and Psyche: A Love Story* tells of how a beautiful princess comes close to destroying the very thing she loves most in the world. Abandoned on a mountaintop by her parents in order to appease the jealousy of the goddess Venus, Psyche finds herself transported to a beautiful palace. By day, she is waited upon by invisible servants who see to her every wish and whim; by night, under cover of darkness, she is visited by a mysterious lover who asks that she never try to discover his identity. At last, overcome by curiosity and egged on by her envious sisters, Psyche conceals a lamp in her chamber. As soon as she feels the stranger's arms around her, she holds up the lamp. Instead of the monster she had feared, she sees the lovely form of Cupid, the god of love. But in her haste, she spills the lamp's boiling oil, gravely burning him. Now Psyche must find a way to undo the wrong that she has done. Like all great myths, the ancient story of Cupid and Psyche is wise about the ways of the human heart. Love is not something that can be taken for granted, it tells us. Instead, love is something that we must earn through loyalty, self-sacrifice, and perseverance. It is our soul—our psyche—that must conform itself to the pattern of love, not vice versa.

D'Aulaires' Book of Greek Myths
Ingri and Edgar Parin D'Aulaire
Doubleday, 1962, 192 pages

THE D'AULAIRES HAVE accomplished something remarkable in this volume: they have made the profusion of Greek myths and their characters accessible and inviting to young minds. The Greeks, of course, invested their gods with human characteristics, including lust, greed, and envy. But most of the Greek myths are permeated by a sense of a moral order. Suffering and defeat are the lot of those who are guilty of pride or arrogance: Icarus falling when flying too close to the sun, Pandora opening her jar and letting vanity, slander, and other evils out to plague mankind, Heracles using not only his strength but also his compassion to do his labors, Oedipus learning, too late, of his blindness to his own pride—these stories are deeply embedded in the Western cultural tradition. The imagination and symbolism in these myths affect children and adults alike at a deep psychological level, shaping our perceptions and judgments. The D'Aulaires recount all of the major Greek myths with unaffected grace. The pastel shades of the color illustrations perfectly capture the otherworldliness of the gods, though they are rendered with recognizable human virtues and vices. This oversized volume achieves a perfect marriage of text and illustration.

Dick Whittington and His Cat
Eva Moore. Illustrated by Kurt Werth.
Clarion, 1974, 61 pages

IF FRANCE HAS its rags-to-riches story in the story of Cinderella, England has its own in the legend of Dick Whittington and his cat. An actual historical figure, who was to become Lord Mayor of London three times in the Middle Ages, Dick Whittington began his life in abject poverty. Lured to London by the popular saying that its "streets [were] paved with gold," Dick soon learns that the truth is very different. Medieval London is a busy, loud, and dirty town and has no time for beggars such as Dick. A kindly merchant finds him on the brink of starvation and gives him a job as his cook's assistant. But life is hard; the cook mistreats him and, aside from Alys, the mer-

chant's daughter, Dick's only friend is a cat. How Dick gener-
ously gives the cat to the merchant to take on a voyage and
how this makes his fortune complete this satisfying story. In
contrast to our own times, Dick's ultimate success is not
founded on hard business sense—he would never have made
Forbes magazine!—but on a willingness to give up everything
he owned to those in need. Throughout his life, the actual Dick
Whittington was renowned for his generosity to the poor and
the homeless. He never forgot that he had been a beggar and
he never forgot the maxim "Do unto others as you would have
them do unto you."

Dragon Slayer: The Story of Beowulf
Rosemary Sutcliff. Illustrated by Charles Keeping.
Puffin, 1966, 108 pages

FAMOUS FOR HER extraordinary ability to breathe life
into the past, Rosemary Sutcliff brings us the ancient Anglo-
Saxon myth of Beowulf. When Beowulf, the renowned warrior
of the Jutes, hears that his old friend King Hrothgar is being
terrorized by Grendel, an inhuman monster in the shape of a
man, he determines to slay him. Years later, after Beowulf has
succeeded King Hrothgar on the throne, he hears of another
ghastly monster roaming the countryside—this time it is Grendel's mother, seeking revenge for the death of her son. Knowing that this will be his last battle, Beowulf dons his armor and
bravely goes in search of the monster's lair. Like most myths,
Beowulf can be read on many levels; it is both an adventure
story, featuring daring feats of courage, and an allegory of the
moral life. Like Beowulf, we must be ever vigilant against the
monsters of hatred, revenge, greed, and pride that inhabit the
dark corners of our hearts. But being aware of them is seldom
enough—like Beowulf, we must also be prepared to do battle
with them.

Heather and Broom: Tales of the Scottish Highlands
Sorche Nic Leodhas
Henry Holt, 1960, 128 pages

IN THE SCOTTISH highlands, where the heather turns the hills purple in the summer months, the people have preserved a rich heritage of storytelling; tales are passed down through the generations like priceless heirlooms. This collection of tales, assembled and retold by Sorche Nic Leodhas, ranges from mythic fantasy to rough peasant humor, but a simple moral code runs through all of the tales. "The Daughter of King Ron" tells of a proud and heartless ruler who loses the bride of his heart when he speaks to her in anger. Transformed by grief into a wise and kind lord, he is eventually reunited with his love. In other tales peasant common sense sets the tone. For example, in "The Lairdie with a Heart of Gold," a young lord is unable to collect rent from his tenants because he is too kind to run out the cheaters and thieves. But when he is kind to a group of dispossessed brownies (a Scottish version of leprechauns), he discovers that one of the wee folk, Lachie Tosh, is willing to be tough on his tenants. Lachie not only whips the bad tenants into shape but brings good luck to the decent folk and a wife to his new master, the softhearted lord. Leodhas also put together another delightful collection of Scottish tales that we recommend: *Thistle and Thyme*.

Island of the Mighty: Stories of Old Britain
Haydn Middleton. Illustrated by Anthea Toorchen.
Oxford, 1987, 80 pages

WHEN WE PEER INTO the ancient past, we look to origins, to the things that give us a particular identity. The legends and folktales of a people or nation dramatize their conflicts, fears, and hopes—they provide a sort of language that later generations use to communicate. Children love legends because they are often about the heroic age, when everything was bigger, bolder, and more intense. The conflicts between good and evil in these legends are stark, but also exciting. The Welsh legends that make up *Island of the Mighty* are among the most entrancing folktales in our heritage. They tell of giants and wizards, kings and fairies, enchanted castles and ships made of glass; they recount the adventures of Old King Cole and the young King Arthur and his knights. In the opening tale, the good king, Bran the Blessed, tries to maintain peace, but his evil brother, Efnisien, commits an abominable crime against a neighboring people. The result of Efnisien's self-destructive passion is war and intrigue, an "original sin" that haunts the British people from that time forward. Most of these stories are about how kings attempt to bring peace and prosperity to Britain. The kingdom, of course, is like the individual soul: if selfishness and a lust for power are kept in check, then freedom and the weal, or well-being, of the people are guaranteed. These Welsh tales possess what William Butler Yeats called a "terrible beauty."

Merlin Dreams
Peter Dickinson. Illustrated by Alan Lee.
Delacorte, 1988, 167 pages

MERLIN DREAMS IS one of the most audaciously original collections of stories in recent memory. Peter Dickinson has taken that mythically potent figure, Merlin, as his inspiration. While the greatest of all magicians sleeps away the centuries beneath the dark earth—imprisoned, some say, by his one-time apprentice, the witch Nenyve—he dreams. Whether they are prophetic insights into what will be, memories of what has been, or figments of his dark imagination, all the "dreams" are rooted in Celtic lore and medieval legend. In the opening story, "Knight Errant," a selfish and cowardly knight is forced to go on a dangerous quest against evil, supernatural forces. Many virtuous knights have failed in this quest. But it is precisely his own awareness of the deceitfulness of the human heart that enables the "knight errant" to overcome his foes. "Unicorn" is a retelling of the legend that this mythical beast could be tamed only by the beauty and purity of a virgin. The wicked Sir Brangwyn seeks to make both men and beasts his possessions, but the virgin Rhiannon and her unicorn teach the evil lord a pointed lesson in family values. The tales are stunningly illustrated with full-color paintings and black-and-white drawings that perfectly embody all the moods and subtleties of the text. For older and more advanced readers.

The People Could Fly: American Black Folktales
Virginia Hamilton
Illustrated by Leo and Diane Dillon.
Knopf, 1985, 178 pages

MYTHS AND FOLKTALES reflect man's attempt to understand both his greatness and his ability to inflict and to endure suffering. The African-American folktales that the Newbery Medal–winning author Virginia Hamilton has brought together in this volume are no exception. Most of these stories, of course, are shaped by the "given" of slavery. Yet the imaginative range of these tales is startling: from comic to grotesque to tragic to mystical. The wiliness and cunning of Brer Rabbit mirror the slaves' urgent need to find ways to maintain dignity and to evade the cruelties of their masters. There are riddle tales that depict slaves outwitting masters whose cruelty has made them stupid. The title story is hauntingly beautiful: it tells of slaves on a plantation who remember the ancient African incantations that enable them to fly. "They didn't shuffle in a circle. They didn't sing. They rose on the air. They flew in a flock that was black against the heavenly blue. . . . Way above the plantation, way over the slavery land. Say they flew to *Free-dom.*" These tales, illustrated by the Caldecott winners Leo and Diane Dillon, are all told in the authentic colloquial idiom of the African-American experience.

Stories for Children
Isaac Bashevis Singer
Farrar, Straus and Giroux, 1990 (1962), 338 pages

THE LATE NOBEL Prize winner Isaac Bashevis Singer was extremely blunt in his opinions about children's literature. He felt that it ought to deal with the most serious and, yes, philosophical questions, such as "Who made the world?" and "Why is there suffering?" He detested books with good "messages," if they were not good stories first. "If all the messages disappeared and only the Ten Commandments remained, we would still have enough messages for the present and the future." All of the wisdom in Singer's magical tales can be found in the Ten Commandments. The tales collected here range from the mystical to the farcical and grotesque; they are often set in the Jewish communities of Singer's Poland. "A Tale of Three Wishes" describes three children and their wishes on the holy night of the Feast of the Tabernacles. The children learn that working for beauty, knowledge, and wisdom is better than merely wishing for it. Stories like "The Fools of Chelm and the Stupid Carp" are set in a town of smug, self-important men and women, who invariably bring grief upon themselves, sometimes in the most hilarious way. "Zlateh the Goat" describes the love between a boy and his goat, and the comfort they bring each other when caught in a terrible snowstorm. "Utzel and His Daughter, Poverty" recounts the life of a lazy man, who wanted his child to work for him. The less he does, however, the larger Poverty grows. Eventually, Utzel realizes the truth of the maxim "Whatever you can do today, don't put off until tomorrow." This collected edition contains the holiday stories collected in *The Power of Light*.

Tales from Silver Lands (N)
Charles Finger. Illustrated by Paul Honoré.
Doubleday, 1949 (1924), 225 pages

AWARDED THE NEWBERY Medal in 1925, *Tales from Silver Lands* is the fruit of the author's travels in South America and the stories he learned from the Indians. Filled with giants, witches, fairy folk, talking animals, and wizards, some of the stories in this collection are close to the traditions of the fairy tale and the cautionary tale. "A Tale of Three Tails" relates how the mouse used to have the tail of a horse and how he lost it as a punishment for his deceitfulness. Other stories have the flavor of myth and legend. In "The Magic Dog," Tlapa, the witch of the Shaking Mud, casts a spell that brings hatred and strife to the once happy kingdom of the Sea-shell King. Only the king's beautiful daughter can restore peace and harmony, by becoming a servant of the man she loves. Strikingly illustrated with original woodcuts, *Tales from Silver Lands* attests to the richly imaginative life of the South American Indians—a life founded on a profound respect for nature and an unshakable belief in the virtue of truth.

The Truthful Harp
Lloyd Alexander. Illustrated by Evaline Ness.
Henry Holt, 1967

FOR THOSE READERS too young yet to enjoy *The Prydain Chronicles* (see page 226) is this delightfully humorous story about how the bard Fflewddur Fflam acquired his extraordinary harp and set out on a journey that eventually leads to his meeting with Taran the Assistant Pig Keeper. Bored with ruling over his kingdom—after all, "he could almost stride across it between midday and high noon"—Fflewddur decides to become a wandering minstrel. With his magic harp in hand, the fledgling bard sets out on his adventures; he gives his cloak to a shivering old man, rescues a young child from drowning, and defends a nobleman from his enemies. But when Fflewddur is thanked for his bravery and kindness, he cannot resist bending the truth just a little. "A Fflam swims like a fish," he tells the parents of the child he has rescued, even though he almost drowned himself. *Twang!* A string on his harp promptly breaks. Before too long, Fflewddur's love of exaggeration—"poetic license" is the way Fflewddur likes to think of it—has reduced his harp to a broken shambles. When asked why he didn't recount all his acts of bravery as they really happened, Fflam replies that they seemed much too dull to be worth telling. But truth, the Chief Bard replies, "is purest gold that needs no gilding." Much like Pinocchio's nose, which grows whenever he tells a lie, Fflewddur's miraculous harp is designed to keep him honest. "Never again will I stretch the truth!" he declares proudly. At this the harp's strings tighten fractionally. " 'That is to say,' Fflewddur adds hastily, 'never beyond what it can bear.' "

Sacred Texts

Some writers sit down to write a book, not because they love the story, but because they are in love with the message it might bring. There is no famine of messages in our time or in any other time. If all the messages disappeared and only the Ten Commandments remained, we would still have enough messages for the present and the future. Our trouble is not that we don't have enough messages but that we refuse to fulfill them and practice them.

—Isaac Bashevis Singer

Younger Readers

The Children's Bible
Hamlyn, 1984 (1964), 518 pages

WE KNOW OF a woman who credits her lifelong love of literature to listening to her grandfather read to her from *The Children's Bible* when she was a little girl. Many years later, the words and pictures of many of the stories are still familiar to her as she shares them with her own children. Filled with unforgettable characters (David and Goliath, Daniel in the lions' den, Moses parting the Red Sea), and illustrated with richly dramatic pictures, *The Children's Bible* is an indispensable introduction to the drama of faith as it is played out in the lives of great men and women.

Days of Awe: Stories for Rosh Hashanah and Yom Kippur
Eric A. Kimmel. Illustrated by Erika Weihs.
Puffin, 1993, 48 pages

THE JEWISH HIGH holy days of Rosh Hashanah and Yom Kippur celebrate the beginning of a new year. While the message of these holidays is to look forward with hope to what lies ahead, there is also emphasis on what the individual has done with his or her life. At the center of this belief in personal accountability are three virtues: charity, prayer, and repentance. Eric Kimmel's *Days of Awe* is a collection of three stories, adapted from traditional folktales, that illustrate these virtues. In "The Samovar," the glovemaker Haskel and his wife, Rivka, are preparing for a humble Rosh Hashanah when a mysterious stranger arrives at their door. A handsome army officer enters, bringing an old samovar (for making tea) that is black with tarnish and cobwebs. Nothing Rivka can do with rags and soap will remove the tarnish, but when she gives a beggar a coin, she notices a small shining patch on the samovar. The samovar helps Haskel and Rivka realize that small acts of charity, even if they are routine at first, can deepen the heart and teach it true compassion. "The Shepherd" tells of a simple soul who prays in the fields, "God, if You were hungry and I had radishes, I would give You half my radishes. And if You were still hungry, I would give You all of them." This prayer annoys a scholarly rabbi, who believes that prayer is valid only in a synagogue, but an angelic visitation proves the rabbi quite wrong. Finally, "Rabbi Eleazar and the Beggar" stresses that asking for forgiveness and forgiving are equally important acts. Eric Kimmel wonderfully balances his explanations of religious traditions with the luminosity of the stories themselves. This is a holiday book to cherish.

Ladder of Angels: Stories from the Bible
Madeleine L'Engle
Illustrated by Children of the World.
HarperCollins, 1979, 128 pages

ONE EXAMPLE OF the crisis of "cultural illiteracy" from which we have been suffering in recent years is the loss of knowledge of the Bible, particularly the enduring stories of the Old Testament. For centuries these stories were central to the moral and psychological development of children: they are incomparable sources for confronting the moral choices and conflicts of life. *Ladder of Angels* is an enthralling and powerful antidote to this crisis of ignorance. Madeleine L'Engle, the renowned author of children's books (whose time travel novels on page 230 we also recommend), has selected dozens of full-color illustrations of Bible stories made by children from around the world and has matched them with her own profound and lyrical meditations. The quality of the children's drawings, their insight into the stories, and their imaginative freedom are truly amazing. L'Engle's poems, monologues, and reflections reveal new facets to the stories of Adam and Eve, Abraham and Isaac, Cain and Abel, Noah's Ark, Moses, David and Saul. Both pictures and text make the familiar stories new, and thus rescue them from being taken for granted. The result of reading this beautiful book, one would hope, would be to lead the reader back to the original.

The Song of the Three Holy Children
Pauline Baynes
Henry Holt, 1986

> *O all ye works of the Lord,*
> *bless ye the Lord:*
> *praise him and magnify*
> *him for ever.*

THUS BEGINS THE joyous hymn of praise sung by three Jewish Babylonian captives. From the Apocrypha, an addition to the Book of Daniel, we learn that three boys—Shadrach, Meshach, and Abednego—were condemned to be burned alive for refusing to worship the Babylonian gods. Shielded from the flames by an angel, they sang this magnificent hymn of praise in thanksgiving for their miraculous deliverance. Accompanied by the sumptuous illustrations of the renowned Pauline Baynes (illustrator of C. S. Lewis's *Chronicles of Narnia*), *The Song of the Three Holy Children* is a moving testament to the power of faith.

Middle Readers

The Book of Adam to Moses
Lore Segal. Illustrated by Leonard Baskin.
Knopf, 1987, 115 pages

THERE HAVE BEEN many attempts to rescue the Bible for modern readers, including children, but they have not always been happy productions. So often the creators of the new illustrated translations feel that the Bible must be turned into a comic book in order for children to respond to it. But by trivializing the images of the Bible, and reducing its soaring language to contemporary slang, they have lost the essence of the thing they want to preserve. Children tend to know when they are being condescended to; in the long run, they would rather be challenged than coddled. *The Book of Adam to Moses* is a new version of the first five books of the Bible, known as the Pentateuch. Lore Segal's supple language is free from the archaic diction of older English translations, but retains the sub-

tle modulations of the original texts. Here are all the great stories: the Creation, Adam and Eve, Cain and Abel, Noah and
the Flood, and the Tower of Babel, along with the great patri-
archs, Abraham, Isaac, Joseph, Jacob, and Moses. Leonard
Baskin, one of America's leading artists, has created a series of
line drawings that evoke the mystery, grandeur, and power of
these stories. As Segal says in her introduction, "The stories
enter your life. It is no wonder the book's been two and a half
thousand years on the best-seller list. How can we bear for our
children to miss this?"

In the Beginning: Creation Stories
Virginia Hamilton. Illustrated by Barry Moser.
Harcourt Brace Jovanovich, 1988, 176 pages

VIRGINIA HAMILTON WAS careful to call this collection
of myths "stories." Why? Because, like all good fiction, myths
are less concerned with factual realism than with the moral
realm of the human soul. Contained within its pages are
twenty-five ancient and contemporary creation myths from
around the world; while each story uniquely reflects the culture out of which it grew, there are many similarities that unite
the stories. In his heart man has always wondered, What
brought sin and death into the world? The ancient Greek myth
of Pandora's box (or jar) and the Old Testament story of Adam
and Eve seek to answer this question allegorically. Who created
the universe? In these creation stories God has many faces and
names: Yahweh, Zeus, Ra, Ulgen, Ta-Aroa. Splendidly illustrated by Barry Moser in strong primary colors that evoke the
very stuff of creation, *In the Beginning* is a marvelous testi-
mony to the power of man's imagination and his perennial
hunger for truth.

The Message:
The New Testament in Contemporary English
Eugene H. Peterson
NavPress, 1993, 544 pages

MANY ATTEMPTS HAVE been made in the last thirty years to make the Bible "relevant" to young people. These paraphrases have not been happy experiments. Too often they reduce biblical language to trite phrases that drain nearly all of the meaning and vibrancy from the original. But a new translation has recently appeared that fulfills all the promise of the attempt at relevance without sacrificing the power of the biblical message. The first part of this translation is the complete New Testament, entitled, aptly, *The Message.* It is the work of one man, Eugene Peterson, a pastor, professor, and outstanding prose stylist in his own right. Peterson has all of the qualifications necessary for this enormous task: a practical knowledge of the way people think and talk, derived from his years as a pastor, along with a thorough knowledge of the biblical languages. As Peterson notes in his introduction, "A striking feature in [the New Testament writings] is that it was done in the street language of the day, the idiom of the playground and the marketplace." He succeeds magnificently in finding a contemporary American idiom adequate to the original; this is not Bible translation by committee. Here is a sample of Peterson's translation of the Sermon on the Mount: "You're here to be light, bringing out the God-colors in the world. God is not a secret to be kept. We're going public with this, as public as a city on a hill. If I make you light-bearers, you don't think I'm going to hide you under a bucket, do you? I'm putting you on a light stand—shine! Keep open house; be generous with your lives." Peterson's translation of the Psalms has recently been published; the rest of the Old Testament will be appearing in the years ahead.

Books for Holidays and Holy Days

To many a youth, and many a maid,
Dancing in a checkered shade.
And young and old come forth to play
On a sunshine holiday.

—John Milton

Younger Readers

Amahl and the Night Visitors
Gian Carlo Menotti. Illustrated by Michèle Lemieux.
William Morrow, 1986 (1951), 64 pages

SINCE ITS FIRST performance in Italy on Christmas Eve in
1951, *Amahl and the Night Visitors* (an operetta by Gian Carlo
Menotti) has become a holiday classic almost as beloved as
The Nutcracker. The story faithfully follows Menotti's libretto
and tells of a poor crippled boy who is given to making up
bizarre tales. When he tells his mother he has seen a strange
new star in the East, she does not believe him; nor does she believe him when he tells her that there are three great kings at
the door seeking shelter. Once they have entered the humble
home and explained their quest, Amahl's mother struggles to
understand how an unknown, mysterious child merits such
rich and exotic gifts when her own lame boy is so needy. In the
crisis that follows, all the people involved learn something
about the nature of love, and they experience a miracle of their
own. Richly illustrated in glowing watercolors, this book enables us to relive the wonder and mystery of that night long ago
when an infant king was born in Bethlehem.

A Gift from Saint Francis: The First Crèche
Joanna Cole. Illustrated by Michèle Lemieux.
William Morrow, 1989

FOR MANY CHILDREN, the Christmas crèche is an essential part of the magic of the season, whether that crèche be a miniature version in their home or a life-size group in front of their church. A crèche makes the Christmas story visible and tangible, the humility of the manger made into something precious. Joanna Cole's book gives the Christmas crèche new meaning by telling us that it came from Saint Francis of Assisi. Children always want to know where things come from (like babies), so this book will have an immediate appeal. Cole begins by telling the story of Saint Francis in simple words, accompanied by the glowing pastel illustrations of Michèle Lemieux. We learn of the rich young man who gives up his wealth to live for the poor and downtrodden. One day, Saint Francis notices a shepherd in the fields outside the town of Grecchio, and is reminded of the story of the Nativity. Francis wants this story to be as real as possible, and so he gathers some of the townspeople and a few carpenters together. That evening, the people of Grecchio go out to the nearby hillside and see a "living" crèche. As they crowd around the crèche, Saint Francis reads to them from the Bible. This book glows with the warmth of Saint Francis's own spirit; it will help children to remember that the essence of Christmas is a celebration of purity, innocence, and love.

Just Enough Is Plenty: A Hannukah Tale
Barbara Diamond Goldin
Illustrated by Seymour Chwast.
Puffin, 1990

THIS IS ONE of the most touching Hanukkah stories we have ever come across. Malka, Zalman, and their family prepare for the Festival of Lights, but money is short, and there may not even be a kopeck left to play with in the traditional

game with the dreidel, a four-sided top. But when Papa lights
the menorah, he reminds Malka that the festival commemo-
rates the miracle when the oil in the temple burned for eight
days, instead of just one. Just as they are about to eat, an old
peddler knocks at the door. Mama says, "Just like Abraham
and Sarah in the Bible, we always have something for the
stranger who knocks at our door." After playing and singing
with them, the old man tells the children stories; their favorites
concern Elijah the Prophet. All the characters in the story make
Malka feel that the house is "filled with guests." But the next
morning the peddler has disappeared, leaving behind a sack
full of presents. Malka decides that the peddler is Elijah himself. The family literally dances for joy. In Goldin's hands the
meaning of Hanukkah is renewed. Seymour Chwast's paintings, with their primitive figures and rich colors, convey the
magic of the story. Winner of the National Jewish Book Award.

The Legend of the Christmas Rose
Selma Lagerlöf. Retold by Ellin Greene.
Illustrated by Charles Mikolaycak.
Holiday House, 1990 (1907)

IN GERMANY, IN the dead of winter, a tiny plant can be
seen pushing up bravely through the frozen ground. It is called
the Christmas rose, and it blooms for only a few short days in
mid-December. Over the centuries, people have turned to stories to explain the flower's miraculous appearance, and this
magnificent retelling brings out all the mystery and joy of that
ancient legend. When a family of outlaws comes to a monastery
to beg, the kindly abbot allows them to wander in the beautiful
monastery garden. But when the robber mother tells him that
the garden is nothing compared with a miraculous garden that
flowers in the Goinge Forest on Christmas Eve, the abbot determines to see it for himself. He is not disappointed; just as the
bells in the village are pealing out the joyful news of Christmas,
the forest around the robbers' miserable cave undergoes a won-
drous transformation: "The snow vanished from the ground,

the moss-turf thickened . . . and the spring blossoms shot their pale-colored buds upwards." Overcome with joy at having witnessed such a miracle, the old abbot vows to secure a pardon from the bishop for the outlaw family. If God has allowed these poor people to witness His glory, he reasons, surely we can forgive them and take them back into the village? By contrast, the lay brother who has accompanied the abbot is filled with dark thoughts. It must be the working of the devil, he says to himself. God would never reveal Himself to robbers. At that very moment, the garden withers and dies. How the abbot keeps his promise to the robber family and how the lay brother comes to repent his lack of faith complete this beautiful story. *The Legend of the Christmas Rose* breathes new life into the meaning of Christmas. Christmas is not about gift giving, it tells us. It is about *receiving*. Without God, our hearts lie in the depths of winter. Only by opening them to the warmth of His grace will they come alive and yield a bountiful harvest.

The Other Wise Man
Henry van Dyke. Retold by Pamela Kennedy.
Illustrated by Robert Barrett.
Ideals, 1992 (1896)

FIRST PUBLISHED IN 1896, *The Other Wise Man* has achieved the status of a classic. As in all great stories, its conception is a simple one: what if there was a *fourth* wise man, who was detained and unable to reach the Christ Child in time? But the simplicity of this plot contains a valuable insight into the moral life. Artaban, the fourth Magus, sells all his belongings for three jewels—a ruby, an emerald, and a pearl. These gems are to be his gift to the newborn king. Rushing to meet the other Magi, Artaban comes upon a man lying ill in the middle of the road. Despite his worry about missing his comrades, he feels that he must stop and save the man's life. When the man recovers, he tells Artaban that the Savior is to be born in Bethlehem. In order to cross the desert, Artaban has to sell his emerald for food and a camel. When Artaban reaches

Bethlehem, he finds that the family has fled to Egypt to escape Herod's wrath. But Artaban is able to save one of the children from Herod's murderous soldiers by using the ruby as a bribe. So it goes for the next thirty-three years: Artaban always missing the king. Then one day he arrives in Jerusalem, only to be told that the one he has sought will be crucified. One last distraction—the saving of a poor woman, with his remaining pearl—prevents him from meeting his king. Just then an earthquake causes a rock to fall on him: as he lies dying, he hears the voice of God tell him he has been a good servant. In helping others, he has given away his worldly wealth and exchanged it for spiritual wealth. *The Other Wise Man* reminds us that searching for a grand ideal is no substitute for our responsibilities to the people around us. That is the ultimate wisdom of the fourth Wise Man.

Petook: An Easter Story
Caryll Houselander. Illustrated by Tomie de Paola.
Holiday House, 1988

IN *PETOOK: AN Easter Story,* the joyful news of the Resurrection is told from an unusual perspective. Petook is a rooster and when he learns that his wife, Martha, has hatched twelve chicks, he is as proud as he can be. Then he discovers a boy's footprints in the earth and, fearing for the safety of his chicks, he flies to the nest. "Boys are sometimes careless," he says to himself. But when he arrives, he sees that the boy is kneeling by the nest with a rapt expression on his face at the miracle of life. This is no ordinary boy, Petook thinks. Many years pass, and one day Petook sees three crosses lifted up on a hillside, little knowing that it is the same boy who is now crucified there to atone for the sins of the world. Three days later, Martha hatches another clutch of chicks and she and Petook watch in wonder as the last one struggles to free itself. With "a splutter of gold fluff" the chick emerges and "the sky [breaks] into a splendor of light." Petook literally crows the good news aloud! It is Easter morning. Illustrated by the incomparable

Tomie de Paola, *Petook: An Easter Story,* in de Paola's own words, "breathes life into the age-old symbol of the Easter egg. . . . Without symbols such as this, Christianity becomes pale." See also *The Clown of God,* by the same author, in the picture book section on page 68.

The Plymouth Adventure
Leonard Weisgard
Doubleday, 1967

BECAUSE HOLIDAYS HAVE become so cluttered with merchandising, it is always worthwhile helping children learn about the original story behind the holiday. Thanksgiving is a case in point. Leonard Weisgard takes the Pilgrims from their days of persecution in England, through their transatlantic journey, to the dangers and challenges that met them when they arrived in the New World. Sustained by their deep religious faith, the Pilgrims endured suffering and privation for the sake of freedom. Before stepping ashore in Plymouth, they signed the Mayflower Compact, the first constitution in America. Their cooperation with the Native American tribes was a model that was not often imitated by other European settlers. After having lost half their number to illness and hunger, the Pilgrims were able to bring in a harvest. The first Thanksgiving is an image of a peaceable world, the American dream in its purest form. See also *Squanto: First Friend to the Pilgrims* (page 261) in the biography section.

The Power of Light: Eight Stories for Hanukkah
Isaac Bashevis Singer. Illustrated by Irene Lieblich.
Farrar, Straus and Giroux, 1980, 87 pages

ELSEWHERE WE RECOMMEND the collected stories of Isaac Bashevis Singer (see page 128), the Nobel Prize–winning writer. But for the Hanukkah season, this special collection is particularly appropriate. Singer's stories affirm the most basic virtues: the ability of faith, hope, and love to triumph over despair, cynicism, and hate. The title story recounts the desperate circumstances of David and Rebecca, two children caught in the hell of World War II in the Jewish ghetto of Warsaw. Hiding in a ruined building, scavenging for food, and avoiding the Nazi troops, the children are almost ready to give in to despair. But one day David returns with a surprise: it is the first day of Hanukkah, and he has found a candle to mark the occasion. The hope symbolized by that light enables the children to find the courage to escape. The story gains a new dimension when we learn, at the end, that it is a true story, one that the author heard from the lips of David and Rebecca themselves. Singer once said that he had five hundred reasons for writing for children. One of them, he said, was that children "still believe in God, the family, angels, devils, witches, goblins, logic, clarity, punctuation, and other such obsolete stuff." In these uplifting tales you will realize that there is nothing obsolete about these timeless truths.

The Story of the Three Wise Kings
Tomie de Paola
G. P. Putnam and Sons, 1983

IN THE BIBLE, the baby Jesus is visited by "wise men"; centuries after the New Testament was written, traditions have grown up around these men: they have been numbered, made kings, and given names—Melchior, Gaspar, and Balthazar. The kings have come to symbolize many things, but in a fundamental sense they represent the human impulse to seek truth and give thanks for the wonder of creation. Tomie de Paola tells the story in few words; he leaves it to his lambent paintings to suggest the meaning. The curiosity and reverence of the kings are contrasted with King Herod's blustering resentment. But the kings manage to find the Mother and Child. These intellectuals and mighty rulers lay down their gifts before a mother and her son. Here power and intellect submit themselves to love. That is the unspoken moral of the story, which nourishes and expands our imaginations. De Paola's style brings out all the spiritual resonance of the story, from his geometrical depictions of the stars to his use of traditional symbols, such as the dove and the pear.

What a Morning! The Christmas Story in Black Spirituals
Edited by John Langstaff. Illustrated by Ashley Bryan. Macmillan, 1987

THERE IS NO better way to capture the universality of the Christmas story than by seeing it through the eyes of different cultures and traditions. In this happy collaboration, the noted singer, educator, and author John Langstaff has brought together a number of black spirituals, which are arranged so as to retell the events of Christ's birth. These spirituals, while simple in spirit, reflect a range of emotions, from exultation to quiet introspection. Included is the well-known "Go, Tell It on the Mountain," as well as less-known spirituals, such as "Sister Mary Had-a But One Child." The refrain from the latter runs: "Sister Mary had-a but one child, Born in Bethlehem / An'-a every time the little baby cried / She rocked him in a weary land." Ashley Bryan's illustrations (stretching across two-page spreads) pulsate with the bright colors of African art; he depicts the characters of the Nativity story as Africans. The piano arrangements are easy to play. John Andrew Ross has added guitar chords to supplement the piano accompaniment.

Yussell's Prayer: A Yom Kippur Story
Barbara Cohen. Illustrated by Michael J. Deraney. Lothrop, 1981

IT IS YOM Kippur, the Day of Atonement, when all Jews go to the synagogue to fast and ask for God's forgiveness. On his way to the synagogue, the rich Reb Meir and his three sons are stopped by Yussel the orphan boy. He begs to be allowed to accompany them but Reb Meir sternly refuses. Yussel is a cowherd and cows, Reb Meir says, do not know that it is Yom Kippur. Besides, adds one of his sons sneeringly, how can Yussel pray when he can't even read? In the synagogue Reb Meir and his sons pray for forgiveness but their hearts are full of pride. In the fields, Yussel prays, "Since I can't give you any words, I give you this tune instead." And he begins to play his reed pipe. At that very moment, the rabbi blows the ram's horn to signal the end of Yom Kippur. When asked by Reb Meir why he did this at that particular time, he replies, "I heard a melody, a simple melody played on a reed pipe. . . . All our prayers went in to God, because he had opened the gates to admit that melody. . . . It was a true prayer." Based on the ancient tradition of the Psalms, *Yussel's Prayer: A Yom Kippur Story* is about the true meaning of prayer. Prayer, it tells us, is not about fancy words or extravagant actions, nor is it about social status. It is about a heart full of humility, gratitude, and love—like Yussel's.

Middle Readers

Angels and Other Strangers
Katherine Paterson
Harper Trophy, 1988 (1979), 118 pages

ANGELS AND OTHER *Strangers* is a collection of stories from the pen of the celebrated Katherine Paterson. With her unerring instinct for discovering "splendor in the ordinary," Katherine Paterson shows how the unremarkable lives of ordinary people can be transformed by a remarkable event long ago—the birth of a child in a stable. In the title story, Julia, the mother of two young children, is happily anticipating a Christmas without the irksome presence of Aunt Patty. But when she gets a call ordering her to pick up Aunt Patty after all, Julia tries to put her selfishness aside and drives off into the night. Meanwhile, Jacob is walking thirty miles to Washington, D. C. Too poor to afford transportation, and too old to be out in the bitter cold, Jacob is nonetheless determined to reach Washington, where a young friend, Marlene, is having a baby all alone. What happens when Julia and Jacob meet on the road and how his kindness transforms Julia's life complete this beautiful story. Julia's four-year-old son says of Jacob, "He's our angel, Aunt Patty. Our Christmas Angel." *Angels and Other Strangers* is a book about the joy and mystery of the Incarnation. Most of us are not kings, it reminds us. We are the humble shepherds in the fields, preoccupied with the struggle of making ends meet, of clothing and feeding our children. The baby in the manger didn't come into the world to be rich, powerful, and self-actualized. Rather, he came in lowliness, in poverty, in *humanity* so that we would recognize and love him. When a little girl in "Many Happy Returns" realizes that Jesus actually *cried,* she says, with more wisdom than she knows, "Happy birthday, Jesus. . . . And many happy *reruns* of the day!"

The Bells of Christmas
Virginia Hamilton. Illustrated by Lambert Davis.
Harcourt Brace Jovanovich, 1989, 59 pages

YOUNG JASON BELL cannot wait for Christmas. He is so agitated with the waiting—wanting the snow to fall and his relatives to arrive—that he sulks. But soon enough Christmas and its joys are upon him. Set in 1890, this story of two African-American families living along the "National Road" in Ohio is told with quiet grace. Jason's family members have lived in their home for a hundred years, and there is a solidity and gratitude in their sense of tradition and family identity. The simpler pleasures of the time recounted in this book can act as antidotes to the commercialized frenzy of the holiday season today. Jason not only gets snow but also the best presents he could want, nearly all of them hand made by members of his family. After the presents are exchanged comes the meal; the day ends with a church service, in which Jason and his sister sing solo parts. Virginia Hamilton, perhaps our greatest chronicler of the African-American experience for children, has written a story that whispers, rather than shouts, its many meanings to us. See also her collection of folktales, *The People Could Fly* (see page 127), and *The Planet of Junior Brown* (see page 212).

The Best Christmas Pageant Ever
Barbara Robinson. Illustrated by Judith Gwyn Brown. HarperCollins, 1972, 81 pages

"THE HERDMANS WERE absolutely the worst kids in the history of the world." This outrageously funny and very moving story of how six diminutive town bullies intimidate an entire congregation into giving them the main parts in the Christmas pageant injects new life into the story of Christ's birth. By humorously exploding stereotypes—instead of acting "quiet and dreamy and out of this world," Imogene Herdman plays Mary "like Mrs. Santoro at the Pizza Parlor . . . loud and bossy," ready to protect her baby come what may—the story asks us to reexamine our perceptions of the relevance of Christmas in our lives. The vigorous realism that the unruly Herdmans bring to their parts—Mary burps the child Jesus before placing him in the manger!—emphasizes the humanity of the Holy Family. "After all [wasn't that] the whole point of Jesus—that he didn't come down on a cloud like something out of 'Amazing Comics,' but that he was born and lived . . . a real person?" In a culture that has reduced Christmas to the level of the checkbook or sentimentalized it to the point of meaninglessness, this is refreshing indeed.

A *Christmas Carol*
Charles Dickens. Illustrated by Trina Schart Hyman.
Holiday House, 1983 (1843), 118 pages

A STORY THIS familiar needs little commentary. Dickens, who had a tendency to lapse into sentimentality when writing about women and children, rescued this story from that fate. The three spirits—of Past, Present, and Future—who visit Ebenezer Scrooge on Christmas Eve pull him out of his miserly solitude and force him to look at the world around him. The spirits act as a substitute for the imagination he has neglected. The final spirit brings the most chilling message: that death is our common lot. Death can be made meaningful and bearable only by a life of virtue and generosity. Scrooge has never risked himself, never made himself vulnerable by loving another. Children believe in Scrooge's transformation, the cracking of the hard shell he has placed around his heart. That is because they see him regain his childlike nature. Children come to love Scrooge because he becomes one of them.

The *Gift of the Magi*
O. Henry. Illustrated by Lisbeth Zwerger.
Picture Book Studio, 1982 (1906)

THE STORY RECOUNTED in O. Henry's classic "The Gift of the Magi" would be unbearably sentimental if not for one thing: the playfulness and irony of its language. Della and James barely survive on $20 a week, but they love each other. On Christmas Eve, Della finds that she has saved only $1.87, and so she decides to sell her long, luxuriant hair in order to buy Jim a watch chain for his beloved timepiece. When she presents the chain to Jim she finds out that he has sold the watch to buy her a pair of tortoiseshell combs for which she has longed. Both have sacrificed their most precious possession for the other. This comedy of errors is told in a wry, engaging style. "She found it at last. It surely had been made for Jim and no one else. . . . It was a platinum fob chain, simple and chaste in design, properly proclaiming its value by substance alone and not by meretricious ornamentation—as all good things should do. It was even worthy of The Watch. . . . It was like him. Quietness and value—the description applied to both." The result is quintessential O. Henry: humor laced with a dose of profundity. Lisbeth Zwerger, an award-winning artist, has produced a series of illustrations that match the tone of the story.

A Gift for Mama
Esther Hautzig. Illustrated by Donna Diamond.
Viking, 1981, 56 pages

WE HAVE SMALL daughters of our own and know how much they love making presents for special occasions. But at a certain age, a young girl yearns to go to the store and *buy* something special. Sara is at just that age. For Mother's Day this year, she has decided that Mama is to have a pair of black satin slippers to go with the black satin robe that Daddy had bought her. The only trouble is that the slippers cost far too much. How is Sarah to find the money? Then she hits upon an idea; if her aunt's college friends pay her to mend their threadbare clothes, she just might scrape up enough. Sarah's devoted industriousness and the lesson it teaches her mother complete this simple story. *A Gift for Mama* reminds us that a child's love is priceless and cannot be reckoned by adult standards alone.

Historical Fiction

In order to find its vitality, we need to constantly step back from the past . . . and one way or another take it by surprise.

—Jean Fritz

Middle Readers

Adam of the Road (**N**)
Elizabeth Gray. Illustrated by Robert Lawson.
Puffin, 1987 (1942)

WINNER OF THE 1943 Newbery Medal, *Adam of the Road* is much more than a panoramic view of medieval England. It is also an enthralling story of a young boy's journey to manhood. With his harp slung over his shoulder and his beloved dog, Nick, at his heels, Adam asks for nothing better than to be on the road with his father, Roger-the-Minstrel. But when his dog is stolen and he is inadvertently separated from his father, Adam soon learns that life is not the endless carnival he had supposed and that people are not always to be trusted. Adam's infectious exuberance for life and adventure makes him the perfect hero for the young reader.

All-of-a-Kind Family
Sydney Taylor. Illustrated by Helen John.
Dell, 1979 (1951), 189 pages

ELLA, HENNY, SALLY, Charlotte, and Gertie are five girls who live in New York's Lower East Side at the turn of the century. Dressed in similar clothes, these sprightly girls are called the "all-of-a-kind family." Taylor's novel is a leisurely depiction of daily life in the predominantly Jewish community of this time. The girls have loving parents who temper their moral lessons with large doses of love. In the little trials and tribulations of everyday life, the girls learn the value of work, responsibility, and generosity. The family members are observant Jews, praying together and keeping the feasts and fasts. The historical dimension of this novel, with its meticulously rendered details, will tell children about a time without many of our modern luxuries, when children lived rich, rewarding lives without television, Barbie dolls, and Nintendo. Among the other titles in this series are *More All-of-a-Kind Family, All-of-a-Kind Family Downtown,* and *Ella of All-of-a-Kind Family.*

Black Beauty
Anna Sewell. Illustrated by John Speirs.
Simon & Schuster, 1982 (1877)

ANNA SEWELL'S NOVEL about the horse called Black Beauty is justly famous. It is not only a heartbreaking exposé of cruelty to animals in Victorian times, but it is also a story containing the timeless themes of friendship, loyalty, and kindness to those more vulnerable than ourselves. Black Beauty tells the story of his life from his days as a carefree colt with loving masters, through his later mistreatment by foolish, drunken, or greedy humans, to his pitiful collapse as an abused London cab horse. By the end of his moving story we feel that we have run the gamut of human nature, that we have seen the best and the worst that is in man. It reminds us that it is the weak and the innocent who must suffer for our vices of cruelty, selfishness, and intemperance. Any child who has grown to love Black Beauty will think twice about tormenting his favorite pet or bullying a younger brother or sister. The lesson of kindness and nobility of heart is the legacy that Black Beauty leaves to his young reader, and it is a legacy that can never be forgotten.

Blue Willow
Doris Gates. Illustrated by Paul Lantz.
Puffin, 1976 (1940), 176 pages

ALL TEN-YEAR-OLD JANEY has known in her short life is wandering. Forced by the Depression to travel from place to place looking for work, the Larkin family has never known a permanent home. Surrounded by hardship, ugliness, and hunger, Janey finds great comfort in one thing: her blue willow plate, left to her by her dead mother. She loves the plate not only for its delicate beauty but for the picture of the little house painted among the gracefully curving willows by the river. It speaks to her of permanence, of a life without traveling, of home. Then her stepmother falls dangerously ill and Janey's father can find no more work. When an unscrupulous ranch hand comes to their shack to demand rent, Janey has made up her mind. She will give him the plate. It is this act of moral courage that finally works to restore what Janey has lost and what she dreams for most of all. The story's solution is simple and satisfying, and its themes of unselfish love and courage in the face of adversity are timeless. Like the plate, Janey's love has "the power to make drab things beautiful, and to a life of dreary emptiness bring a sense of wonder and delight."

The Borning Room
Paul Fleischman
HarperCollins, 1991, 101 pages

TO LOOK AT it, one would not think there was anything particularly special about the small room behind the kitchen in the Lotts' home. It has a bed, two chairs, and, on a bedside table, a Bible and a lamp. But Georgina Lott knows differently. The borning room is the room where all new life begins in the Lott household; Georgina's mother was born there, as well as her mother's children, Georgina included, and Georgina knows that, one day, she too will lie down on the narrow bed to give birth. But if the borning room is the gateway between the hushed world of the womb and the light of day, it is also the threshold between this world and the next. For the borning room is the place where family members go to die—Georgina's grandfather, her parents, and, one day, Georgina herself. Although the story centers on a young girl's coming of age, it is the borning room itself that is the main character in the book. By reminding Georgina of the mysteries of birth and death, it gives meaning to her life. When she lies down in the bed to give birth or embark on her own spiritual journey beyond life, she is comforted by the knowledge that others have done it before her. She is part of an ongoing generation of Lotts. Written with touching simplicity by Paul Fleischman (author of *Saturnalia*; see page 189), and set in nineteenth-century America, *The Borning Room* is not only a compelling story but also a profound meditation on the goodness of life.

Caddie Woodlawn (N)
Carol Ryrie Brink. Illustrated by Trina Schart Hyman.
Aladdin, 1990 (1935), 275 pages

WINNER OF THE Newbery Medal for 1935, *Caddie Woodlawn* is a celebration of the youth and vigor of the American frontier. The heroine of the story, Caddie, is modeled on the author's grandmother, who was raised in western Wisconsin, the fourth child in a large and loving family. Encouraged by her father, Caddie is allowed more freedom than most girls of her time. Along with her brothers, she romps through the fields and forests, makes friends with the local Indians, and rafts on the nearby lakes. But life on the frontier can be hard as well as carefree; we see the uneasy racial tension between the settlers and the Indians, the destructiveness of a prairie fire, and the fragility of life in a barely tamed land. It is only the strong sense of the family and its values of honesty, hard work, and faith in God that allows Caddie to feel protected and enables her to grow into a strong and independent young woman.

The Door in the Wall (**N**)
Marguerite de Angeli
Dell, 1990 (1949), 120 pages

THE FUTURE LOOKS promising for young Robin; he is going to become a knight like his father and win fame and fortune by his valor. But he falls seriously ill, and when he recovers, he finds that he is crippled. With all his boyhood dreams lying in fragments, he falls into despair. But through the guidance of the kindly and wise monks who nurse him through his sickness, Robin comes to learn that one must always seek "the door in the wall"—the chance to learn and to grow. It is this newfound determination and love of life that give him the courage to escape from a besieged castle and go for help. In a culture where wealth and health are talismans of success, *The Door in the Wall* shows us that the worth of a human being lies rather in the virtues of courage, hope, and love.

Dragonwings (**NH**)
Laurence Yep
Harper Trophy, 1975, 248 pages

EIGHT-YEAR-OLD Moon Shadow has never seen his father. All he knows about him is that he is in the land of the Golden Mountain—America—and that he is a maker of kites . . . until the day his father requests that he join him in America. Thus begins Moon Shadow's life in turn-of-the-century San Francisco, or the "land of demons," as the Chinese call it. Moon Shadow soon learns that his father has a great dream—to fulfill his name as Windrider and be the first Chinese man to fly. Moon Shadow dedicates his young life to helping his father achieve his dream and, in the process, makes friends with two "demonesses," old Miss Whitlaw and her niece Robin. In the end it is the friendship and encouragement of these two white women that enable Moon Shadow to rise above his fear and mistrust of America despite prejudice and persecution. *Dragonwings* is one of those rare books that gives true meaning to the often overused term "multiculturalism." Through the eyes of the young Chinese boy—American words in the story are italicized to emphasize their strangeness—we are irresistibly drawn into a culture that would otherwise appear very alien to our own. By seeing life from the reverse perspective we are able to understand the heroism of those first Chinese-Americans, who had the courage to follow their dreams no matter what their personal cost.

A Gathering of Days (**N**)
Joan W. Blos
Aladdin, 1990, 144 pages

"I, CATHERINE CABOT Hall, aged 13 years, 6 months, 29 days . . . do begin this book." Thus begins the journal of a young girl in nineteenth-century New Hampshire. *A Gathering of Days* not only records the hardships of pioneer life but also its many joys. We witness the struggle of Catherine, motherless at an early age, to accept her father's new wife, and we watch as her early resentment blossoms into love. We also share her grief at the untimely death of her best friend—an experience that was tragically common in those days. Despite the intervening century, Catherine's voice comes down to us with all the vigor and hope of a young girl coming of age, but it is a voice with a refreshing difference. As the *School Library Journal* acutely observed, "[Catherine's character is] old-fashioned in the best sense of the word—principled."

Hans Brinker, or The Silver Skates
Mary Mapes Dodge
Dell, 1990 (1858), 320 pages

THE STORY OF how Hans and Gretel Brinker compete for the coveted silver skates has become well known to children throughout the world since its first publication in 1858. Despite their poverty, the Brinkers are a close-knit and loving family.

With their father lying sick after an accident at the dike years before, and their life savings having mysteriously disappeared on that same fateful night, Hans and Gretel must work hard to help their mother make ends meet. But for all the hardships they endure, they are still young and carefree enough to enjoy gliding on the frozen canal outside their home. Then the Great Race is announced, and the prize is to be a pair of silver skates. With only their own clumsy wooden skates to practice on, Hans and Gretel despair of being able to win until, just before the race, one of the straps on Hans's friend's skates breaks. Is this Hans's chance to win the race, or is friendship more important than winning? This is the dilemma that Hans must struggle with while he waits for the race of his lifetime to begin. It is moments like this and the nobility of Hans's ultimate decision that make *Hans Brinker* one of the best-loved children's classics ever written.

The House of Sixty Fathers (NH)
Meindert DeJong. Illustrated by Maurice Sendak.
Harper Trophy, 1987 (1956), 189 pages

EXTREME CIRCUMSTANCES, SUCH as natural disasters and wars, are tests of character. When normality becomes anarchy, how will we react? Without the external order of a peaceful, law-abiding community, can we find order within ourselves? When food is scarce or danger near, will we save our own skins or think of others? *The House of Sixty Fathers* tells of the Japanese invasion of China during World War II. But the terrifying events described in this story—destruction of entire villages, indiscriminate attacks on civilians—could just as easily be set in Bosnia, Central America, Armenia, or the Sudan. War takes its greatest toll on children, and yet children can react to horrifying situations with amazing courage and endurance. DeJong's story tells of a little boy named Tien Pao, who becomes separated from his parents. His attempts to be reunited with them take him through enemy territory, but he is helped by friendly guerrillas, and eventually by American soldiers and airmen. Throughout his long ordeal Tien Pao holds on to his pet pig, Glory-of-the-Republic. His love for the pig is a tangible sign of his refusal to turn in on himself and to despair. Tien Pao survives and is reunited with his parents. De-Jong also wrote the Newbery Award–winning *The Wheel on the School.*

I, Juan de Pareja (N)
Elizabeth Borton de Treviño
Farrar, Straus and Giroux, 1992 (1965), 180 pages

BASED ON A portrait by Velázquez, this inspiring story follows the extraordinary life of Juan de Pareja, a slave who was to become not only the trusted assistant of one of the greatest painters of the seventeenth century, but also an accomplished artist in his own right. Although intensely loyal to his master, Juan has a great secret that he must keep from him; he is a painter but is forbidden to practice his art by Spanish law. The plot hinges on what will happen to him when his skill is discovered. Today Juan de Pareja's canvases hang side by side with Velázquez's in several European museums—a remarkable testament to the victory of inborn skill over social injustice.

Island of the Blue Dolphins (N)
Scott O'Dell. Illustrated by Ted Lewin.
Houghton Mifflin, 1990 (1961), 181 pages

THE LATE SCOTT O'Dell is considered one of the finest historical novelists for young adults. The genius of his books consists not merely in their meticulous evocation of faraway times and places, but in the gripping moral dilemmas faced by each of his heroes and heroines. *Island of the Blue Dolphins* tells the poignant tale, set in the early 1800s, of Karana, an Indian girl living on an island off the coast of California. When her tribe is evacuated from the island, Karana suddenly jumps off the ship when she realizes that her brother has been left behind. Tragically, her brother is killed by wild dogs, and Karana is left alone on the island. *Island of the Blue Dolphins* is, of course, a survival story, with a female Robinson Crusoe for its heroine. But in Karana's solitude, as in Crusoe's, there is time and space for moral growth. Karana's bitterness at the loss of her brother and her people is tempered by the restorative powers of nature. After she heals the wounded leader of the wild dogs, she gains a new companion, whom she names Rontu. When the enemies of her people, the Aleut Indians, come to the island, she hides from them to avoid capture; but she makes a secret friendship with an Aleut girl named Tutok. Her relationships to Rontu and Tutok help her to understand that even among her "enemies" goodness and loyalty may be found.

Johnny Tremain (**N**)
Esther Forbes
Houghton Mifflin, 1971 (1944), 256 pages

THIS CLASSIC TALE of the American Revolution, a Newbery Medal winner in 1944, is a superb evocation of Boston in the 1770s. It is the story of a young silversmith's apprentice and his initiation into manhood. When Johnny's hand is crippled in an accident, he is forced to abandon his beloved trade. His former self-confidence and swagger are destroyed. Near despair and tempted to a life of crime, Johnny finds himself in the circle of patriots resisting the tyrannical policies of King George. Given new direction in life, Johnny plays a small but invaluable role in the stirring events of the Boston Tea Party and the skirmishes at Lexington and Concord that began the American Revolution. More than an adventure story, *Johnny Tremain* is filled with a sense of history and a deep understanding of human nature. Johnny's struggle with despair and his temptation to turn to lawlessness are strikingly contemporary themes, and lift this book above mere sentimental patriotism.

King of the Wind (**N**)
Marguerite Henry. Illustrated by Wesley Dennis.
Aladdin, 1991 (1948), 174 pages

MARGUERITE HENRY RANKS with Anna Sewell as one
of the finest writers of stories about horses in this century. *King
of the Wind* chronicles the adventures of a remarkable Godolphin Arabian and his faithful horseboy, Agba. Born in the sta-
bles of the sultan of Morocco, Sham is sent to the court of
Louis XV of France as a gift worthy of a king. Half starved by
an unscrupulous captain on the terrible sea voyage, Sham and
Agba arrive at the court in pitiful condition and are put to
work by the palace cook. Thus begins a series of adventures
that will eventually take them to England, where Sham is destined to become the father of a long line of famous racehorses.
A favorite from our own childhood, *King of the Wind* is a
touching story about a young boy's devotion and the ultimate
triumph of a horse's remarkable pedigree.

The Little House in the Big Woods
Laura Ingalls Wilder. Illustrated by Garth Williams.
HarperCollins, 1971 (1932), 238 pages

LAURA INGALLS WILDER wrote the *Little House* series
from her recollections of growing up in a pioneer family over a
century ago. Life on the frontier could be hard, especially during the long winter months—Laura recalls wolves howling
around their log cabin at night in the winter. But it was also a
time filled with the simple pleasures of family life, when Pa
would play his fiddle of an evening, or Ma would bake bread.
Filled with the memories of a happy and carefree childhood,
the nine volumes in the *Little House* collection remind us of a
time when a child's first sense of community and society was
fashioned in the loving security of home. The other volumes
(available in a boxed set) are *The Little House on the Prairie,*

Farmer Boy, The Long Winter, On the Banks of Plum Creek, By the Shores of Silver Lake, Little Town on the Prairie, These Happy Golden Years, and *The First Four Years.*

Little Women
Louisa Alcott
Puffin, 1988 (1868), 303 pages

Little Women vies with *The Adventures of Tom Sawyer* and *The Adventures of Huckleberry Finn,* not only as one of the most popular children's novels in American history, but also as one of the most unforgettable. Who does not recall that memorable scene when Jo cuts off her beautiful hair to help her family in a financial crisis? Do we not wish that we too would have such courage and generosity of heart should the circumstances arise? In an age when the needs of the self are exalted far above the claims of the family or the community, *Little Women* continues to remind us that only acts of unselfish love can ultimately bridge the gap between the individual and society at large. We also recommend the novel's sequels, *Little Men* and *Jo's Boys.*

Number the Stars (**N**)
Lois Lowry
Houghton Mifflin, 1989, 137 pages

AWARDED THE NEWBERY Medal in 1990, *Number the Stars* is an inspiring story of a young girl's love for her Jewish friend Ellen, and her determination not to allow the Nazis to take her away. The golden Star of David that Ellen wears around her neck is a symbol of hated otherness to the Nazis, but for Annemarie the star becomes a potent symbol of unity and a sign of God's protection. The story is an eloquent reminder that no matter what our ethnic, cultural, or religious background, we all share a common bond of humanity that must be founded on a respect for the rights of the individual person.

Perilous Pilgrimage
Henry Treece
Criterion, 1959, 158 pages

THIS STORY IS based on one of the most famous, or notorious, incidents in the life of the medieval church—the children's crusade led by the twelve-year-old "prophet" Stephen in the thirteenth century. When the noble-born Alys and her brother, Geoffrey, learn that their father is to remarry, they determine to run away and join the crusade. But their confidence in Stephen's mission is shattered by his failure to part the seas between France and the Holy Land, and by the realization that they have been sold to slave traders by Stephen's evil adviser, a jester who enticed the children to follow them by playing his flute. Aided by their faithful tutor, Brother Gerard, who has followed them to the Holy Land, Alys and Geoffrey come to learn, among other things, that the "pagan" Muslims, like their own Christian countrymen, are composed of good and bad alike and that prejudice based upon the color of skin or the difference of religion is evil and invariably leads to tragedy. A wise story with plenty of adventure to engage the young reader.

Prairie Songs
Pam Conrad. Illustrated by Darryl S. Zudeck.
Harper Trophy, 1985, 167 pages

LOUISA DOWNING AND her younger brother, Lester, are used to the loneliness of the wide Nebraska plains. To them, the endless expanse of land and sky is like a huge coverlet spread over their beds or the unadorned wall of their "soddy" house. It is comforting, predictable . . . home. But to the recently arrived Emmeline Berryman, born and bred on the East Coast, it is a forbidding wilderness. With her nearest neighbors three miles away, and her doctor husband often away on his rounds, the tiny house she lives in seems more and more like a prison. How Louisa and Lester come to know and love Emmeline and how her valiant struggle for survival ends in tragedy complete this moving story. *Prairie Songs* does not sentimentalize pioneer life, a life that was as full of the simple joys of family as it was of terrible hardship. Rather, it leaves us, in the end, with a sense of the heroism of those first pioneers, whose greatest enemy was not the Indians, nor the coyotes, but loneliness.

The Red Badge of Courage
Stephen Crane
Puffin, 1986 (1895), 166 pages

WHEN THE YOUNG Henry Fleming enlists in the American Civil War, his head is filled with dreams of glory and the "red badge of courage." But he soon finds that the reality of war is far different from what he imagined. Caught up in the battle of Chambersburg—one of the bloodiest of the Civil War—he soon learns that courage is not the bright, carefree, and effortless thing he had once thought; rather, it is composed of equal amounts of fear, primitive blood lust, and a dogged determination to do one's duty even in the teeth of enemy fire. Stephen Crane does not sermonize about the horrors of war, nor does he sentimentalize his young hero (Henry has his moments of cowardice and betrayal). Rather, he lays bare the doubts and fears of a young soldier and lets us judge for ourselves. The result is one of the most stirring and humane books about war ever written.

The Red Pony
John Steinbeck. Illustrated by Wesley Dennis.
Viking, 1989 (1945), 131 pages

THE RED PONY is a classic story of a boy's initiation into manhood. John Steinbeck's tale conjures up the emotions, fears, and joys of young Jody Tiflin, who one day receives an unexpected gift. "A red pony colt was looking at him out of the stall. Its tense ears were forward . . . its coat was rough . . . its mane was tangled. Jody's throat collapsed in on itself and cut his breath short." Like all great American heroes, Jody has to learn responsibility and self-reliance against the backdrop of the unpredictable world of nature. Steinbeck's narrative, far from being sentimental, is full of heartbreak as well as joy, loss as well as triumph. This handsome edition is a meticulous reprinting of the limited edition of 1945, with the unforgettable watercolor illustrations of Wesley Dennis.

Sarah, Plain and Tall (**N**)
Patricia MacLachlan
Harper Trophy, 1987, 58 pages

IF JUDGED BY appearances, Sarah is nothing special—she is, as she admits, "plain and tall." But to a lonely widower and his two motherless children, she is the answer to their dreams. Her presence transforms the midwestern farming family; not only is the house once again filled with the sound of song, but her longing for her native Maine enables the children to see anew the familiar land around them. Long grass rippling under a summer storm now suggests the ocean that they have never seen; a haystack becomes a sand dune. This exquisitely written tale is a reminder that, as with Sarah, it is often the most humble part of God's creation that is the most beautiful.

The Secret Garden
Frances Hodgson Burnett
Illustrated by Shirley Hughes.
Viking, 1989 (1911), 240 pages

THE CENTRAL THEME of this perennial children's classic is regeneration—moral and emotional rebirth. Mary Lennox is left an orphan when her parents die of a disease in India.

Mary, who has been spoiled since birth, is sent to live at her uncle's large home, Misselthwaite Manor, on the Yorkshire moors. The dark, gloomy house and the rugged moors do not agree with Mary, who is a petulant and selfish child. But when she discovers an abandoned garden, enclosed by a high wall, she is intrigued. This secret garden was her dead aunt's favorite place, but was locked at her death. Uncle Archibald is a broken man, grief stricken at the loss of his wife and plunged into despair. Archibald's despair is reflected in his sickly son, Colin, whose existence is kept secret from Mary. With the help of Dickon, a high-spirited boy from a poor family, Mary begins to restore the garden. Mary's petulance is replaced by a determination to see life and beauty in the garden. Her stubbornness is now directed toward getting Colin out of his darkened room and into the healthful air. Together, Mary, Colin, and Dickon bring new life to the garden and, ultimately, to Uncle Archibald. This novel has inspired several film versions, as well as a wonderful musical version for the stage. Burnett has been accused of sentimentality, but at her best, as in *The Secret Garden* and *The Little Princess,* she dramatizes the healing power of childlike innocence.

Shades of Gray
Carolyn Reeder
Avon, 1991, 165 pages

IN THE AFTERMATH of the Civil War, Will Page is left an orphan. Taken from his home in the town of Winchester, Virginia, to live in the country with his Uncle Jed and Aunt Ella, Will has a lot of adjusting to do. He discovers that Uncle Jed refused to fight for either side in the war, a choice that appears to Will as either cowardice or a horrible betrayal. When Will receives a letter from the kindly Doc Martin, inviting him to return to Winchester to live with Martin and his wife, Will is thrown into turmoil. On Uncle Jed's farm, Will has learned the value of hard work and a host of new skills. His cousin Meg has been a faithful friend. A violent encounter with a local bully causes Will to seek revenge. But Uncle Jed shows him a different way to react to violence. Suddenly Will begins to see the validity in his uncle's difficult choice and learns something about his own failings. *Shades of Gray* is not a tract in favor of pacifism: Uncle Jed's choice is presented as a painful but far from cowardly option. The focus remains on Will and his need to let go of the resentments and losses of the past. The historical setting of this novel is well researched and thoroughly convincing. Carolyn Reeder has crafted a story with contemporary relevance, an antidote to our own violent times.

The Sign of the Beaver (**NH**)
Elizabeth Speare
Houghton Mifflin, 1983, 135 pages

MATT HAS MIXED feelings as he watches his father disappear among the trees; he is proud that his father trusts him to guard their newly built cabin while he goes to fetch the rest of the family, but he is daunted at the prospect of surviving alone in the wilderness for the entire summer. When his gun is stolen, and his precious supplies destroyed by an inquisitive bear, Matt is forced to hunt for survival and not merely for sport. With an Indian boy as guide he begins to learn the ways of the forest, and he comes to respect and love the life of these Native Americans. Much more than a tale of endurance and a boy's coming to maturity, this compelling story sensitively explores the early pioneer experience from both the Indian's and the settler's perspective.

The Singing Tree (**NH**)
Kate Seredy
Puffin, 1990 (1939), 247 pages

THE SINGING TREE is an inspiring story of one Hungarian family's determination to remain true to its farming and cultural heritage, despite the onset of World War I. When thirteen-year-old Jansi's father is called up, Jansi knows that he has to be the "young master" in his father's stead. Helped by his spirited cousin Kate, he manages not only to run the farm successfully, but also opens his home to six Russian prisoners and a host of German war children. Once again, the large farmhouse is filled with the sound of children's laughter, but tragedy is not far away. Old Uncle Moses, a devoted friend of the family and the Jewish owner of the town's only store, loses two sons to the war. Hans, one of the German refugees, learns that his father has been killed. But the watchword on the Nagy farm is "comrade." Despite their cultural and religious differences, despite the war that is tearing Europe apart, the people on the farm are united by their common humanity. A story that Jansi's father tells when he returns from the war eloquently articulates this miracle of brotherhood. "Ahead of us and behind us lay a devastated forest with only skeletons of trees . . . barbed wire, broken guns, empty cartridges, empty tins. . . . And then . . . we saw one tree. One single apple tree . . . alive with birds." It is difficult to impart the horrors of war to children without simultaneously offering them hope for the future. *The Singing Tree* does just that. We also recommend *The Good Master,* a story of how the irrepressible Kate came to live on the farm and how the Nagy household was never to be the same again.

The Slave Dancer (**N**)
Paula Fox
Dell, 1975, 127 pages

WHEN THIRTEEN-YEAR-OLD Jessie is kidnapped in the dead of night from the streets of New Orleans he little suspects that he has been shanghaied onto an illegal slave trading ship. At first Jesse can think of no reason why he has been taken on board *The Moonlight;* he has never set foot on a ship before and is too small and weak to man the sails. The only thing that he can do is play the flute and this, he soon learns, is precisely what is required of him. He is to be *The Moonlight's* slave dancer; dancing was a macabre practice intended to keep the slaves healthy for the slave auction. As he watches the manacled bodies moving in slow agony to the notes of his flute, he is filled with an intense hatred for the sailors who profit in the misery and degradation of others. He forms a bond with one of the slave boys but is powerless to help him until, one night, a great storm arises and threatens to destroy the ship. Compellingly told through the eyes of a young boy, *The Slave Dancer* is a haunting evocation of one of the most brutal chapters in American history.

Smith
Leon Garfield
Dell, 1987 (1967), 192 pages

IF THERE IS ANYONE who could step into the shoes of that master storyteller, Charles Dickens, it is Leon Garfield. With the deftness of a truly great writer he conjures up haunting scenes of eighteenth-century London, ranging from the darkest cellar in the most notorious alehouse in the city to the sparrows huddled on the dome of Saint Paul's. From their vantage point high over the teeming streets, the sparrows see a small figure dodging in and out of the crowd. His name is Smith; he is twelve years old and he is a pickpocket. After stealing a document from an old gentleman, Smith then witnesses his brutal murder. Unable to read but filled with pity for the murdered man, Smith determines to get to the bottom of the mystery, and is inexorably dragged deeper and deeper into a complicated and horrifying web of intrigue. Part Artful Dodger and part Oliver Twist, Smith journeys into London's criminal underworld, which forces him to choose between his own greed and justice, between good and evil. Packed with adventure and peopled with unforgettable characters, *Smith*, like all great mystery novels, is built upon the wise maxim "Truth will out."

Sounder (**N**)
William H. Armstrong
HarperCollins, 1992 (1969), 116 pages

THE TRAGIC VISION in this novel encapsulates all the evils visited on African-Americans in our history. But like all great tragedies, *Sounder* has a universal significance, beyond time and place. The story is told in a spare, understated style that echoes the restrained stoicism of its characters. A black sharecropper steals some food for his starving family and is caught. As he is taken away, his hunting dog, Sounder, runs after him and is shot. We follow the story from the point of view of the eldest boy in the family, whose love for Sounder echoes his love for his missing father. The boy and his family learn to live with the loss of their father. He finds comfort in the stories his mother tells from the Bible, particularly the story of Joseph, who endures suffering and captivity before his wisdom and goodness triumph. The boy's mother reminds her son, "You must learn to lose, child. The Lord teaches the old to lose. The young don't know how to learn it. Some people is born to keep. We was born to lose, I reckon." As the boy spends the ensuing months and years searching rock quarries and chain gangs to find word of his father, he manages, through his persistence, to learn to read. This achievement is a form of liberation and is the sign that hope may be found even in tragedy. But the lasting image that will remain with every reader of this book is the noble coon dog Sounder, maimed but never without dignity or the patient love that endures all things.

Treasure Island
Robert Louis Stevenson. Illustrated by N. C. Wyeth.
Charles Scribner and Sons, 1981 (1883), 273 pages

TREASURE ISLAND WOULD have been a rather lackluster adventure story had not the mysterious and charismatic pirate Long John Silver burst out of Robert Louis Stevenson's imagination and onto the book's pages. When a battered old seadog arrives at the Admiral Benbow tavern, young Jim Hawkins's life is changed forever. The seaman brings trouble with him, including murder, treasure, and pirates. When a treasure map is located, Jim finds himself on an expedition to recover the loot, led by the local aristocrat, Squire Trelawney. Trelawney and Dr. Livesey are adults who are ostensibly good, but who are really foolish and greedy. In the thick of his adventures, Jim comes to rely on his own ingenuity and sense of morality. But Long John Silver remains an enigma. Ruthless and yet charming, Silver is like a chameleon: his colors change depending on his environment. Jim cannot find it in him to utterly condemn this cunning pirate, who is more appealing than the squire and the doctor. Jim's courage and resourcefulness, along with the efforts of the long-suffering Ben Gunn, ultimately save the day. Stevenson's ironies do not intrude on the swift pace of the story, but they are there, just below the surface, like buried treasure.

The True Confessions of Charlotte Doyle (**NH**)
Avi
Avon, 1990, 232 pages

THE CHARLOTTE DOYLE who boards the *Seahawk* one day in 1832 is a young lady who is quite sure of her privileged place in the world. The daughter of a wealthy shipowner, she is confident that she will be able to teach the rough sailors a little breeding and she is encouraged in this mission by the gentlemanly Captain Jaggery. But when she disembarks in Boston, months later, the captain is dead and her world will never be the same again. Charlotte's story, told through her own eyes, challenges our preconceptions about life by posing certain questions. Is a person to be accorded more respect than a black cook just because he wears fine clothes, as Captain Jaggery does? Or is it nobility of heart that constitutes real worth? It is only when Charlotte foils a mutiny, betrays the culprits to Jaggery, and witnesses his cruelty firsthand that she realizes that the cook Zachariah is more of a gentleman than the captain, because he has told her the truth. In atonement for her treachery and against all the codes of ladylike behavior, Charlotte cuts her hair, exchanges male clothing for her fine silks and petticoats, and takes to the rigging. *True Confessions* is not a book that recommends rebellion for its own sake, but a book that reinforces one of the guiding principles of the founding of America—namely, that all men and women are created equal in the sight of God and that any rule that contradicts this truth should be strenuously opposed. It is no coincidence that, by the end of the voyage, it is Zachariah, a poor black man, who has become Charlotte's truest friend.

The Trumpeter of Krakow (**N**)
Eric Kelly
Collier, 1973 (1928), 239 pages

SET IN FIFTEENTH-CENTURY Poland, *The Trumpeter of Krakow* is the story of a young boy's admiration for the bravery of a long-dead youth and how this encourages him to remain loyal to his country in the face of great danger. Forced to abandon their farm to the invading Tartars, Joseph Charnetski and his parents flee to Krakow with the only thing that they managed to salvage—a priceless family heirloom called the Great Tarnov Crystal. Reputed to have strange magical powers that will guarantee victory to anyone who possesses it, the Crystal must be delivered to the king before it falls into the wrong hands. Only the inspiring example of the young trumpeter of Krakow, who met his death when he alerted the city to an invasion by the Tartars, gives Joseph the courage he needs to complete his mission. *The Trumpeter of Krakow* is a dramatic example of how stories can be powerful incentives to virtue in our young, virtues that might well lead to the transformation of our society and the healing of its many ills.

Twenty and Ten
Claire Huchet Bishop
Illustrated by William Pène du Bois.
Puffin, 1978 (1952), 76 pages

SET DURING THE German occupation of France, *Twenty and Ten* is the story of how twenty schoolchildren had the courage to hide ten Jewish children from the Nazis. Sent to a remote school in the mountains run by the kindly Sister Gabriel, the children lead happy and secure lives, safe from the horrors of their war-torn country. Then, one day, Sister Gabriel comes to the children and explains that they must hide ten Jewish refugee children, and warns them, "We can never betray them, no matter what the Nazis do." Inspired by the story of Mary and Joseph, a Jewish family that successfully escaped the persecution of King Herod, the children readily agree. But when soldiers come to the school, the children must have the courage to stand by their convictions. Simply but movingly told, *Twenty and Ten* is a story that reminds us that, no matter what our religious convictions, we are all children of God.

Under the Hawthorn Tree
Marita Conlon-McKenna
Puffin, 1992, 124 pages

UNDER THE HAWTHORN TREE is the tender and moving story of how three children manage to survive the famine in nineteenth-century Ireland. Abandoned by their parents and forced to go to a children's work house, the O'Driscoll children decide to run away to distant Castletaggart, where their great-aunts live. But the journey is long and arduous, and the children have to battle starvation, fatigue, and illness. It is only their love for one another and the courage and resourcefulness of Eily, the eldest girl, that save them from sharing the terrible fate of many of their countrymen. An inspiring story of family love, *Under the Hawthorn Tree* is also a vivid reminder of one of the most tragic episodes in Irish history.

The Writing on the Hearth
Cynthia Harnett. Illustrated by Gareth Floyd.
Viking, 1973 (1971), 318 pages

WHEN YOUNG STEPHEN encounters a well-dressed stranger on a horse in the forest, he is at first immensely impressed. The man is not only learned and courteous, he also turns out to be Roger Bolingbroke, a master of arts at Oxford University, the very place to which Stephen aspires to go someday. But when Master Bolingbroke asks Stephen to lie about having seen him, the boy's suspicions are instantly aroused. A gentleman does not lie, he tells himself. And when Stephen accidentally discovers a secret letter implicating Bolingbroke's patron, Duke Humphrey, in a plot against the king, he knows that it is up to him to prevent treachery from disrupting the life of his quiet village and that of the entire nation. Set in fourteenth-century England and filled with scenes of medieval Oxford and London, *The Writing on the Hearth* follows Stephen's struggle to choose between his own ambition and loyalty to the crown.

Older Readers

The Adventures of Huckleberry Finn
Mark Twain
Penguin, 1986 (1884), 336 pages

IN THE FAMOUS "Notice" at the beginning of *The Adventures of Huckleberry Finn,* Mark Twain warns that anyone "attempting to find a moral" in the novel "will be banished." As usual, Twain was being humorously ironic, since this American classic is shot through with profound moral dilemmas. It is full of adventure and high comedy, of course, but this novel is far more complex and thematically rich than its predecessor, *The Adventures of Tom Sawyer.* When Huck and the runaway slave Jim head out on the Mississippi on their raft, they encounter a series of events that shows the corruption and hypocrisy of what is often called "respectable" society. Huck, a child, and Jim, a slave—the weakest members of this society—are forced to use their wits to survive. Like other writers of satire, such as Jonathan Swift, Twain points out the rot in society because he wants to assert a more just moral order— the world as it should be. *Tom Sawyer* should be read first, as a preparation for the more subtle ironies of *Huckleberry Finn*.

Billy Budd, Sailor
Herman Melville
Penguin, 1983 (1924), 466 pages

MUCH LIKE HIS contemporary, Nathaniel Hawthorne, Herman Melville dedicated his fiction to asking the great questions: What is the nature of evil? How can a man know what is the right thing to do? Is all suffering meaningless? When Billy Budd, a sailor of uncommon physical beauty and moral innocence, is falsely accused by the evil master-at-arms, Claggart, he acts the only way he knows how—he strikes him down and inadvertently kills him. Now the captain of the ship faces an excruciating moral dilemma; should Budd hang for murder or should he be allowed to go free because of mitigating circumstances? Beautifully written by one of America's greatest masters of prose, *Billy Budd* presents us with a world in which the struggle for right action and moral justice must always be attempted, however imperfect the result. For older readers who enjoy a challenge, we also recommend *Moby Dick*. (See page 182.)

The Call of the Wild
Jack London. Illustrated by Martin Gascoigne.
Puffin, 1988 (1903), 124 pages

BUCK—HALF GERMAN shepherd, half Saint Bernard—is a thoroughly civilized dog: he rules over an extensive California raisin farm owned by Judge Miller. But a greedy, unscrupulous servant kidnaps him and sells him to pay for his gambling habit. Buck is sold to men who have raced to the frozen Yukon, "because men, groping in the arctic darkness, had found a yellow metal." Soon Buck is caught up in the famous Klondike gold rush. In the frigid North he learns the "law of club and fang," and in the service of masters both compassionate and cruel he experiences love, loyalty, and betrayal. London tells the story from Buck's point of view, ironically commenting on the bestiality of the men obsessed by the yellow metal. He is at times savage but ultimately he possesses a dignity, a wisdom, and even a sort of moral code that is so often lacking in the human world. The "call of the wild" that Buck hears draws him to the wolf pack, where all members of the pack work together for the common good. Jack London's gripping tale is a moving and challenging tale for older children.

David Copperfield
Charles Dickens
Bantam, 1988 (1849), 817 pages

THIS IS THE most nearly autobiographical of all Dickens's works and, along with *Oliver Twist,* contains some of his most deeply felt scenes of childhood misery and his most enduring themes: innocence versus cynicism, simplicity versus hypocrisy, and good against evil. When David is abused by his merciless stepfather, then sent to a boarding school presided over by a tyrannical and sadistic headmaster, he feels as if his young life has come to an end. Then he meets some unexpected friends—the comical Mr. Micawber, the amiably mad Mr. Dick, Aunt Betsey Trotwood, and the kind and hospitable Peggotty family. Their love and humor help to restore David's faith in life and to balance the host of evil characters that teem within the pages of this book—the loathsome Uriah Heep and the corrupt aristocrats of the Steerforth family. When he grows up, David Copperfield, much like the young Charles

Dickens himself, credits his salvation to a love founded on the humane maxim "Do unto others as you would have them do unto you."

Dr. Jekyll and Mr. Hyde and The Body Snatchers
Robert Louis Stevenson
Illustrated by Gerard Gibson.
Bedrick, 1989 (1886), 125 pages

FROM THE PEN of Robert Louis Stevenson comes this chilling story of addiction and moral decay. All his life the brilliant and wealthy Dr. Jekyll has led a double life. Outwardly, he is the picture of staid Victorian respectability; secretly, he has pursued a life of self-indulgence and moral turpitude. Now he has devised a potion that, once drunk, will separate these contradictory elements in his soul. By day, he is the kindly Dr. Jekyll; by night, he becomes the monstrous Mr. Hyde, roaming the streets and instilling terror and loathing into everyone he meets. But as in all cases of addiction, what begins as a controlled experiment rapidly starts to get out of hand. Like a moral cancer, the evil Mr. Hyde is beginning to take over his better self. This is the logic of all addiction, the story tells us. We begin by convincing ourselves that we can master our compulsions, then realize that we have become enslaved by them. As Dr. Jekyll writes in his confession before his death, "The powers of Hyde seemed to have grown with the sickliness of Jekyll. . . . He [Jekyll] had now seen the full deformity of that creature . . . and was co-heir with him to death." Living as we do in a culture increasingly dominated by drugs, alcohol, gambling, and sex, Dr. Jekyll and Mr. Hyde is an impassioned and timely plea for moral responsibility. Its companion story, The Body Snatchers, tells of a pair of scientists who repeatedly violate the sanctity of the grave in order to pursue their experiments, and what happens when their crimes finally catch up with them. Like Dr. Jekyll, the body snatchers find that science divorced from ethics is ultimately soul destroying. These stories are for the advanced reader.

Emily of New Moon
L. M. Montgomery
Bantam, 1983 (1923), 339 pages

L. M. MONTGOMERY, author of the celebrated *Anne of Green Gables* series, brings us another spirited heroine. When Emily Starr, orphaned at the death of her father, goes to live at New Moon Farm, she thinks that she will never be happy again. Aunt Elizabeth is stern and forbidding and Cousin Jimmy is a boy who cannot possibly share a lonely girl's passion for reading. But Emily is in for a few surprises. Not only does she come to love and respect her aunt for the order and security that she brings to her life, but she finds that Jimmy is enthusiastic and encouraging of her emerging talent as a writer. As she learns to trust the household at New Moon Farm, Emily finds that she is more and more capable of generosity and love. This, combined with her quickness of mind, enables her to solve a mystery that gives a lonely man the chance to love again. Set in nineteenth-century America, the *Emily* trilogy (*Emily Climbs* and *Emily's Quest* are the sequel books) allows us to share Emily's adventures, loves, and hopes as she grows to womanhood. She is living testament to the fact that all a child needs to fulfill his or her potential is a loving environment founded on encouragement and discipline. We also highly recommend the *Anne of Green Gables* series.

Flambards
K. M. Peyton. Illustrated by Victor G. Ambrus.
World, 1968, 206 pages

ORPHANED AT AN early age, thirteen-year-old Christina Parsons has spent most of her young life being shuttled from one relative to another. Now she has come to live at Flambards, a decaying mansion in the heart of the English countryside, and she thinks that, at long last, she has found a home. But Flambards, she soon discovers, is no ordinary household. Embittered by a horse-riding accident that left him permanently crippled, Uncle Russell is determined to live vicariously through his two sons, and Christina finds herself caught up in the ensuing conflict. Set in Edwardian England at a time when horses are being replaced by the automobile and the airplane, *Flambards* is a novel about the misunderstanding between the generations in a rapidly changing culture. Uncle Russell is trapped in an outmoded way of life, whereas Christina and the boys find themselves in a world on the brink of World War I. Their struggle to shake off the old world and come to terms with the new is a challenge that the young must face in any age. K. M. Peyton explores this theme with sensitivity and great moral insight. We also recommend the other books in the *Flambards* series: *Thunder in the Sky, The Plan for Birdmarsh,* and *The Maplin Bird.*

A Girl of the Limberlost
Gene Stratton Porter
Puffin, 1992 (1909), 413 pages

FATHERLESS AND NEGLECTED by her grieving and embittered mother, Elnora Comstock has learned early to take care of herself. With her usual independence, she puts herself through high school, and pays for her books and tuition by collecting rare species of butterflies in the swampy forest near her home. It is here, among the trees of the Limberlost, that Elnora finds not only solace for her loneliness but the key to understanding her own soul. As she watches the delicate unfurling of the butterflies' wings from the confining shell of the chrysalis, she realizes that if she is to bring her mother's heart back to life, she must first break through the protective shell of her own resentment and pride. Compassionately written and filled with scenes of haunting natural beauty, *A Girl of the Limberlost* is a moving story about the transforming power of love.

The Grapes of Wrath
John Steinbeck
Viking, 1989 (1939), 592 pages

AN INSTANT CLASSIC since its first publication in 1939, *The Grapes of Wrath* is the story of one family's struggle for survival during the Great Depression. Forced to abandon their poor sharecropping farm by unscrupulous landowners, the Joad family sets out, along with thousands of other Oklahoma families, in search of the "Golden West." But when they arrive in California, they find that it is not the "land of plenty" that they had been led to suppose. Instead, they encounter widespread hostility, brutal living conditions, and, worst of all, the willful destruction of crops in order to keep prices high. The Joad family must now struggle with "the grapes of wrath" in their own souls, a process of dehumanization as threatening as the terrible conditions in which they are forced to live. John Steinbeck has been called one of the greatest socialist writers of this century, but his achievement goes far beyond this. Filled with passages of savage moral indignation as well as of great lyrical beauty, *The Grapes of Wrath* is a haunting testament to the dignity of the human spirit in the face of injustice.

Great Expectations
Charles Dickens
Puffin, 1992 (1860–61), 464 pages

FROM THE PEN of the great Charles Dickens comes this powerful story about the vanity of human wishes. Encouraged by the mad but aristocratic Miss Havisham to believe that she is his secret benefactress and that one day he is destined to marry Estella, her beautiful but spoiled niece, Pip shuns the poor but honest couple who raised him and turns his back on all his former friends. Then one day Pip is shattered to learn that it is Magwitch, a reformed ex-con, who has been supporting him all these years. Thus begins Pip's painful reassessment of his life, a moral journey that will ultimately lead him to reject his false values and adopt Magwitch as his spiritual father. Perhaps one of the greatest of Dickens's later novels, *Great Expectations* explores the theme of redemptive love, a theme that was to recur again and again. Along with Pip, Dickens invites us to reexamine our own values and discover the source of society's greatest wealth—the power of the human heart.

The Great Gatsby
F. Scott Fitzgerald
Charles Scribner and Sons, 1980 (1925), 182 pages

WE CAN ANTICIPATE someone wondering why we would include this book, long a staple of college literature courses, in this guide to books for children. Isn't it too advanced or subtle? We recommend it for the same reason we have selected books by William Faulkner, Ernest Hemingway, and other great authors: because a brilliantly written work should not be kept from older children because it is somehow "reserved" for college courses. Fitzgerald's novel is about the decadence of the Jazz Age, an indictment of a hollow society preoccupied with money and the conspicuous display of wealth. But in that world there is someone who stands out: the enigmatic Jay Gatsby. The story is told by Nick Carraway, a transplanted midwesterner who believes that Gatsby is motivated by a strange kind of hope and innocence that shines brightly. Though Gatsby has become fabulously wealthy, he cares little for his riches, except as a means for attracting his lost love, Daisy. But the tragic thing about Gatsby is that he idealizes Daisy and refuses to come to terms with the real world. Gatsby's ability to rise above the materialism of his generation elicits our admiration, but his tendency to live in a dream world is less commendable.

Jane Eyre
Charlotte Brontë
Signet, 1960 (1847), 461 pages

WRITTEN BY CHARLOTTE Brontë, one of three extraordinary literary sisters, *Jane Eyre* is considered one of the greatest Romantic novels to come out of nineteenth-century
England. When the orphan Jane Eyre arrives at Mr. Rochester's
stately but gloomy home to take up the position of governess,
she soon begins to suspect that the house contains a dark secret. Mr. Rochester's strangely erratic behavior seems to indicate a troubled conscience and when Jane hears screams
coming from a remote wing of the house, her suspicions are
confirmed. Thriller, mystery, and love story all rolled into one,
Jane Eyre is the compelling story of how a lonely, brooding man
is transformed by a young woman's courage and steadfast love.

Kim
Rudyard Kipling
Dell, 1992 (1901), 312 pages

IT HAS TO be said, straight off, that this book is only for the
most advanced readers. The language and the style are not easy
to pick up, because they are studded with foreign and obsolete
words and phrases. But for the confident reader, *Kim* is an experience not soon forgotten. We have had a great deal of talk
about "multiculturalism" in recent years, but Kipling was interested in the subject a long time ago. Though he is often considered a mindless supporter of imperialism and racism,
Kipling was a more complex figure than that. In *Kim*, he wrote
a novel that positively revels in the cultural diversity of India. It
is set in the nineteenth century, when Britain's rule was challenged by uprisings and invasions. An orphan, the son of a
British soldier who has died of drink, Kim survives in the
streets of Lahore through his wits. He speaks the native tongue
and is so tanned that he passes for an Indian boy. This comes in
handy for those engaged in the political intrigues of the day,
for Kim makes a perfect spy. Inconspicuous, multilingual, intelligent—Kim can gather information, transmit messages,
and steal. When he encounters a Tibetan monk, Kim becomes
his disciple. The monk is on a quest to find a sacred river that

will bring healing and forgiveness. As the novel unfolds, Kim moves from the cynical world of spying to the idealistic religious vision of the monk. Though he recognizes that the monk is slightly crazy, Kim is, at heart, more sympathetic to the quest for the sacred river than to the business of spying for the British government and its allies. Kim is open to the good in all the diverse cultures that coexist in India; his multiculturalism is something bred in the bone, not in political tracts.

The Last of the Mohicans
James Fenimore Cooper
Signet, 1962 (1826), 430 pages

LIKE HUCKLEBERRY FINN and a number of the other great American literary heroes, James Fenimore Cooper's Natty Bumppo is a rebel against the corruption in society. His morality is more true to the historical and practical realities of life than that of the representatives of "civilization" around him. *The Last of the Mohicans* takes place during the French and Indian Wars in 1757. Natty is a hunter and frontier scout who travels with his adopted Native American father, Chingachgook, and his son, Uncas. Risking their lives, they escort two young women to a British fort under siege by French forces. However, that is just the beginning of their troubles. Cooper is our early American master of the adventure story, and this novel can be appreciated on that level alone. But Natty's philosophy, which draws on Native American reverence for nature, stands as a moral challenge to the social order. Natty and his comrades have to convince the Europeans that they are underestimating the reality of evil. The trappings of civilized power can give men the illusion that they are all-powerful, invulnerable. Natty's moral realism undercuts that sort of pride. His relationship to Chingachgook and Uncas is a romantic dream of the brotherhood between Native Americans and the European settlers that was seldom realized in practice. Other recommended novels featuring Natty Bumppo are *The Pioneers, The Deerslayer, The Pathfinder,* and *The Prairie.*

A Man for All Seasons
Robert Bolt
Vintage, 1962, 95 pages

HERE IS ANOTHER example of a book that is known primarily in its film version, starring Paul Scofield. In this instance, the film itself is a classic that does ample justice to Robert Bolt's stage play. Thomas More, a brilliant humanist scholar, becomes Lord Chancellor of England under King Henry VIII. But when Henry divorces his first wife in order to remarry, More, a staunch Catholic, cannot publicly approve of the king's actions. Though he resigns his office and attempts to remain silent, this is not enough for Henry, who needs More's public acquiescence. More cannot do this, and is executed. Bolt's play is rich with believable characters and More's incisive vision. More explains to his daughter why he cannot take an oath approving the king's divorce: "When a man takes an oath, Meg, he's holding his own self in his own hands. Like water. And if he opens his fingers then—he needn't hope to find himself again." He continues, "If we lived in a State where virtue was profitable, common sense would make us good, and greed would make us saintly. . . . But since in fact we see that avarice, anger, envy, pride, sloth, lust and stupidity commonly profit far beyond humility, chastity, fortitude, justice and thought, and have to choose, to be human at all . . . why then perhaps we *must* stand fast a little—even at the risk of being heroes." Bolt is not interested in More as a Catholic, but as a deeply moral individual, a hero for all seasons.

The Master of Hestviken
Sigrid Undset
Knopf, 1973 (1925–27), 994 pages

SINCE ITS FIRST publication in the late twenties, Sigrid Undset's compelling saga of thirteenth-century Norway has become a classic in its own right. Betrothed to each other at the age of seven, Olav and Ingunn have no other thought than that they will, one day, be married. Then Ingunn's father dies when she is fifteen and her uncle refuses to honor the betrothal. Olav and Ingunn are now faced with a cruel dilemma; do they obey their families and allow themselves to be separated, or do they take matters into their own hands and become man and wife without the blessing of the Church? They little suspect that their choice will set them on a path that will not only lead them to betray each other but will also result in murder. Although nearly eight centuries separate us from Olav and Ingunn, we feel that they are not strangers; like us, they are neither wholly good nor wholly bad; like us, they struggle to live out their lives according to their own lights. And, like us, their hearts are not so hard that the seeds of grace cannot still take root in the landscape of their souls. Much more than a masterful evocation of medieval life, *The Master of Hestviken* is a profound and moving study of the human conscience. This book is a one-volume edition that includes the text of four novels: *The Axe, The Snake Pit, In the Wilderness,* and *The Son Avenger.* We also recommend another epic by Nobel Prize–winner Undset: *Kristin Lavransdatter.*

Moby Dick
Herman Melville
Penguin, 1986 (1851), 1,112 pages

ARGUABLY THE GREATEST American epic ever written, *Moby Dick* is also one of the most psychologically realistic portraits of megalomania in the history of literature. Since losing his leg to a white whale, Captain Ahab is consumed by hatred and a desire for revenge. He will stop at nothing to kill the whale, and is willing to sacrifice everything in the process—his ship, his men, even his own soul. But Captain Ahab, like Moby Dick, is no mere monster; although Ahab is eaten up by pride, hatred, and vengefulness, Melville allows us to glimpse the last vestiges of his essential nobility, thus bringing home the full tragedy of a soul gone awry. A superb adventure story, as well as a fascinating re-creation of the vanished days of whaling under sail, *Moby Dick* is a profound and complex study of good and evil. Like *Billy Budd* by the same author (see page 172), we recommend *Moby Dick* to those older readers who enjoy a challenge. An abridged edition is acceptable for those not able to read through Melville's many fascinating digressions.

My Ántonia
Willa Cather
Houghton Mifflin, 1988 (1918), 238 pages

IT IS DIFFICULT TO say enough about this wonderful book! Long considered a masterpiece of American literature, *My Ántonia* is an unforgettable portrait of a pioneer woman living in nineteenth-century Nebraska. We see Ántonia through the eyes of Jim, her lifelong friend, and we watch as she grows from a little girl, newly arrived from Bohemia, to a strong and independent woman with a family of her own. We come to see how her extraordinary strength of character is somehow part of the land on which she lives, that she "had only to stand in an orchard . . . to make you feel the goodness of planting and tending and harvesting at last." No one who has met Ántonia in the pages of this book will be tempted to take the grandeur of this country for granted or to forget the courage and endurance of the first pioneers, whose legacy it is.

One Corpse Too Many
Ellis Peters
Fawcett, 1985, 224 pages

MOVE OVER, SHERLOCK Holmes! Enter Brother Cadfael, medieval super-sleuth extraordinaire. Written by the notable British author Ellis Peters, and filled with authentic sights and sounds of medieval England as well as brain-teasing plots, the Cadfael mysteries are among the best we have found. Brother Cadfael, former crusader, now lay brother in a Shrewsbury monastery, is no stranger to the darker side of human nature. But he is no cynic. With a rigorous sense of justice tempered with compassion, he tracks down criminals, restores peace and order, and comforts the innocent. All this without once resorting to violence. Since we are living in an age that is more and more inclined to admire justice when it is administered down the barrel of a gun, it is refreshing indeed to come across an individual whose only weapon is his robust faith in God and human nature. *One Corpse Too Many* is the first of nearly twenty Brother Cadfael mysteries; we recommend them all.

A Parcel of Patterns
Jill Paton Walsh
Farrar, Straus and Giroux, 1992, 137 pages

BASED ON THE true story of how the plague came to the English village of Eyam in the seventeenth century, *A Parcel of Patterns* is a poignant tale told by one of the few survivors, a young woman called Mall Percival, and how that devastating experience was to change her life forever. When a parcel of the latest London patterns is delivered to the village tailor one spring evening, no one can guess the terrible secret it contains. But when the tailor suddenly dies with the markings of the plague upon him, the villagers know that the angel of death has come to Eyam. The village is cut off from the rest of the countryside for fear of contagion, and the plague forces the villagers to choose between self and neighbor, cowardice and heroism, faith and despair. Beautifully written by one of today's foremost children's authors, *A Parcel of Patterns* is the moving story of a girl's heroism in the face of suffering and loss.

The Plague
Albert Camus
Modern Library, 1948 (1947), 278 pages

WHEN ALBERT CAMUS was awarded the Nobel Prize in Literature in 1957, the official citation praised his works for "[illuminating] the problems of the human conscience in our times." Considered his most profound work of fiction, *The Plague* is a symbolic exploration of the human conscience when faced with its greatest challenge—death. The citizens of Oran are like any other townsfolk—they go about their business by day, raise their families, and gossip in the cafés by night. Then, one spring, rats are seen pouring out of the cellars and sewers and dying by thousands in the streets. At the same time, a doctor named Rieux notices that more and more people are dying of a mysterious affliction. At last the prefect of the town can ignore the statistics no longer: He proclaims Oran in a state of plague and seals the city. Those condemned to remain in the city now face an agonizing decision; do they volunteer to help those stricken by the plague and risk infection themselves or do they turn their backs and try to save themselves? The crisis forces them to look deep into their own souls and discover what kind of people they really are. Masterfully written and filled with scenes of poignant heroism, *The Plague* articulates some of the great questions of the twentieth century and remains one of the most important novels to have come out of postwar Europe. This novel is only for more advanced readers.

The Power and the Glory
Graham Greene
Penguin, 1991 (1940), 222 pages

FOR THE OLDER, more mature reader, *The Power and the Glory* can be an unforgettable experience. The moral wisdom of this novel is not written in neon lights, but it is there for the finding. The story is set in Mexico in the 1930s, when some provincial governments had become violently anticlerical and had prohibited priests from carrying out their duties, on pain of death. The story centers on the "whisky priest," a weak, cowardly cleric who has fathered a child and has a drinking problem. Though he is filled with a sense of unworthiness and guilt, he nonetheless decides to administer the sacraments in violation of the laws. He often doubts his decision but manages to continue to fulfill his priestly duties. Betrayed by a Judas-like figure, the whisky priest goes on to meet his death. As the novel progresses, the reader comes to the realization that, for all his many failings, the whisky priest does show compassion and risks his life to bring others the message of salvation. It is his very humility, his searing honesty about his own faults, that convinces us that he has indeed achieved a kind of holiness.

Pride and Prejudice
Jane Austen
Penguin, 1982 (1813), 396 pages

JANE AUSTEN'S *Pride and Prejudice* has been captivating readers since its first publication, in 1813. From the moment the witty and spirited Elizabeth Bennet appears on the scene, we know that we are not involved in just another ordinary love story filled with stock characters. Elizabeth's determination to humble the proud Darcy fills the pages with sparkling dialogue and finely tuned emotion—their intellectual duels reveal an equality of mind that any feminist would find supremely satisfying. But beneath the dazzling surface of their encounter lies a more profound theme. *Pride and Prejudice* is as much about the relationship between the individual and society, and the responsibilities to others that this implies, as it is about romantic love. Since we live in an age that regards romantic love as an end in itself, Elizabeth's realization that authentic love can be built only upon considerable self-sacrifice is not only refreshing, it is almost revolutionary. We also recommend *Northanger Abbey* and *Emma* by the same author.

The Prisoner of Zenda
Anthony Hope
Puffin, 1984 (1894), 170 pages

WHAT DOES IT take to get a handsome young man to abandon his frivolous, self-centered life and learn something about duty, self-sacrifice, and love? In the case of the wealthy rake Rudolf Rassendyll, it takes international intrigue, kidnapping, and murder. Anthony Hope's romantic adventure is hardly serious reading, but it does trace Rudolf's development from rake to hero. Traveling in Europe, Rudolf visits the nation of Ruritania, where some of his distant relatives once lived. Suddenly he finds people who think he is the king; he is almost an identical twin. The king's power-hungry brother, Black Michael, has kidnapped the king and plans to pull off a coup d'état. Rudolf, before he fully realizes the implications of the situation, is enlisted by men loyal to the rightful king. Forced to play the role of king, he begins to learn kingly virtues. In fact, his valor and decisiveness surpass that of the king, who was himself something of a rake. Also he finds himself falling in love with Princess Flavia, the king's intended, surprising her with his ardor and chivalry. Midnight raids on dungeons and secret trysts follow. In the end, Rudolf saves the day, but then he must perform his most heroic deed—giving up his crown and his love. In the sequel to this novel, *Rupert of Hentzau,* Rudolf once more rises to the occasion.

Robinson Crusoe
Daniel Defoe. Illustrated by N. C. Wyeth.
Charles Scribner and Sons, 1983 (1719–20), 368 pages

HERE IS THE granddaddy of all adventure stories, and after nearly three hundred years, it remains one of the best. In addition to being an adventure—the standard by which all survival stories are judged—it is a deeply moral narrative as well. Unfortunately, the moral dimension of *Robinson Crusoe* is often cut out in the many abridged children's editions. It's true that the narrative slows down considerably in the middle, where Crusoe describes in minute detail his methods for farming, hunting, and self-defense; in the pretelevision age, these chapters had an educational function. But it is also in these chapters that we learn of Crusoe's moral and spiritual development. Perhaps the best answer is to give younger children an abridged edition but to encourage them to read the full version (illustrated by the incomparable N. C. Wyeth) when they are ready. Crusoe is a restless young man, who fights with his father and will not settle down to a conventional way of life. He takes to a life at sea and despite misfortune refuses to return home. Even when he becomes a prosperous merchant on an inhabited island he is struck by wanderlust and sails on the fateful voyage that strands him on a Caribbean island. Forced to fend for himself, Crusoe lurches from despair to hope. He learns to be grateful for his life and for the abundance of nature. When he suspects that another human is on the island, however, his paranoia and fear remind us that solitude is not the best environment for full moral growth. His relationship with Friday helps him to recover his inner balance and to build a readiness for returning to civilization.

Roll of Thunder, Hear My Cry (**N**)
Mildred D. Taylor
Puffin, 1991 (1976), 276 pages

MILDRED D. TAYLOR joins Virginia Hamilton and Walter Dean Myers as one of the best chroniclers of African-American experience today. Whereas Myers chooses to focus on the problems of black youngsters growing up in the inner city, Taylor's masterful trilogy follows the lives of four black children growing up on a farm in rural Mississippi during the Depression. Looking through the eyes of nine-year-old Cassie Logan barely fifty years after emancipation, we realize that the conditions of blacks have hardly changed. In the story, they are not allowed to use the same restrooms as whites or even the same water fountains. And it is only the white children who are lucky enough to ride a bus to school, whereas Cassie and her brothers have to get up before dawn in order to walk the three miles there and back each day. Cassie feels the pain of this inequality keenly, but it is the loving context of her tightly knit family that saves her from ultimate despair. Cassie's parents teach her that it is the value of the human person that counts, not the color of one's skin. By their loving, though firm, example, they teach her that it is honesty, integrity, and perseverance that will win out in the end, not resentment, hatred, and revenge. Taylor is unflinching in her portrayal of the outrage of white supremacy, but she tempers it with an unshakable belief in the capacity for human virtue and justice. Any child who has met Cassie Logan and shared her growing up can never be indifferent to the problems of racial inequality. Cassie is too real for that.

Saturnalia
Paul Fleischman
HarperCollins, 1990, 113 pages

FROM AUTHOR OF *The Borning Room* (see page 151) comes a haunting evocation of seventeenth-century Boston, a city divided by separate castes of master and servant, Christian and heathen. William, an Indian captive turned printer's apprentice, is the only character in the novel who inhabits both worlds. By day he sets the type for his kindly master, Mr. Currie; by night he roams the streets playing his heron-bone flute and searching for his brother and his Narrangansett past. With a Dickensian flair for breathing life into a multiplicity of characters, Fleischman shows us the suffering, absurdity, and inherent dignity of human life as it is played out in the Puritan town. As the festival of Saturnalia approaches, that ancient Roman holiday in which masters and slaves exchanged places for a day, all the characters are challenged to overcome their limitations in one way or another. There is no overt moral to *Saturnalia,* but it is one of those rare novels that challenges us to look at our past in a new light and to reevaluate its triumphs and failures simply by showing it to us in rich, unforgettable prose.

The Scarlet Letter
Nathaniel Hawthorne
Penguin, 1983 (1850), 282 pages

IN OUR PERMISSIVE society, the young reader who encounters *The Scarlet Letter* may be inclined to ask, "What is all the fuss about?" The notion that an act of adultery could lead to the social ostracism of a good woman and her child, and the destruction of the man, must appear to such readers as bizarre. And there are those who are inclined to use this novel to argue how far our civilization has progressed since those early, repressive times. We believe that such a simplistic attitude reveals a tremendous loss of moral wisdom. Hawthorne, of course, did intend to indict the harsh and inhuman moralism of the Puritans, but not because he believed Judeo-Christian morality to be obsolete. To Hawthorne, both the Puritans and modern secularists, represented in the novel by Chillingworth, had lost the true understanding of compassion and forgiveness. Chillingworth tries to dispense with morality, but is left with the bitterness of revenge. Dimmesdale is wracked by guilt, but he is so conscious of his public role that he cannot confess and risk his position in society. Hester alone learns that her suffering can lead to a deeper knowledge of love. Hester is not a proto-feminist in the political and ideological senses of the term, but her feminine "heart-knowledge" is contrasted with the brittle and untrustworthy "head-knowledge" of the other characters in the novel. Properly understood, *The Scarlet Letter* can enable a young reader to move beyond the superficial attitudes that have become so prevalent in our society. For more advanced readers, we also recommend *The House of Seven Gables*.

The Scarlet Pimpernel
Baroness Emmuska Orczy
Bantam, 1992 (1905), 264 pages

EVERYTHING SEEMS TO be going according to plan for the leaders of the French Revolution until a letter is received bearing the device of a blood-red flower—the dreaded symbol of the Scarlet Pimpernel. Dreaded, that is, by all who would persecute their fellow human beings for the sake of an abstract and bloody ideology. It is this mysterious figure who masterminds the daring escape of French nobles condemned to die by the guillotine. What is this man's true identity? That is the burning question of the time. Some say he is an exiled French nobleman wreaking revenge for the death of his family; others, that he is an English lord risking his life for the sheer sport of it. A man of many disguises and infinite daring, he eludes capture until the beautiful Lady Blakeney is blackmailed by the evil spy Chauvelin into betraying him. *The Scarlet Pimpernel* is not only a first-rate adventure story but also a compelling story of one man's courage in the face of the notorious Reign of Terror.

Shakespeare's Stories: Comedies
William Shakespeare
Retold by Beverly Birch
Illustrated by Carol Tarrant.
Bedrick, 1988, 126 pages

THE ONLY OBSTACLE that stands between older children and their enjoyment of Shakespeare is the difficulty posed by Elizabethan language, with the archaic vocabulary and unfamiliar syntax. One way to break down this barrier for young readers is to give them the story first, and then to expose them to the original language. In the early nineteenth century, Charles and Mary Lamb wrote prose versions of Shakespeare's plays, which introduced children to the Bard for generations. For our own time, Beverly Birch has translated Shakespeare into vigorous prose, interspersed with many direct quotations from the plays. The narrative thread that Birch weaves in these retellings is extremely close to the spirit of Shakespeare's plays. His comedies take aim at human vanity and the complexities of romantic love; his histories trace the destruction brought about by power lust and ambition; his tragedies plumb the depths of depravity and the heights of self-sacrifice. The other two volumes in this series are called *Shakespeare's Stories: Histories* and *Shakespeare's Stories: Tragedies*. The selections in these three volumes contain most of the major plays, including *A Midsummer Night's Dream, The Tempest, Henry IV, Julius Caesar, King Lear,* and *Hamlet*.

Silas Marner
George Eliot
Penguin, 1981 (1861), 265 pages

THIS BEAUTIFUL STORY is perhaps the closest George Eliot came to writing a moral fairy tale. Set in an early-nineteenth-century village in the north of England, *Silas Marner* is a story about the resurrecting power of love. When the linen weaver Silas Marner is unjustly convicted of stealing, he vows never again to have anything to do with his fellow human beings or with God, who has betrayed him. He lives in this state of spiritual death for many years until, one stormy night, his house is broken into and robbed. When he returns after his futile search for the thief he discovers a tiny child with golden hair lying in the very spot where he had hidden his gold. Convinced that the child has been given to him in restitution for his lost treasure, he determines to raise her as his own. As she grows, Eppie's unconditional love and trust for the man she believes to be her father brings Silas's heart slowly back to life. Masterfully written by one of the greatest English novelists, *Silas Marner* reminds us that "love is stronger than death," and that no one, however hard his heart, is beyond hope.

Three Famous Short Novels
William Faulkner
Viking, 1958

"HE WAS SIXTEEN. For six years now he had been a man's hunter. For six years he had heard the best of all talking. It was of the wilderness, the big woods, bigger and older than any recorded document. . . . " *The Bear,* William Faulkner's classic story of a boy's initiation into manhood, is more than a story about hunting. The hunt for the ancient, indomitable bear known as "Old Ben" is merely the plot; the theme is the conflict between pride and humility in the human heart. Young Ike McCaslin learns to respect the wilderness as something sacred and not to be raped and plundered by human arrogance. The hunt for Old Ben is like an ancient dance, where hunter and hunted move in a complicated series of motions, each attuned to the rhythms of nature. Ike's companions are representative of the human condition: some are wise in the ways of nature, others are arrogant and selfish. Faulkner's prose is densely poetic, so it is not for a casual reader. But when one learns the rhythm of his language, it is richly rewarding. The bear represents something that men fear, and the attempt to kill it is a sign that in the modern era something has been lost, something that cannot easily be recovered.

Typhoon and Other Tales
Joseph Conrad
Oxford, 1990 (1903), 324 pages

YOUNG PEOPLE ARE extremely conscious of the image they project to others. Because they have not yet established their own identities, they tend to cultivate a "cool" surface image, shaped by peer pressure. For boys, coolness is, more often than not, an extension of machismo; right and wrong are irrelevant categories here. The best books for teenagers are about the struggle to discover one's identity, and the difference between appearances and reality. Joseph Conrad, one of the twentieth-century's greatest novelists, did not write for children. But some of his stories of the sea contain powerful insights into the moral life. In his novella *Typhoon,* we encounter a rather dull, simple man, Captain MacWhirr, whose appearance is "ordinary, irresponsive, and unruffled." To his shipmates, MacWhirr is something of a joke. But when his ship is caught in a typhoon (the Oriental name for a hurricane), MacWhirr's moral qualities begin to shine, and the weakness and cowardice of his shipmates are revealed. His ship contains a large number of coolies—poor Chinese laborers—and only MacWhirr considers their welfare in the midst of the storm. In this test of character, MacWhirr comes off better than the cool young bucks on his crew. Conrad is a master of irony, which requires a fairly advanced reader, so *Typhoon* may not be for every young person. But for strong readers with a taste for adventures at sea, this tale, and the others collected in the same volume, will be deeply rewarding.

The Witch of Blackbird Pond (N)
Elizabeth Speare
Dell, 1978 (1958), 276 pages

THE FIRST SIXTEEN YEARS of Kit Tyler's life have been spent on her grandfather's luxurious Barbados plantation, where she was allowed to run virtually wild. Now he is dead and Kit is forced to travel across the ocean to live with her aunt and her Puritan household in seventeenth-century Connecticut. The transition is anything but smooth. Kit is expected to perform such menial tasks as baking bread and dipping candles and has to exchange her fine silks and laces for plain homespun. At first resentful and rebellious, Kit comes to realize the importance of hard work and sharing, and that friendship is to be prized above material wealth. She is helped to this understanding by a harmless old woman who lives on the edge of Blackbird Pond but who has been branded a witch by the Wethersfield community. Kit's defense of her friend causes herself to be accused of witchcraft and she is eventually brought to trial. *The Witch of Blackbird Pond* is an honest book. It does not cover up the darker side of Puritan New England, when superstition and suspicion of witchcraft were rife and led to the persecution of the innocent, but neither is it blind to the simple virtues and strengths of the community. Kit's ability to understand this by the end of the novel signals the beginning of womanhood.

Contemporary Fiction

My job is to tell a story—a story about real people who live in the world as it is. And I dare to believe that such stories, even when they are painful, have a power to illumine the reader in the way that a nice tale with exemplary characters does not.

—Katherine Paterson

Middle Readers

Cracker Jackson
Betsy Byars
Puffin, 1986, 146 pages

JACKSON HUNTER, WHOSE nose is always running, is in trouble. He receives an anonymous letter consisting of a single sentence: "Keep away, Cracker, or he'll hurt you." It doesn't take long for him to figure out who sent the letter: the only person who ever called him Cracker is Alma, his former baby-sitter. Alma is being physically abused by her husband, and Cracker feels that something must be done about it. The worst of it is that Alma's baby, Nicole, is in danger too. But Alma fears for Cracker's safety and begs him not to tell his parents. He tries to honor her request, but in doing so he breaks other rules and promises. Byars contrasts Cracker's increasing seriousness with the childish pranks of Cracker's friend, Goat. Even Cracker's father, who calls him from a business trip, plays silly games that Cracker no longer enjoys. Byars has not written a "problem novel" about wife beating but a portrayal of a boy's moral quandary in the face of a complex, adult situation. Cracker's choices may not always be right, but he struggles to do the right thing, and we can't help but admire him.

Dear Mr. Henshaw (N)
Beverly Cleary. Illustrated by Paul O. Zelinsky.
Dell, 1984, 134 pages

TOLD ENTIRELY THROUGH letters and diary entries, *Dear Mr. Henshaw* is the story of a sensitive boy who learns to cope with life's problems through his love of reading and writing. Leigh Botts writes his first letter to an author of children's books when he is a second grader. Over the next few years he continues to write and eventually Mr. Henshaw answers. When Leigh asks a series of questions for a book report, Mr. Henshaw answers facetiously and asks the boy a set of his own questions. Leigh is compelled to express his thoughts and emotions in a series of letters. He writes about his parents' divorce, his troubles in school, and, unconsciously, about his loneliness and love of stories. Mr. Henshaw does not so much offer advice as he encourages Leigh to continue writing, through a diary as well as through letters. Slowly Leigh becomes more self-sufficient, his diary entries becoming longer, more observant, and wiser. He writes Mr. Henshaw again, asking for help with a story that he is writing for a competition. Leigh is stuck because his story goes nowhere. Mr. Henshaw reminds him that a good story must involve a character who solves a problem or changes in some way. Leigh abandons his fictional story and tells a true story, simply and well, winning an Honorable Mention in the competition. In *Dear Mr. Henshaw* Beverly Cleary has crafted a moving novel about the way stories enable us to make sense of our experience. Leigh's writing enables him to understand and forgive his parents, cope with his problems at school, and grow into a more independent and loving boy.

The Diddakoi
Rumer Godden
Viking, 1972, 147 pages

KIZZY LIVES WITH her Great Great Gran and their beloved old horse, Joe, in a tumble-down caravan in the corner of an orchard owned by Admiral Twiss. Though they are often hungry, they are happy together. Kizzy—unbathed, untaught, wild—runs free. She is a tinker, a Gypsy, a *diddakoi*. But when Gran dies, the law of Romany dictates that her possessions must be destroyed, and the caravan is burned. Kizzy's freedom is suddenly curtailed. She becomes a "social problem" to be dealt with by the villagers, young and old alike. But Kizzy's unique personality defies all conventional attempts at charity and the little English village soon learns that if the villagers are to help Kizzy at all they must first respect her Romany heritage. By placing her spirited heroine in a dilemma that, in these days of increasing homelessness, has a special relevance to our own time, Rumer Godden reminds us that authentic social action should always be based on a profound respect for the individual.

A Dog on Barkham Street
Mary Stolz. Illustrated by Leonard Shortall.
HarperCollins, 1985 (1960), 184 pages

NINE-YEAR-OLD EDWARD Frost at 21 Barkham Street has two problems. The first is Martin Hastings, who lives next door, at number 23, and bullies him at every available opportunity; the other is that his mother does not think he is responsible enough to own a dog. He wonders when he will have enough courage and responsibility. Probably never, he glumly concludes. Then his charming but irresponsible uncle Josh comes to visit and brings with him the answer to Edward's prayers—a dog named Argess. At first, Edward is infatuated with Uncle Josh's wandering lifestyle, until the morning when he wakes up to discover that Uncle Josh has left without saying good-bye and that he has taken Argess with him. Heartbroken and thoroughly disillusioned, Edward decides to run away. Many hours and much trouble later, Edward has come to appreciate his father's steady reliability over the fecklessness of Uncle Josh. A sensitive and humorous book, *A Dog on Barkham Street* reminds us that love and responsibility must always go hand in hand if we are to truly care for others. We also recommend its sequel, *The Bully of Barkham Street.*

Maniac Magee (**N**)
Jerry Spinelli
Harper Trophy, 1990, 184 pages

MANIAC MAGEE IS the story of how a twelve-year-old boy was able to transform an entire Pennsylvania town and become a legend in the bargain. Everyone knows that there is an invisible line that divides the East and West sides of Two Mills, and that this line should never be crossed. Everyone, that is, but Maniac Magee. He is a stranger in town, a runaway without a home, and is naively ignorant of the differences between East and West, black and white. He is also unaware that people just don't *do* the things that he does—run on the rails of the track, hit the first-ever "frogball" for a home run, score forty-nine touchdowns in a single game, and venture boldly into the garden of the notorious neighborhood ogre, Mr. Finsterwald. This last feat alone is enough to give him the name "Maniac." But perhaps the most courageous thing he does is heal the division between the East and West sides of town. Hugely entertaining and peopled with unforgettable characters, *Maniac Magee* is the moving story of how one boy's simplicity and courage brought about the most miraculous thing of all—an end to racial prejudice in Two Mills.

On My Honor (**NH**)
Marion Dane Bauer
Dell, 1986, 90 pages

PROMISES ARE HARD to keep. Why else make a promise in the first place? For children, promises are sometimes the only link between their parents' concern for their safety and the dangers of the world outside the front door. When a child is with other children, promises are even harder to keep. This short, harrowing novel is a sensitive dramatization of these themes. Joel's friend Tony is a daredevil and he wants Joel to climb the cliffs at the state park. Joel thinks this is foolish, but Tony does not take no for an answer. Joel asks his father permission to ride to the state park, without telling him of Tony's dangerous plan. His father is worried about the long bike ride to the park, but he doesn't want to be overly restrictive. He gets Joel to promise, on his honor, that he will go directly to the park and not stop anywhere else. But halfway there, Tony stops and tells Joel that he wants to swim in the swift-moving river by the road. Joel tries to argue him out of this, too, but then he reasons that it must be safer than climbing the cliffs. Tony plunges in. Joel joins him, but when he emerges from the water Tony is gone. Most of the novel is about Joel's reaction to Tony's drowning. Stunned, wracked by guilt, and in a state of shock, Joel blames himself and fears the blame of others. He returns home, avoiding his father and lying about Tony's whereabouts. But when his father tells Tony's parents that he is an honorable boy, Joel tells the truth. He is not perfect but he feels pain precisely because he has a conscience. Joel cannot be blamed for Tony's recklessness, but he learns, to his cost, just how real are the dangers his parents worry about.

Other Bells for Us to Ring
Robert Cormier. Illustrated by Deborah Kogan Ray.
Dell, 1990, 136 pages

ROBERT CORMIER, PERHAPS best known for his dark, controversial novel, *The Chocolate War* (see page 204), is a writer of many talents. *Other Bells for Us to Ring* is not a dark novel; it affirms the power of love, though it is, in parts, heartbreakingly sad. The story is set during World War II. Darcy Webster's parents have moved into a town in Massachusetts near a military base. For Darcy, whose parents are vaguely Unitarian, this town, dominated by Catholic French Canadians, is an exotic and mysterious place. The shy Darcy is soon befriended by an outgoing Irish Catholic girl, Kathleen Mary

O'Hara. Kathleen comes from a large family, dominated by an alcoholic father given to violence. The two girls complement each other perfectly. But life soon becomes complicated. Darcy's father is missing in action in Europe, and Kathleen and her family suddenly move away from town. Left in uncertainty, Darcy ponders her friend's Catholic faith, which seems to make everything so physical and external. Eventually she visits an ancient nun, Sister Angela, who is reputed to be a miracle worker. Sister Angela speaks to Darcy of the daily miracles that surround us and our need to seize the opportunities for love. At the novel's end, Darcy hears two pieces of news, one wonderful and one tragic. But her sadness is surrounded by Sister Angela's words about the daily miracles of love.

The Saturdays
Elizabeth Enright
Dell, 1987 (1941), 175 pages

THE MELENDY CHILDREN are not the type of kids you forget in a hurry. For a start, they are extremely noisy, as their beloved housekeeper, Cuffy, is always remarking. Rush, who wants to be a concert pianist, bangs out marches on the nursery piano, Mona is a budding young actress who delights in reciting Shakespeare at the top of her lungs, Randy dreams of being a ballerina and pirouettes all over the house, and Oliver, the youngest, loves sounds of any variety so long as they are *loud*. Bored by a succession of rainy stay-at-home weekends, the children decide to pool their allowances to enable one of them to go and do something special with the money each Saturday. Challenged to spend their time and money well, all of the children end up learning something unexpected about themselves—Mona, for instance, goes to a beauty parlor and learns that it is not looks that count so much as the person underneath. In an age where the most often heard complaint from kids is "I'm bored," despite more entertainments than ever before, the Melendy children are a refreshing example of how much fun can be had with just a little imagination. An adventuresome and resourceful lot, they are definitely not your usual television zombies.

The Summer of the Swans (N)
Betsy Byars
Puffin, 1981, 142 pages

UP UNTIL SARA'S fourteenth year, her life seems to have glided by without a hitch. Now everything in Sara's life has suddenly become inexplicably complicated; she finds herself fighting with her Aunty Willie, envying her older sister's beauty, and resenting her absent father. But, most of all, she is at war with herself: one moment she is laughing, the next she feels like crying. Worst of all, she can't stand the sight of herself; her feet are too big, she's too tall, and, to cap it all, she is decidedly plain. The only person who can draw her out of herself is her younger brother, Charlie, brain damaged at the age of three by a serious illness. Charlie's vulnerability elicits from Sara an unconditional love that goes beyond the everyday struggles of adolescent life. And when he is missing one night, Sara is the only person who knows where to find him. He has gone to look for the swans, a powerful and moving symbol of the innate beauty in all of us. *The Summer of the Swans* is founded on the belief that each and every one of us is an "ugly duckling" ready, at any minute, to turn into a graceful swan. That is the truth that Sara discovers when she is finally re-united with Charlie—that, despite physical or emotional handicaps, everyone is uniquely precious—Charlie, Aunty Willie, her sister, her father, even Sara herself.

Thank You, Jackie Robinson
Barbara Cohen. Illustrated by Richard Cuffari.
Lothrop, 1974, 125 pages

SAM GREENE IS a fanatic. In the mid-1940s he follows every game the Brooklyn Dodgers play. He not only knows the names of the players and their statistics, he can remember every single game, down to the minutest detail, for several years. A shy, withdrawn boy, he lives in an inn, run by his mother. He finds in the Dodgers a way of concentrating his emotions, learning all of the virtues that sports can teach. When a new cook is hired at the inn, Sam discovers a new friend. Davy, a sixty-year-old black man, is also a Dodgers fan; his hero is Jackie Robinson, the first great African-American baseball star in a sport dominated until that time by white men. Together they travel to all the stadiums in the Northeast to watch the Dodgers. Cohen's depiction of this shy Jewish boy and his African-American friend could easily have become a sentimental sermon on two groups that have experienced prejudice in America. They do encounter moments of prejudice, but Cohen's interest is focused on the way the two find a bond that transcends their racial identities. When Davy becomes seriously ill with a heart condition, Sam goes to a Dodgers game and begs Jackie Robinson to sign a baseball as a gift to Davy. After Davy's death, we see Sam in a thoughtful moment, for once giving only part of his attention to the Dodgers game on the radio.

Older Readers

Bridge to Terabithia (**N**)
Katherine Paterson. Illustrated by Donna Diamond.
Crowell, 1977, 128 pages

TO MOST CASUAL observers in the rural town where they live, Jesse and Leslie look like a teenage version of the "odd couple." Jesse comes from a poor family, Leslie from affluent, cultured parents. But there is something that binds them together; it is a shared imaginary kingdom called Terabithia lying deep within the woods. When tragedy strikes, Jesse is able to find comfort in the world of the imagination and the mind. He comes to realize that Terabithia is Leslie's legacy to him, a gift of friendship that enables him to come to terms with her death. Inspired by C. S. Lewis's imaginary world Narnia, *Bridge to Terabithia* reminds us that the realm of the imagination is not an escape from life's complexities but often a means of coping with them.

The Chocolate War
Robert Cormier
Dell, 1986 (1974), 191 pages

MAKE NO MISTAKE about it: this is a dark, disturbing novel that is only for the most mature and discriminating reader. Ever since *The Chocolate War* was published in 1974 there have been critics who have seen it as a bleak, nihilistic story, without redeeming features. But we beg to differ. This novel is essentially a tragedy and can be understood only in that light. Like Shakespeare's *Hamlet,* it depicts a world where things are rotten to the core. Its hero, like Hamlet, struggles to make sense of an amoral world and is finally crushed by it. Why read such a story? Because tragedy is a part of life, and works of this kind, though terrifying, serve as cautionary tales. Jerry Renault attends Trinity School, a New England Catholic prep school run by an order of brothers. The school is dominated by a gang—the Vigils—that is led by Archie Costello, a boy who has a genius for humiliating and intimidating other boys. The school itself is run by the cruel Brother Leon, who is morally linked with Archie. When Brother Leon announces the annual Trinity fund drive, which involves selling boxes of chocolates, Archie sees a way to assert his power in the school and crush Jerry Renault's spirit. Archie induces Jerry to refuse to sell chocolate, an act that incenses Brother Leon. But when Archie tells Jerry to begin selling the chocolate, Jerry refuses; he is determined to show that he will not be bullied by either Archie or Brother Leon. Jerry, whose mother has recently died, attempts to cope with these problems by channeling his energy into football, where violence is kept in bounds by rules and plays. But in the end, Archie entraps Jerry, and Jerry gives in to the very violence that he once protested. Like Hamlet, Jerry cannot break out of the cycle of evil. Though the story is set in a Catholic school, Cormier does not place the blame on the Church itself: there is a good brother, Jacques, who tries to intervene, but he is powerless to stop Archie and Brother Leon. This novel is powerful medicine, a warning about the way evil gains power when members of a community give in to it. For a novel on a similar theme, see *The Lord of the Flies* by William Golding on page 208.

The Chosen
Chaim Potok
Simon & Schuster, 1967, 284 pages

HERE IS A NOVEL that depicts the spiritual and intellectual quests of two teenage Jewish boys, a story that makes us believe in the passion and urgency of their search for meaning. Very few children today have a conception that the spiritual and intellectual life can be as exciting and compelling as the glories of athletic success, movie stardom, or corporate wealth and power. Reuven Malter, the son of a reformed Jewish scholar and activist, meets Danny Saunders, the son of an Orthodox rabbi, on the baseball field. Reuven is injured by Danny in the game, but this ultimately brings them together as friends. Reuven is introduced to the strange ways of the Orthodox, finding Danny's father, Reb Saunders, harsh, rigid, and authoritarian. Danny, who is expected to succeed his father as rabbi to the close-knit Orthodox community, is fascinated by Sigmund Freud and struggles with his desire to pursue a career in psychiatry. As World War II ends, life for Jews around the world becomes more painful and complex. The horror of the Holocaust, the effort to found the state of Israel, and other events within the Jewish world parallel the tensions in Reuven's and Danny's personal lives. Reuven comes to see that Rabbi Saunders is not merely an "ultraconservative," but a man of intense faith and moral convictions who loves his son in the only way he knows how. Reuven's own father comes to the same opinion and shares his wisdom with his son. "A man must fill his life with meaning, meaning is not automatically given to life. It is hard work to fill up one's life with meaning."

Dicey's Song (N)
Cynthia Voigt
Atheneum, 1983, 196 pages

DICEY'S SONG IS the story of a character we meet only briefly in *A Solitary Blue* (see page 213). Thirteen-year-old Dicey Tillerman thinks she is used to hanging on. After all, she managed to keep her family together on the long journey by foot from Provincetown to Gram's house on a small Chesapeake Bay island. Dicey knew she had no choice when her mother began to show signs of mental illness. Now Gram must take steps to adopt the grandchildren she has never seen and Dicey feels that, at long last, her responsibilities are over. But when Gram tells Dicey that Maybeth is failing third grade and that six-year-old Sammy is acting strangely at school, Dicey knows that she has to do something about it. As Gram tells her, "You've got to hold on. Hold on to people. They can get away from you . . . but if you don't—hold on—then you lose them." *Dicey's Song* is about holding on—holding on to those you love with courage and perseverance. Movingly shown through the eyes of a girl on the brink of adolescence by one of today's foremost children's book authors, *Dicey's Song* will leave you feeling that, however hard it might be, keeping a family together is perhaps the most important thing we can do in life.

Hatchet (NH)
Gary Paulsen
Puffin, 1988, 195 pages

SURVIVAL STORIES MAKE for riveting reading, especially when they are about children. How will the boys or girls adapt to the life-and-death situation they suddenly find themselves in? Will they find food and avoid vicious predators? When will rescuers come? But the most absorbing part of a survival tale is the internal, rather than the external, story: the development of the survivor's character. Thirteen-year-old Brian Robeson is flying in a small plane to visit his father, who works in the oil fields of northern Canada. The pilot of the plane has a heart attack, but Brian manages to guide the plane to a lake and emerges from the plane unhurt. The plane sinks to the bottom of the lake and Brian has nothing but the clothes on his back. Alone in the vast forests of Canada, Brian, a typical suburban boy, learns to survive; his only teacher is grim necessity. Eventually he makes a fire, spears fish, and hunts ruffled grouse with bow and arrow. His emotions veer from despair to exultation. But he learns patience, self-reliance, the value of hard work, and a respect for nature. There is never any question that his situation is desperate; Paulsen does not for a moment inject a note of sentimentality in the story. Even if this novel is read in the comfort of a library or a home, the wilderness and the moral challenges it offers will enter the reader's heart.

Jacob Have I Loved (**N**)
Katherine Paterson
Harper Trophy, 1990 (1980), 244 pages

"JACOB HAVE I loved. . . ." Louise does not have to listen to the rest of her grandmother's taunt to understand its full implication. Louise has grown up in the shadow of her beautiful and talented twin sister, and her whole life has been one long reenactment of the biblical quotation: ". . . but Esau have I hated." Like the biblical Esau, who was robbed of his birthright by his younger brother, Louise has always seemed a pale second in the eyes of her family. Literally from the moment of her birth, Caroline has carelessly deprived Louise of her friends, her hopes for schooling, even her name. The only thing Louise can turn to on the tiny Chesapeake island on which she lives is the life of the waterways. She begins to learn the secrets of the watermen who prong for oysters and cull for crabs, and dreams of a time when she can work alongside her father in his fishing boat. It is Louise's struggle to come to terms with her hatred for her sister and her deep resentment of God for having cursed her at birth that make this story so exceptional. There is no question about it; Louise has been wronged! But Katherine Paterson is too insightful about human nature to leave it at that. She shows that Louise has to overcome her self-pity and anger if she is to blossom into the strong and compassionate woman that she eventually becomes. Winner of the Newbery Medal, *Jacob Have I Loved* is a book that looks suffering squarely in the eye and refuses to give easy answers. Its unflinching honesty is a quality that any adolescent will appreciate. We also recommend *The Great Gilly Hopkins,* about an embattled girl growing up in the rootless environment of foster care.

Lord of the Flies
William Golding
Perigee, 1954, 208 pages

THIS IS AN ugly book (though beautifully written), and for those who dislike looking at ugliness, it is something to be avoided. But if the ugliness in *Lord of the Flies* is related to something deep within human nature, how can we afford to look away? Golding's novel forthrightly confronts the reality of evil. It suggests that what we call civilization is a very thin layer of order covering passions and emotions that could easily rip it apart. A plane crash on a tropical island leaves a group of British schoolboys stranded. A power struggle between Ralph, a decent if far from perfect boy, and Jack, a bully, leads to death and betrayal. The fat, shortsighted Piggy is the one who most consistently utters the truth, but no one will listen to him. Without the protection of the adult generation, the older children find themselves drawn into all the sins of their parents' world: ambition, vanity, greed, hate. *Lord of the Flies* is a cautionary tale, meant to shock us into an awareness of the fragility of moral and political life. Golding firmly believed that evil was located in the human heart, not in political systems. Of this novel he once said, "The theme is an attempt to trace the defects of society back to the defects of human nature. The moral is that the shape of a society must depend on the ethical nature of the individual and not on any political system however apparently logical or respectable." Older, more advanced readers will find this a tough but rewarding book.

The Mozart Season
Virginia Euwer Wolff
Henry Holt, 1991, 249 pages

IF THIS NOVEL had to be categorized, it would go under the heading "musical competition story, for girls." But that would be to diminish a novel of astonishing beauty and richness. The plot of *The Mozart Season* moves through the preparation of twelve-year-old Allegra Shapiro for a violin competition, but that is not what the book is about. It is about an extraordinary child's initiation into adulthood, and the way she learns responsibility, self-control, empathy for human suffering, and the way art can embody all of these themes. As Allegra prepares for the competition, her relationship to the Mozart violin concerto mirrors her moral and spiritual growth. She is a prodigy, but she is not the skittish type. Resilient and curious, she is able to learn from her mistakes. From the famous singer (and family friend) Deirdre, she discovers that a performer can be a nervous wreck and yet a consummate performer. From a retarded, homeless man who dances at all the outdoor concerts Allegra attends, she learns that music can bring joy and meaning to anyone, regardless of his or her cultural sophistication. Allegra's Jewish grandmother teaches her the importance of memory and loyalty in love. Above all, from her struggle to become one with Mozart, she finds her own individuality. Of course, this novel will appeal to girls who play musical instruments, but its readers should be legion.

The Old Man and the Sea
Ernest Hemingway
Macmillan, 1986 (1952), 127 pages

IN A TECHNOLOGICAL age, the realm of nature comes to
be dominated by the machine. Machines provide us with the
sense that we can manipulate nature to our own ends. But
when we lose the sense of nature's inherent wisdom, and our
need to respect that wisdom, a host of dangers follow, including pollution and the specter of genetic engineering. That is
why stories like *The Old Man and the Sea* are so crucial to the
formation of the moral imagination. The old man of the story
is a Cuban who has earned a meager living as a fisherman all
his life. One day he goes out alone and catches a huge marlin.
The fish is enormously powerful and drags the old man farther
and farther out to sea. His epic struggle with the fish reveals
not only the grandeur of nature but the courage and sensitivity
of the human spirit. The old man loves and admires the fish.
" 'I'll kill him, though. In all his greatness and glory.' Although
it is unjust, he thought." Enduring pain, hunger, and mortal
danger, the old man catches the fish, but on his way back to
port all of the fish except the head is completely eaten by
sharks. But tragic though the loss of the fish is, something important has been proved. "[M]an is not made for defeat. . . . A
man can be destroyed, but not defeated." The old man's lonely
combat with the marlin is a triumph of the human spirit.

One Day in the Life of Ivan Denisovich
Aleksandr Solzhenitsyn
Signet, 1963 (1962), 160 pages

THE SOVIET UNION may no longer exist, but that does not
diminish the power or relevance of Aleksandr Solzhenitsyn's
writings. There are many places in our world where totalitarian
rule and the abrogation of human rights are still the order of
the day. This "slice of life" story concerns a single day in the
Soviet gulag, a prison camp in a remote and frigid Siberian

wasteland. Ivan Denisovich is not an extraordinary man; his day is like that of thousands of others. In the gulag the prisoner is stripped of everything: freedom, possessions, health. But as Solzhenitsyn himself found out, when a man is stripped of everything, he discovers that there is one thing left that cannot be taken away: his soul. There is a powerful scene in this novel where Ivan stays late at a work site, trying to finish a brick-laying job. Even though the other prisoners are marching back to their barracks, Ivan works hard to do the job well—a mark of his decency and an assertion of his human dignity. When this book was published in the Soviet Union (during a brief lull in the censorship laws), it shook the entire nation. It should be read both as a reminder of the continuing plight of political prisoners and as a humane celebration of the moral and spiritual dimensions of human nature.

Onion John (**N**)
Joseph Krumgold. Illustrated by Symeon Shimin.
Harper Trophy, 1984 (1959), 248 pages

ONION JOHN IS a story about the unusual friendship between a twelve-year-old boy and a man who spends most of his time going through the dump in the little town of Serenity, New Jersey. But Onion John (named for the magnificent onions he grows and likes to eat for breakfast!) is no mere vagrant (he has lived in Serenity for twenty-five years), he is just *different*. The language he speaks is unintelligible and he has decidedly peculiar ideas—peculiar, that is, to the modern faith in facts and figures. Up until now, Andy Rusch has treated Onion John like the rest of the town does, but after a ball game, when he scores the winning run, something changes. He not only finds that he can understand what Onion John is saying, but he discovers that there is a good deal of sense in it. Raised by his father to pursue a career in engineering, Andy finds Onion John's more intuitive way of looking at the world intriguing. But when Mr. Rusch extends his control over his son's future to include his best friend's way of life, Andy knows that he has to act if he is to save them both. *Onion John* is a profound study on the theme of parental and civil responsibility. How far should Mr. Rusch go in dictating his son's future? Should the town try to change Onion John's way of life just because it is different? By the end of the story these questions have been put to the test and humanely resolved. Not only are the bonds between Andy and his father immeasurably strengthened, but the town comes to a greater appreciation of Onion John's uniqueness. The town of Serenity has at last grown into its name! We also recommend . . . *And Now, Miguel!*, a Newbery Medal winner, by the same author.

The Planet of Junior Brown
Virginia Hamilton
Macmillan, 1971, 240 pages

THIS IS THE story of how three lonely and gifted people came together to create their own "solar system" of friendship and support. Each of them has been marginalized by society in some way—Junior Brown because he is a musical prodigy, Buddy because he is homeless, and Mr. Pool because his teaching methods were considered unorthodox. Together they construct a solar system in the basement of the boys' school where Mr. Pool is now janitor, and they spend long hours watching the slow and stately revolution of the planets. It is this solar system that becomes the central metaphor of this remarkable story, for it comes to symbolize the harmony that should exist between one individual and another. As Mr. Pool says, each planet cannot "be measured alone, but only in relation to one or more of the others." Buddy himself knows this in a special way; he is the leader of a "planet"—a hideout for young homeless boys—and, like the sun that keeps all the lesser planets in orbit by its steady gravitational pull, Buddy teaches the boys how to survive on the street without resorting to crime. By introducing us to the unique worlds of her characters, Virginia Hamilton makes an eloquent and impassioned plea for compassion, tolerance, and charity—all the virtues that should bind our world (or planet) together. As one reviewer in *Black World* put it, "There is so much in *The Planet of Junior Brown*, it could be . . . a prayer."

Scorpions (**NH**)
Walter Dean Myers
HarperCollins, 1990, 216 pages

SCORPIONS IS THE name of a street gang, consisting mainly of young teens, in New York City. With his father gone, his mother working nights, and his older brother behind bars for murder, the lure of the gang becomes almost unbearable for fourteen-year-old Jamal. It seems to promise him protection from the streets as well as prestige among those who bully him at school. But when he accepts a gun from one of its members, he also accepts the laws of violence and intimidation that it represents and is deaf to the entreaties of his best friend, Tito, for him to get rid of it. Jamal's refusal to do so leads to the breakup of their friendship, but in a way that neither of them could have imagined. *Scorpions* is a realistic and often harrowing book. Its unflinching portrayal of the loneliness and despair of life on the street reminds us that as long as our hearts love violence above peace, lawlessness above responsibility, we will never solve the problems of the inner cities, let alone safeguard the futures of youngsters like Jamal and Tito. As one of the characters in the story says to Jamal, "You ain't got nothing to back you up 'cept what you got in your heart."

A Solitary Blue (**NH**)
Cynthia Voigt
Scholastic, 1993, 307 pages

A SOLITARY BLUE (by the author of *Dicey's Song;* see page 206) is the moving story of a young boy's experience of divorce and his painful coming of age. Abandoned by his mother when he is seven, Jeff grows up a solitary and lonely child in the company of his coldly distant father. His only comfort is his unshakable faith in his beautiful mother's love for him. Unshakable, that is, until he is invited to spend a summer with her in Charleston. There he begins to learn that his mother's commitment to her own freedom and self-expression far outweighs her love for him. Wounded by her selfishness and insincerity, Jeff seeks solace in the creeks and waterways around Charleston and sees, for the first time, a great blue heron. Naturally solitary and suspicious of human contact, the bird not only becomes a powerful symbol for how Jeff feels but also becomes the means by which Jeff comes to understand that his father's aloofness is an expression of his own private pain and not a lack of love for his son. *A Solitary Blue* is not just another book about divorce (and many of them abound); rather, it is a powerfully realistic story about the sacrificial and ultimately redemptive nature of love. As Jeff's father says, "It's so easy to fall in love . . . but living love is a different thing."

Fantasy and Science Fiction

The hero cannot grow if he or she is shielded from the very elements that create growth. So acceptance of the call to adventure represents the great rite of separation: the cutting of the apron strings.

—Natalie Babbitt

Middle Readers

At the Back of the North Wind
George MacDonald. Illustrated by Lauren A. Mills.
Godine, 1988 (1871), 307 pages

GEORGE MACDONALD AND Lewis Carroll, the author of *Alice's Adventures in Wonderland*, were good friends, but they had very different attitudes toward children. Carroll was intrigued by puzzles, absurdities, and nonsense, and there have been children who have found the antics in his stories delightful. But MacDonald was far more interested in the actual sufferings and moral challenges of childhood, and wrote stories that encouraged children to believe that life was meaningful. *At the Back of the North Wind* tells of a poor boy named Diamond who lives in the hayloft above a stable. There he is visited by the North Wind, who appears in the form of a beautiful woman. North Wind takes Diamond on many journeys both far and near. Each of these journeys enables him to be more kind and helpful to his family, but they are paralleled by a weakening of his physical health. Here, as in all his fantasies, MacDonald makes goodness interesting and believable, a force that is so enchanting as to be contagious. The ending, though sad, is also full of hope, for Diamond is able to live forever in the land at the back of the North Wind.

The Borrowers
Mary Norton
Harcourt Brace Jovanovich, 1981 (1953), 200 pages

BENEATH THE FLOORBOARDS of a large English country house lies the miniature world of the Borrowers. In past times the house was home to many a Borrower—the Harpsichords, the Overmantles, the Drainpipes (even their names were borrowed from their locations!)—but now only Pod and Homily Clock and their daughter, Arietty, remain. Wanting nothing better than to live in harmony with the "human beans" above the floorboards, the Clocks discover that they are regarded as vermin by everyone in the house except a young boy. And when a dog is brought in to ferret them out, they know that they must do the unthinkable—they must move. A delightful story in itself, *The Borrowers* contains an important message: that any form of discrimination is, at best, foolish; at worst, destructive of other people's lives. Any child who gets to know the Borrowers on their own terms will intuitively understand this and carry away with her an important lesson for life.

Charlotte's Web
E. B. White. Illustrated by Garth Williams.
HarperCollins, 1952, 184 pages

WHO HASN'T HEARD of that rotund little pig, Wilbur, and his near escape from being turned into somebody's breakfast by the ingenuity of his friend Charlotte the spider? E. B. White is a master at portraying an animal world that is often more humane than our own world. Charlotte gladly expends her last ounce of energy weaving a masterpiece of a web in order to save Wilbur's life. In *Charlotte's Web*, pacifism is transformed from a mere political statement to a belief founded on the unique value of the individual.

The Chronicles of Narnia: The Lion, the Witch, and the Wardrobe; Prince Caspian; The Voyage of the Dawn Treader; The Silver Chair; The Horse and His Boy; The Magician's Nephew; The Last Battle
C. S. Lewis. Illustrated by Pauline Baynes.
Macmillan, 1988 (1950–56)

WHEN LUCY PEVENSIE is drawn by the strangely carved wardrobe in the home of Professor Kirke, she opens a door to a new world. C. S. Lewis's beloved *Chronicles of Narnia* have, since their first publication, commanded the loyalty of millions of children. What makes these fantasies so compelling? Perhaps it is Lewis's respect for the child's imagination, his ability to portray goodness without making it sugary, and evil without making it merely grotesque. Then there are the characters: the children, some good, some naughty, but almost all achieving nobility in the end; the talking animals, like the chivalrous Reepicheep, homely Mr. and Mrs. Beaver, and the down-to-earth Marshwiggle, Puddleglum; above all, there is the mighty but loving figure of Aslan, the great Lion. Lewis has been accused of being moralistic, but there are few examples of that in *The Chronicles*. At his best, Lewis can create scenes that embody, mythically, the moral challenges we all must face. When Eustace Scrubb turns into a dragon in *The Voyage of the Dawn Treader,* he has to learn that he cannot rely on his own power to shed the evil dragon's skin and resume his normal shape. Digory Kirke, in *The Magician's Nephew,* finds the allure of the evil queen Jadis intoxicating; only when he sees the desolation she brings can he snap out of his enchantment. Lewis has a wonderful sense of the normal: of the simple joys and pleasures of home and hearth, of the decency of ordinary people who are motivated by love. In this sense, Lewis is far from a moral elitist. These are the qualities that have turned so many of us into the loyal subjects of Narnia.

The Curse of the Blue Figurine
John Bellairs
Dial Books for Young Readers, 1983, 200 pages

BELIEVE IT OR NOT, horror novels are one of the most popular genres among children today. The level of gore and violence in these novels is on the increase and their literary value is negligible. But children like scary stories, and there is nothing inherently wrong with this instinct. The problem is to direct them to the books with the highest literary and moral qualities. Elsewhere we recommend classics from the tradition of the Gothic novel, including *Frankenstein* (see page 235) and *Dr. Jekyll and Mr. Hyde* (see page 174). One of the best contemporary writers in this genre is John Bellairs. While his books are quite frightening, they are well written and undergirded by a moral vision. In *The Curse of the Blue Figurine,* we meet Johnny Dixon, whose mother has recently died of cancer, and whose father is flying bombing missions in the Korean War. Left with his grandparents, Johnny meets the funny, eccentric Professor Coote, who lives across the street, and together they discover an ancient Egyptian figurine in the basement of a church. Soon after Johnny meets the mysterious Mr. Beard, who gives him a magical ring. The ring gives Johnny the power to defeat bullies and anyone else who crosses him. But the ring is evil—like the ring in Tolkien's fantasies, it corrupts its user. With the professor's help, Johnny eventually defeats Mr. Beard, but not before he has learned something about his own susceptibility to dark forces. Among Bellairs's other novels are *The House with a Clock in Its Walls*, *The Figure in the Shadows*, and *The Letter, the Witch, and the Ring*.

Elisabeth and the Water Troll
Walter Wangerin, Jr. Illustrated by Deborah Healy. HarperCollins, 1991, 64 pages

THIS IS A HARD book to summarize: it is longer than a picture book but shorter than a novel. Though it is similar to the story of *Beauty and the Beast,* its tone is closer to one of the melancholy, ancient ballads. Wangerin, author of the prize-winning fantasy novel *The Book of the Dun Cow* (see page 233), here tells of a little girl's sorrow and of a water troll whose heart is awakened by wounded innocence. Near the town of Dorf, a girl named Elisabeth comes to a well known as Despair. Inconsolable because her mother has died, she throws her mother's hair combs into the well. The water troll, who lives in a cave inside the well, becomes fascinated by Elisabeth. That night he steals into the town and kidnaps her. When she awakens, she is frightened: his loving words sound like snarls. But when she falls down the well, the water troll rescues her, and she begins to understand his love. Meanwhile, in the town, Elisabeth's father tries to find her. The townspeople want revenge; the sheriff, a partisan of violent methods, vows that he will kill the kidnapper. In the climactic scene, the water troll returns Elisabeth to her father, but he pays the ultimate price. This story is about death and loss, and the hope that can be found even within the depths of despair. Suffering can be eased, Wangerin seems to be saying, when it is shared.

Five Children and It
E. Nesbit
Dell, 1990 (1902), 208 pages

IN THIS COMIC tour de force, set in Edwardian England, four children learn that getting one's wish is not always as delightful as it may sound. Robert, Anthea, Cyril, and Jane are playing one day in a sand pit near the country home they are visiting. They dig out of the sand a small furry creature with eyes on the ends of long stalks. This creature declares that it is a Psammead, a sand fairy who has lived for thousands of years. Psammeads, more common in the era of dinosaurs, grant wishes to people. Naturally the children cannot wait to make their dreams come true. In a hilarious series of misadventures, the children's wishes get them into scrapes and binds that land them in no end of trouble. They wish to be as beautiful as the day, but then no one recognizes them. They desire gold in abundance, and almost get arrested as robbers. They ask for their baby brother to be able to grow up, and they find that he is no longer interested in them. They acquire the ability to fly, but get stuck on a church steeple. Wishes are always tempting because they promise a better life. But learning to appreciate the blessings one has is really more important. Thanks to the Psammead—and the literary genius of E. Nesbit—the children learn that truth in the funniest possible way. Nesbit also wrote two equally delightful sequels: *The Phoenix and the Carpet* and *The Story of the Amulet*.

The Gammage Cup (**NH**)
Carol Kendall. Illustrated by Erik Blegvad.
Harcourt Brace Jovanovich, 1987 (1959), 221 pages

THE MINNIPINS ARE a sober people living secure, orderly, and, to be honest, rather dull lives in an isolated valley. The trouble begins when several of their neighbors begin wearing different colored cloaks—orange, blue, and gold—instead of the sensible green worn by the majority. Outlawed from the village for nonconformity, the five exiles learn that the Minnipins' ancient enemy is preparing to attack. Instead of resorting to a tit-for-tat mentality—despite the fact that the elders of the village contemptuously refuse to believe their warning—the courageous exiles determine to save the village themselves. *The Gammage Cup* teaches the valuable lesson that authentic unity—whether familial, civil, or national—springs from selfless service, not conformity.

The Golden Key
George MacDonald. Illustrated by Maurice Sendak. Farrar, Straus and Giroux, 1976 (1867), 86 pages

THIS IS THE most perfectly conceived and moving fantasy story for children ever written. It strongly influenced such twentieth-century writers as G. K. Chesterton, W. H. Auden, C. S. Lewis, J. R. R. Tolkien, and Madeleine L'Engle. To read it is akin to waking up from the most beautiful and comforting dream imaginable. *The Golden Key* is an allegory of life. It concerns two children, Mossy and Tangle, who find a golden key and search for the lock that will open and lead them into the "land from which the shadows fall." Along the way Mossy and Tangle become separated. They travel to strange seas and deep beneath the surface of the earth. They meet infinitely wise children who are also infinitely old. They pass through fire and cool baths, until they are eventually reunited as adults. Though their separation and their journeys involve pain and uncertainty, the children are guided by benevolent forces and find themselves at the base of the rainbow. Though there is no question in this tale of good versus evil, the allegory is about the faith, hope, and love necessary to sustain one's journey through life. This special edition was created and illustrated by Maurice Sendak, one of our greatest illustrators for children.

Gulliver's Travels
Jonathan Swift. Illustrated by David Small.
William Morrow, 1983 (1726), 96 pages

GULLIVER'S TRAVELS IS a classic that a child can grow
with. A small child can enjoy the absurdity and fun of Gulliver's visit to Lilliput, while a young adult can read all four
parts of the book and relish Swift's biting satire against politi-
cians, scientists, and just about everyone else. Swift took the
genre of adventure stories about voyages to exotic lands (popular in the eighteenth century) and used it to create kingdoms
of giants and pygmies, of insane scientists and talking horses.
The tiny size of the Lilliputians, of course, symbolizes their
pettiness and their ridiculous pretensions to pomp and power.
The war between Lilliput and Blefescu, Gulliver learns, was
started over an argument about how to break eggs. In his next
adventure, Gulliver is the midget, pushed around by the giants
of Brobdingnag. Their size indicates their coarseness and
greediness. Older, more advanced readers will want to continue with the final two parts. The scientists and philosophers
of Laputa are bizarre, running experiments like trying to ex-
tract sunbeams from cucumbers. The final book is about a trip
to the land of talking horses known as Houyhnhnms. It contains a devastating portrait of human beings reduced to their
lowest passions in the apelike creatures known as Yahoos.
Swift's humor, ranging from the mild to the savage, has intrigued and challenged generations of readers. Choose the edition that's right for your child.

The Hobbit
J. R. R. Tolkien
Houghton Mifflin, 1987 (1937), 317 pages

"IN A HOLE in the ground there lived a hobbit." So begins
the tale that introduced the world to the mythical realm of
Middle Earth. Bilbo Baggins, like all hobbits, loves the comfort

of hearth and home, but he is not allowed to live a retired life. He finds himself called upon to do something extraordinary, to reach into himself and discover whether he can become a hero. *The Hobbit* is a classic quest story, in which Bilbo and his companions seek to end the dragon Smaug's reign of terror. But this quest is full of temptations, including the most dangerous temptation of all—the ring of power Bilbo takes from Gollum. The cantankerous dwarfs who take him on the quest are more concerned about their people's gold, which Smaug sits upon, than protecting the country from a dragon. When the chief dwarf, Thorin Oakenshield, lies dying, he tells Bilbo, "There is more good in you than you know. . . . Some courage and some wisdom, blended in measure. If more of us valued food and cheer and song above hoarded gold, it would be a merrier world!" Bilbo learns that the most lethal enemy is not the dragon but the enemy within, the capacity of the human heart to prefer the self to the good of others. This is the core of Tolkien's moral imagination, dramatized so hauntingly in this unforgettable world of elves and goblins, enchanted forests and misty mountains.

Hounds of the Morrigan
Pat O'Shea
Holiday House, 1987, 469 pages

PIDGE (SHORT FOR P. J., short for Patrick Joseph!) and his young sister, Brigit, seem to be the most puny opponents of evil that one could imagine. How can two children from rural Ireland prevent the wicked sorceress, the Morrigan, from destroying the world? But as is often the case in fantasy, it is always the weakest and most insignificant members of society that succeed against evil where stronger forces have failed. This is because all great fantasy writers know that it is the nature of evil to be proud; to be so filled with schemes of power and world domination that it cannot conceive that it can be brought down by the weak and the humble. And that is precisely the Morrigan's undoing. Challenged by a cast of characters so unusual, so comic, and so seemingly harmless, the wicked sorceress does not suspect the children until it is too late. As the children are pursued across Ireland by the hounds of the Morrigan, their ultimate triumph is all the more satisfying for the tremendous odds against them.

The Indian in the Cupboard
Lynne Reid Banks
Avon, 1983, 182 pages

WIDELY REGARDED AS among the very best of recent children's fiction, *The Indian in the Cupboard* gives a whole new meaning to that rather shopworn phrase "the dignity of human life." When Omri, an English boy, receives a small plastic Indian and an old medicine cabinet for his birthday, he is disappointed. But disappointment soon turns to excitement when he discovers that by locking the Indian in the cabinet, it magically comes to life. After the initial thrill wears off, however, Omri is confronted with the sobering responsibility of taking care of his fiercely independent new friend, Little Bear. When Omri's friend Patrick introduces a cowboy, an old chief, and horses to the tiny cast of characters, Omri finds that he has a full-scale war on his hands. Realizing that they have inadvertently resurrected ancient rivalries and sensing that playing God with the lives of others is profoundly wrong, Omri scolds Patrick: "They're people, you can't use people." Unlike Patrick, Omri has realized that relative size and power provide no justification for tampering with the lives of others, that might is almost never right. Exciting, absorbing, and thought-provoking, this story, like the Indian in the title, is alive with magic. The series continues with *The Return of the Indian* and *The Secret of the Indian*.

Mrs. Frisby and the Rats of NIMH (**N**)
Robert O'Brien
Atheneum, 1971, 232 pages

MRS. FRISBY, A widowed field mouse, becomes involved in the lives of a colony of remarkable rats who have escaped from a nearby laboratory. Though timid by nature, she braves terrors and strange adventures in her determination to save her children's lives. Spring is coming and, unless she moves her family out of the field in which she lives, their home will be torn up by the plow. This absorbing, and often harrowing, fantasy asks us to choose between an inhuman technological society and a simpler life, rooted in the rhythms of nature. In an age that has seen widespread experimentation on both animals and humans, *Mrs. Frisby and the Rats of NIMH* reminds us that life must be respected in all its forms. After O'Brien's death, his daughter, Jane Conly, continued the series with two fine novels, *Racso and the Rats of NIMH* and *R-T, Margaret, and the Rats of NIMH*.

The Phantom Tollbooth
Norton Juster. Illustrated by Jules Feiffer.
Random House, 1964 (1961), 256 pages

"THERE ONCE WAS a boy named Milo who didn't know what to do with himself—not just sometimes, but always." Thus begins *The Phantom Tollbooth*, one of the most delightful fantasies about the life of the mind ever written. Milo's boredom and time-wasting ways are suddenly challenged when a tollbooth mysteriously appears in his home. In his special car, Milo crosses into the Kingdom of Wisdom. His adventures lead him to Dictionopolis, ruled by King Azaz the Unabridged, a city nestled in the Foothills of Confusion. In his attempt to rescue the Princesses Rhyme and Reason, Milo stumbles upon many adventures of the mind. *The Phantom Tollbooth* has been compared to Lewis Carroll's *Alice* books because both authors love words, numbers, and logic, and the ways they can enlighten and vex our brains. Juster's story is packed with quirky humor, scintillating wordplay, and brain teasers galore. For instance, Milo arrives at the Island of Conclusions in an unusual fashion—he jumps, of course. The child who becomes entranced by this tale will get a taste of the wonder, mystery, and excitement of the well-tempered intellect.

The Princess and the Goblin
George MacDonald
Illustrated by Jesse Wilcox Smith.
William Morrow, 1986 (1871), 208 pages

IT IS OFTEN SAID that in literature evil characters are usually more interesting than good ones. This is undoubtedly true: it is extremely difficult to prevent good characters from seeming too saccharine or remote. One might think that children's literature would be an exception to this rule, but in many instances it is not. (Which character in *Treasure Island* is more intriguing—Squire Trelawney or Long John Silver?) But George MacDonald, the nineteenth-century Scottish writer, knew how to create characters whose intense goodness and love remain deeply etched in the memory. In this novel, the central characters are the young Princess Irene and a miner boy named Curdie. It is up to Curdie to foil the plans, made by the goblins who live under the castle, to kidnap the princess. There is one character, however, who presides over the story: Irene's great-great-grandmother. The old lady lives in a turret at the castle's highest point. She appears to be incredibly old and beautifully youthful; she only appears to a few people. Her fireplace contains burning roses that never consume themselves and her spinning wheel hums with the sounds of summer. This lady is not only loving and compassionate, but also strong and decisive, calling on the princess to overcome her fears and to behave courageously. MacDonald wrote a sequel, equally good, entitled *The Princess and Curdie*.

The Prydain Chronicles: The Book of Three; The
Black Cauldron; The Castle of Llyr; Taran Wanderer;
The High King (**N**)
Lloyd Alexander
Dell, 1980 (1964–68)

HAVING ONCE CROSSED the borders into the imaginary
kingdom of Prydain, ruled over by Math the High King, any
child will want to return again and again. There you will meet
Taran, Assistant Pig-Keeper to the wizard Dallben, who is destined to become one of the greatest heroes Prydain has ever
known. His adventures begin when Hen Wen, the oracular pig,
runs away in terror from some strange force and Taran pursues
her into the forest. He cannot know that before Hen Wen is
found again he will have been called upon to face the dread
warlord, the Horned King, with his host of the Cauldron-
born, warriors who cannot be killed because they are already
dead. How he meets up with his companions-in-arms, the
great protector of Prydain, Prince Gwydion, the beautiful and
headstrong Princess Eilonwy, Gurgi, part beast and part man,
and Fflewddur the bard, is told in *The Book of Three,* the first
in the series. Each volume in this magnificent series chronicles
the adventures of the companions as they battle against the
forces of evil. In the final volume, *The High King,* Taran and
his friends are forced into a final confrontation with the malev-
olent Lord Arawn, the outcome of which will decide the fate of
Prydain forever. Younger children will enjoy *The Truthful
Harp* (see page 129), a brief, illustrated tale about Fflewddur.

Redwall
Brian Jacques. Illustrated by Gary Chalk.
Philomel, 1986, 351 pages

AS A NOVICE monk at Redwall Abbey, Matthias the mouse
has dedicated himself to the service of peace. But when his
beloved abbey is besieged by Cluny, the vicious one-eyed rat,
and his horde, Matthias gradually learns that, sometimes, it is

virtuous to defend oneself and those one loves. He sets off on a hazardous quest in order to recover the long-lost sword of Martin the Warrior. As ancient legend tells, once the weapon is found a champion will appear to defend Redwall in its greatest need. Set in medieval times and packed with brain-teasing riddles, humor, and pathos, *Redwall* and its companion volume, *Mossflower,* are compelling tales of courage and daring in the face of adversity.

The Reluctant Dragon
Kenneth Grahame. Illustrated by Ernest H. Shepard.
Holiday House, 1966 (1898)

A HUMOROUS EXPLODING of fairy tale stereotypes, *The Reluctant Dragon* is the delightful story of a dragon who prefers making up verses in his head rather than rampaging around the countryside. A problem arises when the terrified villagers enlist the help of a knight to rid them of this "monstrous bane." Now the boy who has befriended the dragon and knows perfectly well that it wouldn't hurt a fly, let alone a knight, must somehow make sure that the knight and the dragon both come out of the battle without loss of face. Like *The Story of Ferdinand* (see page 83) and *The Griffin and the Minor Canon* (see page 72), this whimsical tale reminds us that it is not always wise to judge by appearances.

The Shining Company
Rosemary Sutcliff
Farrar, Straus and Giroux, 1990, 293 pages

SET IN ANCIENT Britain, fifty years after the death of Arthur Pendragon, *The Shining Company* is a story about a young boy's dream of following in Arthur's footsteps. His wish comes true when a young chieftain makes Prosper his shield bearer. Prosper and his faithful body servant, Conn, find themselves riding into battle with warriors whom the king, Mynyddog the Golden, has named The Shining Company, after Arthur's Knights of the Round Table. In the course of their adventures both boys discover that courage is not the only mark of a hero, but also the virtues of loyalty, love, and perseverance.

Tom's Midnight Garden
Philippa Pearce. Illustrated by Susan Einzig.
Harper Trophy, 1992 (1958), 229 pages

THIS NOVEL IS widely considered to be one of the masterpieces of children's literature, and we heartily endorse this judgment. It is a story of astonishing richness and heartbreaking beauty. The critic Humphrey Carpenter has noted that *Tom's Midnight Garden* is, in essence, a reversal of *Peter Pan*. In Pearce's novel, a boy has to come to terms with the fact that time cannot be stopped, that change and growth and loss are part of human existence. At the same time, Pearce celebrates the joys of childhood and the way memory can preserve the fleeting moments of joy and understanding in our lives. Tom Long's brother Peter has measles, and so Tom is forced to spend the summer in the suburbs with his aunt and uncle. Tom is furious, because he doesn't like his aunt and uncle, and can't stand being cooped up in their apartment. Then one night he hears an old grandfather clock strike thirteen. When he goes down to investigate he decides to step outside, and he discovers himself in a beautiful garden rather than a paved driveway. In this magical midnight garden, Tom meets a pretty young girl named Hatty. Each night he goes into this garden, but he is puzzled by the changes he finds there. Slowly he begins to realize that each visit occurs at a different point in time in Hatty's life. Though he experiences Hatty's world every night, she perceives him as a ghost who appears only after long absences in her life. Pearce resolves these mysteries in a satisfying and moving conclusion. Tom's experiences cause him to leave his angry, self-preoccupied life behind, and learn something about love, time, and the importance of memory.

Tuck Everlasting
Natalie Babbitt
Farrar, Straus and Giroux, 1988 (1975), 139 pages

MOST OF US fear death, but would we really want to live forever? Cursed, or blessed, with eternal life after drinking from a magic spring, the Tuck family must now wander the earth so that no one will discover its fearsome secret. Until one day ten-year-old Winnie Foster stumbles upon the spring and learns of its power. Forced to choose between mortality and everlasting life, Winnie now faces a compelling moral dilemma. She is helped in her choice by the friendship of the Tucks and Pa Tuck's sobering and wise words: "Us Tucks are stuck. We ain't part of the wheel no more. Dropped off, Winnie. Left behind." At the heart of this beautiful book lies a profound truth, that the cycle of life and death is a wheel that has been set in motion by the Creator and that we tamper with it at our peril. Winnie must come to understand this if she is to protect the spring from those who would use it for their own selfish ends.

Westmark
Lloyd Alexander
Dell, 1982, 192 pages

FROM THE PEN of that masterful children's author, Lloyd Alexander, comes this spirited tale of adventure set in the mythical kingdom of Westmark. Unjustly accused of killing a man, Theo is forced to flee his country and lead the life of an exile. His travels bring him into the company of an assortment of characters: Las Bombas the mountebank, who, for all his trickery, nevertheless has a good heart; Mickle, a girl with a mysterious past; and Carrabus, the evil adviser to the king. Although innocent, Theo is haunted by the knowledge of his own murderous hatred for the man he is supposed to have killed, and when his adventures lead him to oppose Carrabus's plot to usurp the throne, he is troubled by the violence that ensues. It is Theo's profound moral questioning of whether the end can ever truly justify the means that sets this story far above others of its genre.

The Wind in the Willows
Kenneth Grahame. Illustrated by Ernest H. Shepard.
Aladdin, 1989 (1908), 259 pages

RATTY, MOLE, BADGER, and Toad need no introduction. Their adventures on the river and the country roads of Edwardian England are part of our cultural memory. We know of no book for children that can match *The Wind in the Willows* for its timelessness, its air of endless summer afternoons by the riverbank. The love of good fires, good talk, and an occasional song, which Ratty, Mole, and Badger embody, is enhanced by Toad's quest for thrills and spills. Grahame is a consummate comedian: it is impossible not to laugh at Toad's sudden enthusiasms and anarchic escapades. But we also sympathize with Ratty and Mole as they struggle to rescue Toad from the consequences of his actions. Above all, *The Wind in the Willows* is about friendship and loyalty, shared pleasures and shared responsibilities. All of these themes are brought together in the climactic retaking of Toad Hall from the mean-spirited weasels and ferrets who attempt to claim squatter's rights. It is impossible to think of Grahame's classic without Ernest Shepard's immortal illustrations—perhaps the most perfect collaboration in the history of children's literature.

A Wrinkle in Time (**N**)
Madeleine L'Engle
Farrar, Straus and Giroux, 1962, 211 pages

MADELEINE L'ENGLE'S fantasies reveal an imagination that is able to see harmonies and connections where we usually see only categories and conflicts. Science and mysticism, the ordinary and the extraordinary, sorrow and hope—these divisions are healed in L'Engle's soaring vision. *A Wrinkle in Time* begins her fantasy series about the Murry and O'Keefe families. In this story we meet the sensitive adolescent Meg Murry, her brother, the boy genius Charles Wallace, and their famous scientist parents. With Meg's friend Calvin O'Keefe the children are swept into uncharted areas of the universe, where they confront the powers of good and evil. Modern physics, with its richly metaphoric language about space and time, matter and energy, provides L'Engle with an opportunity to link the grand abstractions of science with the concrete moral and spiritual problems of young people. As a writer, she never loses sight of her child protagonists' personal dilemmas and aspirations; rather, she weaves them into her tales. In this story, the protagonist is Meg: only her love for her know-it-all brother can rescue him from the clutches of IT, a disembodied, evil intelligence that knows nothing of love or imagination. Meg is forced to confront her own faults and fears, and to triumph over them; though she has love and support from others, she must face IT alone. The other novels in this series follow in the same model, maintaining a high standard of literary excellence. They include *The Wind in the Door, A Swiftly Tilting Planet, Many Waters,* and *An Acceptable Time.*

Older Readers

Animal Farm
George Orwell
Signet, 1986 (1945), 128 pages

FROM THE PEN of one of the twentieth century's greatest critics of political ideology comes this trenchant satire of totalitarianism. When the animals on an English farm finally expel their tyrannical master, Farmer Jones, they believe that, at last, they are going to be able to establish the animal utopia they have always dreamed of. To commemorate their great victory, they inscribe on the wall of their barn the seven "command-ments" of their new political order. The last and greatest of these is "All animals are equal." But the pigs have an altogether different agenda. With the help of their "secret police"—a pack of vicious mastiffs—they gradually take over the running of the farm. Now the only commandment is "All animals are equal. But some animals are more equal than others." A former radical socialist and witness to the atrocities of both Stalinist Russia and Nazi Germany, George Orwell had no illusions about the deadly nature of totalitarianism. He intended *Animal Farm* to be a vivid reminder of the well-known statement "Power corrupts, and absolute power corrupts absolutely."

Antar and the Eagles
William Mayne
Delacorte, 1989, 166 pages

WHEN A BOY named Antar starts to climb the scaffolding on the church in his village, he doesn't want to go very high. But his feet seem to propel him to the very top of the bell tower. Suddenly, in a flash of wings and beaks, he is lifted into the air by powerful eagles and carried off into the mountains. Thus begins a strange but compelling fantasy by one of Britain's leading authors of children's books. Summoned to the aerie of the Great Eagle, Antar is told that he must perform a danger-ous mission to ensure the survival of this noble race of birds. He is to rescue a very special egg—the egg containing the next Great Eagle—from a greedy human king who has taken it as a trophy. Antar also discovers that he must learn to fly in order to carry out his mission. He learns to live as an eagle, eating raw meat, flying, and speaking a new tongue. This initiation into a new life teaches him the fierce courage and undying loyalty of these magnificent lords of the sky. By the time he completes his quest and returns home, he is no longer the fearful boy who climbed the church tower.

*The Arthurian Trilogy: The Light Beyond the Forest,
The Sword and the Circle, The Road to Camlann*
Rosemary Sutcliff
E. P. Dutton, 1980–82

ROSEMARY SUTCLIFF'S masterful retelling of the legend
of King Arthur still has the power to elicit shivers of terror and
awe as the hand rises out of the lake and holds Excalibur aloft.
Steeped in the magic of the Druids, the Britain that Sutcliff depicts is filled with a brooding mystery that suggests a world in
which anything might happen; a poor squire may become the
greatest king that his country has ever seen, while the noblest
knight in the kingdom might one day betray his lord. This trilogy begins with the circumstances of Arthur's birth and follows his fortunes, including the quest of the Holy Grail, until
his death at the hands of Mordred. A tale that has inspired the
imagination of many great poets throughout the ages, the legend of Arthur continues to remind us that nobility of soul far
outweighs the transient glories of pomp and circumstance.

The Book of the Dun Cow
Walter Wangerin, Jr.
HarperCollins, 1989 (1978), 241 pages

ONCE, LONG AGO, when the sun still orbited the earth
and the animals had the gift of speech, there lived a rooster
named Chauntecleer. He ruled over his roost, and his hens and
all the other animals were pleased with him. But under the
earth stirred Wyrm, embodiment of all evil. Chauntecleer and
his fellow creatures did not understand that their mission in
life was to contain Wyrm within his dark dungeon. So when
Wyrm attempts to break through they are unprepared for the
apocalyptic conflict to come. Walter Wangerin won the American Book Award for this strikingly original animal fable, reminiscent of Richard Adams and J. R. R. Tolkien. There is never

any question in this story of which forces represent good and evil. The subtlety of the tale involves the moral struggles inside Chauntecleer and his friends, Mundo Cani Dog and John Wesley Weasel. Though we sympathize with Chauntecleer, we hope that he will rule wisely, avoiding vanity, rashness, and complacency. He is helped not only by the Dog and the Weasel, but by his beautiful consort, Pertelote, and the mysterious figure of the Dun Cow, who moves silently through the story. The final conflict between Chauntecleer's subjects and the minions of Wyrm teaches the creatures, through suffering and pain, that they are the Keepers of the Wyrm. The sequel to this novel is *The Book of Sorrows,* which we also recommend.

The Dark Is Rising sequence: *The Dark Is Rising* (**NH**); *Over Sea, Under Stone; Greenwitch; The Grey King* (**N**); *Silver on the Tree*
Susan Cooper. Illustrated by Alan Cober.
Aladdin, 1987 (boxed set)

IN *THE DARK IS RISING,* the first in the sequence, eleven-year-old Will Stanton discovers that he has been chosen to stand against the great forces of the Dark. His mission begins on Christmas Eve when a local farmer suddenly warns him that "the Walker is abroad" and then gives him a mysterious iron ring to wear, the first of Six Signs. How Will meets Merriman the wizard, and how he becomes an "Old One," one of the greatest warriors of the Light, is told in this first volume. In subsequent books, Will teams up with four other children in order to combat the Dark, a battle that will test each child's capacity for loyalty, truthfulness, and courage to the utmost. *The Dark Is Rising* series confirms Susan Cooper as one of this century's most accomplished writers of fantasy. Like Tolkien, C. S. Lewis, Lloyd Alexander, and Ursula Le Guin, Cooper is able to depict a world in which the forces of evil, however terrifying, are ultimately seen as hollow and valueless in comparison to the forces of good. She is remarkable in her ability to make virtue the most exciting adventure of all.

The Dream Time
Henry Treece. Illustrated by Charles Keeping.
Meredith, 1968, 114 pages

SET IN PREHISTORIC times, this novel has the quality of a
dream, as Rosemary Sutcliff says in her afterword. The characters in the story live at the dawn of time, when what it is to
be a human being is still unclear. Crookleg is a boy who has
suffered a broken leg that did not heal properly. He is expected nonetheless to take part in his tribe's raids on neighboring tribes in order to steal food. On one such raid his
father is killed, and Crookleg runs away. He meets a girl
named Blackbird, whose family has also been killed. Together
they set off to find a way to live—an odyssey in which they will
discover their humanity. Crookleg, who is given the new name
of Twilight, is really an artist, gifted with the ability to scratch
pictures into copper. Yet even his ability to make beautiful
things becomes an occasion for jealousy and violence. As Twilight continues his search, he thinks about what separates
people. "He wished that all people, the men and women and
horses and owls and dogs could agree to speak the same
words. Then all things would be easy, to speak and be understood. Perhaps no one would fight then." The almost mythic
quality of this book will communicate with the deepest part of
your child's imagination.

Frankenstein
Mary Shelley. Illustrated by Charles Keeping.
Bedrick, 1988 (1818), 222 pages

BEFORE THE ADVENT of the modern horror movie, with
its gore-for-gore's-sake mentality, the great writers of ghost
stories and Gothic novels explored a deeper and more profound realm of the human spirit. In classic works like
Frankenstein, older children encounter the reality of evil, and
the dangers of curiosity untempered by common sense and
moral restraints. *Frankenstein,* though it has been debased by

endless films, cartoons, spoofs, and toys, remains one of the most potent myths of the modern era. At the heart of this myth is the pride of the scientist who would take God's place and become a Creator in his own right. What Mary Shelley dramatizes so vividly is that man cannot create something new; he can only re-create from the materials around him. But this process of re-creation involves him in dangers and mysteries that are beyond his power to control. The monster in this story is the dark alter ego of Dr. Frankenstein, the image of his own moral twistedness and illicit desires. *Frankenstein* is a tragic story, a cautionary tale. At the close of the twentieth century, what story could be more relevant to our society, given the increasing power wielded by scientists and businessmen over genetics and human life? At the beginning of the modern era, Mary Shelley, with an artist's prophetic imagination, reminded us what it is like to be a human—and less than human. This edition, chillingly illustrated by Charles Keeping, preserves the original, unabridged text. For advanced readers.

The Hero and the Crown (**N**)
Robin McKinley
Ace, 1987, 227 pages

PRINCESS AERIN IS an unlikely heroine; she is clumsy, not particularly beautiful, and, worst of all, her mother is reputed to have been a sorceress. In short, she is the ugly duckling at the court of Dalmatia. But like Frodo of *Lord of the Rings* (see page 237) and Taran the Assistant Pig-Keeper in the *Prydain Chronicles* (see page 226), it is often the weakest and most insignificant character who is called upon to do the bravest things. When her country is threatened by the forces of the evil wizard Gonturan, Aerin knows that if she is to defeat him, she must first conquer her own pride and selfish desires. Helped by Luthe, a young magician who taught her mother, and armed only with her love of truth, Aerin journeys to Gonturan's Dark

Tower. There she will be tempted not only to betray her country but also herself. Like all great works of fantasy, *The Hero and the Crown* does not merely deal with mythical events and characters. Instead, it involves us in the timeless drama of good against evil, a battle that must be waged, first and foremost, in the heart and soul of the protagonist.

The Lord of the Rings: The Fellowship of the Ring,
The Two Towers, The Return of the King
J. R. R. Tolkien
Houghton Mifflin, 1967 (1954–55)

TOLKIEN'S EPIC STORY of Middle Earth, which began with *The Hobbit* (see page 221), continues in the three books that constitute *The Lord of the Rings*. As in *The Hobbit,* the hero is a hobbit, named Frodo, who must contend with the evil ring of power found by his uncle Bilbo. Now the whole fate of Middle Earth is at stake, for the evil lord Sauron has sent his forces out to seek the ring and gain ultimate power. Frodo sets out from his home to join the Companions, the dwarfs, elves, and men who must accompany him on his quest to destroy the ring. Aided by the wizard Gandalf and his homely hobbit friend, Sam Gamgee, Frodo struggles to overcome his own temptations. In the epic scope of these books, many tales are told in addition to the central narrative, including the odyssey of Boromir, whose desire to regain his throne causes him to go mad with ambition. Even the pathetic Gollum, first met in *The Hobbit,* makes a reappearance. Frodo comes to understand the moral weakness of Gollum, and shows him compassion as well as judgment. Tolkien's ability to embody these moral conflicts in the landscape, characters, and history of Middle Earth has often been copied but never surpassed. For children who become completely absorbed in Middle Earth, Tolkien's other chronicles of this world—including denser, more challenging novels such as *The Silmarillion*—may serve to extend their delight.

Pilgrim's Progress
John Bunyan. Retold by Mary Godolphin.
Illustrated by Robert Lawson.
Lippincott, 1939 (1678–84), 120 pages

NEXT TO THE BIBLE, *Pilgrim's Progress* was the most read and revered book for generations of Americans. What made it so absorbing was not merely its religious message, but its imaginative use of allegory. Though allegory works by personifying abstract ideas, John Bunyan knew how to dramatize his allegorical figures, endowing them with very recognizable human traits. As Christian makes his way from the City of Destruction on the dangerous journey to the Celestial City, he encounters a number of friends and foes, including Obstinate, Mr. Worldly Wiseman, the Giant Despair, Mr. Love-ease, and Mr. Great-heart. Christian battles evil, overcomes deceptions and mistakes, and achieves the goal of his pilgrimage. Bunyan's story emerges from an intense religious sensibility, but it is not necessary to share his doctrinal positions to delight in the moral wisdom of his allegory. Because the original text of the book is too long and its language too obscure, the best edition we have found for children is the one retold by Mary Godolphin and illustrated by Robert Lawson.

Something Wicked This Way Comes
Ray Bradbury
Bantam, 1990 (1962), 215 pages

RAY BRADBURY IS one of America's literary treasures, a writer who transcends the categories of science fiction and fantasy. This novel, a dreamlike fantasy, is a profound exploration of the moral life. Two boys, Jim Nightshade and Will Halloway, go to a carnival, "Cooger and Dark's Pandemonium Shadow Show." There they find the mysterious Mr. Dark, who has the power to grant everyone's secret desire. But the price of that offer is dreadful, a devil's bargain that can end only in madness and destruction. The boys are alternately tempted and repulsed by the carnival. They are helped by Will's father, Charles Halloway, a melancholy but wise man. He warns them not to judge by appearances, and to remember that the moral life is a daily struggle. "Oh, it would be lovely if you could just *be* fine, *act* fine, not think of it all the time. But it's hard, right? with the last piece of lemon cake waiting in the icebox, middle of the night, not yours, but you lie awake in a hot sweat for it, eh? . . . [I]t never ends, never stops, you got the choice this second, now this next, and the next after that, be good, be bad, that's what the clock ticks, that's what it says in the ticks." When Jim gives in to temptation, Will and his father rescue him through the power of laughter. Only in laughing at the pretentiousness and self-importance of evil can we flush it out of our systems. Bradbury's moral imagination can also be found in such classics as *Fahrenheit 451* and *The Martian Chronicles,* which we also recommend.

The Space Trilogy: Out of the Silent Planet, Perelandra, That Hideous Strength
C. S. Lewis
Macmillan, 1990 (1944–46)

IN THE MODERN era, we have experienced both the benefits of scientific technology and its ability to unleash unimaginable horror. Before C. S. Lewis wrote *The Chronicles of Narnia,* he became concerned with an ideological frame of mind he called "scientism." According to Lewis, scientism was the belief that technology would liberate mankind from the moral traditions of the past; the end result would be the elevation of certain scientists to the status of godhood, with the power of life and death over the whole human race. Recent news reports about the cloning of human embryos and other genetic experiments ought to convince us that Lewis's worries were neither paranoid nor fanatical. The three novels that constitute *The Space Trilogy* dramatize the conflict between scientism and the moral tradition of the West. A Cambridge University scholar named Ransom accidentally stumbles onto a scheme in which two men—one a scientist and the other a huckster with intellectual pretensions—prepare to travel to Mars and plunder its rich and strange culture. In the second novel, Ransom is brought to Venus, where he finds a new Adam and Eve, who are being tempted by the evil scientists from the first novel. Finally, in *That Hideous Strength,* the cosmic struggle between good and evil takes place on earth, as a scientific institute comes close to asserting its power over the world. In each of the novels, the decent characters have to overcome their own fears and weaknesses to do battle with the forces of scientism. Ultimately, according to Lewis, it is the moral tradition of the West that best illuminates our understanding of the universe, and not the utilitarian logic of science.

Watership Down
Richard Adams
Macmillan, 1974, 444 pages

WATERSHIP DOWN IS the real thing: an original and compelling story that blends elements of fantasy, epic, and nature writing into a powerful and unforgettable narrative. In depicting a group of wild rabbits in the English countryside, Adams has created a coherent world, complete with its own myths, legends, and heroes. When Fiver, a mystic, foresees that the developer's bulldozer will destroy the warren, he asks his friend Hazel to lead a band of rabbits on a perilous journey to a new home. Their trek and the struggles they encounter in establishing a better way of life, relate not only to the troubles of our technology-dominated environment but to the timeless problems of justice and peace. At the heart of the novel is the theme of self-sacrifice, the hero's willingness to take decisive action on behalf of the community. Advanced readers will discover in the novel insights into the nature of political order, but all readers will be swept up in the epic sweep of this exodus to a new, promised land. *Watership Down,* a work in the tradition of Tolkien and Kenneth Grahame, presents us with characters who are true both to their animal natures and to the best and worst of the human spirit.

The Wizard of Earthsea tetralogy: *The Wizard of Earthsea, The Tombs of Atuan, The Farthest Shore, Tehanu*
Ursula K. Le Guin
Atheneum, 1968–90

WHAT MAKES A wise man wise? This is the question that Ged, the hero of this popular tetralogy, must discover. Originally desiring the great powers of wizardry, Ged learns painfully that a true magician is one who places his power in the service of others rather than the self. As a result of a foolish boast in the first volume of the series the young Ged summons a spirit from the dead. This one act of false pride is to set in motion a chain of events that will ultimately threaten to destroy the kingdom of Earthsea. In the remaining volumes Ged must undo the wrong that he has done; in the process, he is elected Archmage of Roke—the greatest wizard of all. Ursula Le Guin is like Tolkien in her uncanny ability to create a believable, self-contained world peopled by characters who engage us by the heroism of their undaunting search for truth in the face of almost overwhelming odds.

Biography

There is no heroic poem in the world but is at bottom a biography, the life of a man; also, it may be said, there is no life of a man, faithfully recorded, but is a heroic poem of its sort, rhymed or unrhymed.

—Thomas Carlyle

Note: In this section, books are listed in alphabetical order according to the name of the subject of the biography.

Younger Readers

Barry, The Bravest Saint Bernard
Lynn Hall. Illustrated by Antonio Castro.
Random House, 1992 (1973), 48 pages

DOGS EMBODY TWO of the most important virtues a child can ever learn: courage and loyalty. Here is the story of the Saint Bernard monastery and the dogs the monks bred to help them with their primary mission in life: rescuing travelers in the snow-capped Swiss Alps. Here, in the days before automobiles and highways, a special dog named Barry became known as the greatest Saint Bernard of all time. The story is told through the eyes of a boy named Werner, who loves Barry deeply. They grow up together—the puppy becoming a great rescuer and the boy becoming a monk in charge of the dogs. Among Barry's feats of heroism were the thwarting of a robbery and carrying a baby on his back to safety after the child's mother died. Author Lynn Hall and illustrator Antonio Castro depict the bonds of trust and love between Brother Werner and Barry. After Barry's death, the monks maintained a tradition of calling their best rescue dog Barry.

Thomas Alva Edison: Great Inventor
David A. Adler. Illustrated by Lyle Miller.
Holiday House, 1990, 48 pages

AS PARENTS, WE know that there are days when your child seems to ask at least fifty questions too many. But before you stifle your child's barrage of questions, consider the example of Thomas Edison. He exasperated both his teachers and his father with incessant questions; only his mother realized that he needed more individual attention. When she began to teach him at home, he was so grateful that he vowed never to disappoint her. His boyish experiments burned down a barn and got him into frequent trouble, but his thirst for knowledge couldn't be quenched. One of his first inventions was an automatic vote recorder for legislators, but they did not want to use it. After this experience, Edison made another vow: never to make something that was not useful. In later years, after he had invented the electric light bulb, the phonograph, and the first machine that could show motion pictures, Edison said that his inventions were not simply happy accidents. "Genius is one percent inspiration and ninety-nine percent perspiration," Edison averred. During World War I he helped the American war effort with several inventions, but he was always proud that he never invented anything that would kill. By the time of his death, he had been granted more than a thousand patents for his inventions.

St. Francis: The Poor Man of Assisi
Tomie de Paola
Holiday House, 1982

THOUGH IT WAS Thomas More who was called "a man for all seasons," the same could be said for Saint Francis of Assisi. Over the centuries, this holy man has had a universal appeal: his joyous spirit, love of nature, abundant charity, and lack of all pretension have endeared him to millions. Born in 1182, Francis was a typically wild young man, running with a fast crowd, drinking, and carousing. But after becoming a prisoner of war and enduring a long illness, Francis took to praying in the fields around his home. One day, in the church, he addressed Christ on the crucifix, asking what the Lord wanted of him. "Francis," a voice said, "rebuild my church. It is falling down." He decided to give up his possessions and live the life of poverty. This embittered his father, who angrily disowned his son. Soon Francis became known as "un pazzo"—a crazy man. "I am God's Fool," he said. It wasn't long before Francis's foolishness attracted many followers. Francis founded the religious order of Friars Minor (meaning the humblest of friars), known today as the Franciscans. The friars, who kept no possessions, wore a coarse, brown woolen robe, with a simple belt made of rope. Francis touched people's hearts because he asked them to lay down their fears, resentments, and possessiveness; in return, they would gain peace and a sense that all men and women were brothers and sisters. He began the tradition of the Christmas crèche (see *A Gift from St. Francis,* page 137). His love of nature is embodied in stories such as those of his preaching to the birds and his taming of the wolf of Gubbio. For this, Pope John Paul II named Francis the patron saint of ecology. But Francis was not merely a medieval flower child; his method for changing society was to ask each individual to change his own behavior first. The rest, he believed, would follow. Tomie de Paola's text and illustrations are thoroughly Franciscan in spirit.

The Boy Who Loved Music
David Lasker. Illustrated by Joe Lasker.
Viking, 1979

BEFORE THE ROMANTIC era, musicians were not considered geniuses whose bad tempers and enormous egos should be tolerated for the sake of art. Before Beethoven and his generation came along, musicians were the employees of aristocrats, often treated no better than a butler or gardener.

Franz Josef Haydn worked for the music-loving Prince Ester-
hazy, the richest nobleman in Hungary. The prince enjoyed his
summer estate, Esterhaza, so much that he tended to stay there
later and later in the year. Unfortunately, this meant that his
musicians, who all lived in Vienna, were forced to stay away
from their families for as much as seven months. Told from the
viewpoint of young Karl, a horn player in the prince's orchestra, the story reminds us that the musicians had few rights. But
Haydn comes up with an ingenious way to humor the prince
into letting the musicians go home: he composes the
"Farewell" Symphony, which concludes with the members of
the orchestra slowly leaving the stage. The power of Haydn's
musical imagination works its magic on the prince, and Karl is
reunited with his family.

Hello Amigos!
Tricia Brown. Photographs by Fran Ortiz.
Henry Holt, 1986

SET IN AN inner city Hispanic family and told predominantly through the use of photographs, *Hello Amigos!* is a
heartwarming account of a day in the life of a little boy. Today
is Frankie's seventh birthday. But first, Frankie has to go to
school. We accompany him throughout the day—on the
school bus, in the classroom, at recess—and then we follow
him home, where his mother is busy preparing a traditional
Mexican meal in honor of his birthday. Later that evening,
friends and family gather to celebrate and break open the large
piñata that Frankie's mother has hung from the living-room
ceiling. One look at his shining face is enough to tell you that
he has had the happiest day of his life! But the true culmination
of the day comes when his father takes him to the church to
light a candle before the altar and encourages Frankie to count
his blessings. With its themes of close family ties and gratitude
for the gift of life, *Hello Amigos!* is the perfect starter biography for the very young child.

Keep the Lights Burning, Abbie
Peter and Connie Roop
Illustrated by Peter E. Hanson.
Houghton Mifflin, 1989, 40 pages

THIS IS A SIMPLE but true tale about the courage of a young girl who is determined to keep her father's lighthouse lights burning while he is away on the mainland, despite a great storm that threatens to sweep their little house into the sea. Abbie doesn't regard herself as especially heroic. All she can think about is the ships on the dark ocean without the saving light of the beacon; her sick mother, who must be kept warm and fed even while their food and fuel supplies are running perilously low; and her chickens, which are in danger of being swept away by the lashing rain. Illustrated with washes of watercolor that evoke the very essence of the sea, *Keep the Lights Burning, Abbie* brings new and invigorating meaning to the concept of duty.

The Microscope
Maxine Kumin. Illustrated by Arnold Lobel.
HarperCollins, 1984

SIMPLY AND HUMOROUSLY told through verse and handsome half-tone illustrations, *The Microscope* is the story of Antonie van Leeuwenhoek, the seventeenth-century Dutchman credited with the discovery of bacteria. A shopkeeper by trade, Leeuwenhoek was fascinated by the invisible-to-the-naked-eye world of the microscope, a new invention at that time. His friends and neighbors thought him crazy and laughed at his outlandish assertion that there were little "bugs" in drinking water. It wasn't until nearly two centuries later that his discovery was linked to the transmittal of disease and to the beginnings of medicine as we know it today. By sharpening the focus on the past, *The Microscope* reminds us that curiosity and patience have as much, if not more, to do with great scientific discoveries than sheer intelligence, and that we should not mock that which we do not understand.

Louis Pasteur: Enemy of Disease
Carol Greene
Children's Press, 1990, 45 pages

WHEN LOUIS PASTEUR was eight years old, a mad wolf rampaged through his French town, biting people. He saw someone putting a hot iron into a neighbor's bite; he noticed that his neighbor did not die of rabies and he never forgot that moment. Later, when he was a successful scientist, he discovered the existence of microbes, or germs. He not only invented the technique of pasteurization but also introduced the idea of vaccination. Author Carol Greene writes in a simple, lucid style, but she also knows how to highlight the human side to Pasteur's career. The death of several children from disease prompted him to even more intense scientific research and experimentation. For Pasteur, helping others included his own beloved family members.

The Story of William Penn
Aliki
Prentice-Hall, 1964

THE STORY OF the founding of Pennsylvania ought to be told as often as that of the Pilgrims. William Penn was a wealthy Englishman who nonetheless lived a humble and modest life because of his Quaker convictions. The Quakers were a peaceful sect, but England in those days did not practice religious toleration. Penn endured persecution and jail sentences for proclaiming his beliefs. But the king, who owed large sums of money to Penn, decided to pay it back in the grant of a large territory in America. When Penn and his followers emigrated, they called their new city Philadelphia, the City of Brotherly

Love. Penn wanted to live in peace with everyone, and he was able to prove this when he met the Native Americans who lived in Pennsylvania. He signed a treaty with them and bought their land, rather than stealing it from them. His fairness earned him their trust.

Peter the Great
Diane Stanley
Four Winds, 1986, 32 pages

IF HISTORY IS made up of true-life stories of the past, then it follows that it should be as entertaining as it is educational. For what is more entertaining than real-life stories? *Peter the Great* fits this description perfectly. Not only is it an accurate historical account of seventeenth-century Russia, it is also an exciting adventure in exploration. Crowned a czar when he was only a boy, Peter determined then that his life's work lay in bringing his country out of the past and into the present. But before he insisted that his country modify its cultural standards, he set out to teach himself all that seventeenth-century Europe had to offer. Meticulously researched and filled with sumptuous full-color paintings, the story of Peter the Great's life is a vivid overturning of the oft-repeated phrase "Do as I say, not as I do."

Middle Readers

Jim Abbott: All-American Pitcher
Howard Reiser
Children's Press, 1993, 46 pages

"I DO NOT BELIEVE that I should be looked upon as anything special, merely because I was born with one hand," says Jim Abbott. "Everyone has challenges to overcome." Ask any of the major league batters in the American League whether Jim Abbott has overcome his challenges and the answer will be an emphatic yes. Abbott is one of the best young pitchers in the majors. As he pitches, Abbott rests a baseball glove on his right wrist; after he delivers the ball, he slips the glove onto his left hand. He is an outstanding fielder and an asset to his team. Abbott's attitude toward those who make a fuss about him is remarkably refreshing. "People say I am courageous. But I do not pitch to be courageous. I pitch to win." Like most boys, Abbott began playing in Little League, and became a star on his high school and college teams. He went on to pitch the winning game for the United States at the 1988 Olympic Games. He is one of only fifteen men who have gone straight to the major leagues, without spending any time in the minors. Jim Abbott's quiet, self-effacing character stands in contrast to those sports heroes who spend most of their off-duty time promoting products and their own careers.

Clara Barton: Founder of the American Red Cross
Susan Sloate
Fawcett, 1990, 119 pages

SHYNESS IS NOT an illness, but in extreme cases it can cripple you. Children understand this. Children are naturally shy in situations where they lack confidence, such as meeting new people and going to a new school. The life of Clara Barton has much to offer young readers by way of inspiration. But it contains a special message for those who struggle with shyness. Born ten years after her brothers and sisters, Clara grew up in a sheltered environment. When she finished her schooling, Clara had to find an occupation. Options for women in the mid–nineteenth century were limited, so she decided to become a teacher. Facing an audience of any kind, much less forty raucous schoolchildren, can be daunting, but Clara managed to overcome her shyness and gain a reputation as a fine teacher and disciplinarian. Her ability to bring discipline to schools was based on gentleness rather than violence and punishment. But Clara did not have the emotional energy to continually fight political battles with town and school authorities. Once again she challenged herself, going to Washington to work in the male-dominated environment of a government office. With the Civil War, however, Clara found her true vocation: she became a nurse and medical organizer, legendary for her tireless charity. Perhaps her efforts to save the mutilated bodies strewn about the battlefield were the ultimate test of her shy nature. If so, she passed the test with flying colors. After the war, she spearheaded the effort to locate missing soldiers and brought a European organization, the Red Cross, to America, becoming its first president.

Louis Braille:
The Boy Who Invented Books for the Blind
Margaret Davidson
Scholastic, 1971, 80 pages

A CHILDHOOD ACCIDENT left little Louis Braille blind in both eyes. In nineteenth-century France, blind children like Louis had little help and few hopes. But when a kind priest, Father Jacques Palluy, gives Louis lessons, he is amazed at his intelligence and eagerness to learn. With his parents' permission, Father Palluy succeeds in enrolling Louis in the Royal Institute of Blind Youth in Paris. Thrust into a new and frightening environment, Louis is lonely and depressed. In time, however, he finds friendship and encouragement. When his hunger for learning once more asserts itself, Louis is frustrated by the institute's lack of books in raised print. He also finds the symbols in raised print confusing. So he sets out, at twelve years of age, to invent his own system. After three years he perfects the method, but he encounters indifference and hostility when he tries to convince the world that his system is better. Even with the support of the institute's director, Louis is told again and again that he is too young to have created a workable alphabet for the blind. Years pass. Louis grows older, is made a teacher at the institute, and becomes a fine organist, always hoping that his method will find acceptance. But Louis's health is frail. While he lies in bed, dying of tuberculosis, he hears that the first steps are being taken to popularize his system. Though he did not live to witness it, Louis's alphabet became the universal method. His courage and hunger for knowledge enabled him to triumph over disability and disease and open new worlds to future generations.

Rachel Carson: Who Loved the Sea
Jean Lee Latham. Illustrated by Victor Mays.
Garrard, 1973, 80 pages

RACHEL CARSON, who became one of the most compelling writers about the sea, grew up near Pittsburgh, Pennsylvania, and never even saw the ocean until after she graduated from college. A talented English major in college, she shocked everyone when she switched her course of study to science. After struggling to make her way as a marine zoologist in a male-dominated profession, Rachel found a way to combine her writing skill with her love for the teeming life of the sea. Despite having to take on extra jobs to support herself and several other family members, Rachel managed to write *The Sea Around Us,* which became an international best-seller. Late in her life, she learned about the deadly effects of the pesticide DDT. She spent her final years fighting the use of DDT, publishing a book, *Silent Spring,* that helped to end the use of the chemical.

Columbus
Ingri and Edgar Parin D'Aulaire
Dell, 1955, 59 pages

IN RECENT YEARS there has been a great deal of controversy about Christopher Columbus and the European colonization of the Americas. In this beautifully illustrated and well-researched biography, the husband-and-wife team of In-

gri and Edgar Parin D'Aulaire have done justice to a complicated figure. They depict the inspiring side of the story: the boy
who dreamed of becoming a sailor, his persistence in trying to
organize a voyage to the West, his ability to rouse his men to
sail on despite their fears and grievances. But the D'Aulaires
also make plain that Columbus was vain and grasping, and at
the end of his life, bitter and resentful that he did not discover
the way to China. Though not so vicious as some of his men,
Columbus was not a paragon of moral virtue. But his story is
an essential one for Americans: the flawed but heroic figure of
Christopher Columbus is part of our history.

Frederick Douglass: Voice of Freedom
Eric Weiner. Illustrated by Steven Parton.
Dell, 1992, 107 pages

PRIOR TO THE Civil War, there was one thing that slave
owners did not want their slaves to possess: the ability to read.
Reading constituted a pathway out of ignorance and silence: it
brought an inner freedom that would not stand for institutional slavery. Young Frederick Douglass, separated from his
family like so many other slaves, was given as a present to a
Baltimore family. Having been raised on a farm, Douglass
found it difficult to adjust to city life. But the mistress of the
house, Mrs. Auld, took an interest in him and began to teach
him to read. When Mr. Auld found out about this, he forbade
her to continue. But the seed was planted. Over the years, Douglass pursued the prize of reading whenever he could. As a
young man, he became rebellious and even a "slave-breaker"
could not break his will. In 1838 Douglass escaped to New
York and freedom. When asked to address an antislavery meeting, he stepped to the podium nervously, but the power of his
oratory overwhelmed the audience and he was soon in demand
as a speaker. He wrote and published his autobiography, a
book that caused an enormous stir around the country. His
way with words was now helping to bring freedom to others.
After the Civil War, Douglass held a number of major govern-

ment posts, including marshal of the District of Columbia and ambassador to Haiti. A few decades after Douglass's death, he inspired another African-American with a powerful command of language: Martin Luther King, Jr.

Amelia Earhart: Pioneer of the Sky
John Parlin. Illustrated by Wayne Alfano.
Dell, 1962, 69 pages

FROM THE EARLIEST age, Amelia Earhart was irresistibly drawn to flying. At the age of seven she constructed a roller-coaster in her backyard so she could feel the thrill of hurtling off the end! And when her father took Amelia and her sister to a fun fair, she screamed with delight as the Ferris wheel swooped toward the ground. Amelia Earhart has been called a feminist, but this label tends to obscure rather then define her unique personality and her tremendous contribution to aviation. Like all truly great pioneers, whatever she did, she did for the sheer love of it and not for any abstract ideological reason. And if she managed to fulfill that dream by becoming the first woman to fly solo across the Atlantic—well, so much the better. "Women must try to do things as men have tried. When they fail, their failure must be but a challenge to others." These were Amelia Earhart's last words in a letter she left to her husband in case she never returned from her courageous round-the-world attempt. Amelia disappeared over the Pacific Ocean in 1937, but her prophetic words live on today.

Homesick: My Own Story (NH)
Jean Fritz. Illustrated by Margot Tomes.
G. P. Putnam and Sons, 1982, 163 pages

MOST OF US are familiar with Jean Fritz for her spirited re-creations of the lives of historical figures, but in *Homesick: My Own Story* she trains her biographer's eye on her own life. Born and raised in China, the daughter of American missionaries, Jean grew up with a yearning for the country she had never seen. In school, she refuses to sing the British national anthem until her father convinces her that she can sing "America the free" to the same tune. And she faithfully carries on a loving correspondence with the Pennsylvanian grandmother she has never met. How she copes with her infant sister's death and how her family survives the Communist takeover in China to arrive, safe and sound, in America, complete this absorbing chronicle. *Homesick: My Own Story* is filled with a ten-year-old child's recollections of early-twentieth-century China. But more than that, it is filled with a sense of the vitality and independence of a little girl who was to grow up to become one of America's most celebrated authors of children's books.

Martin Luther King, Jr.: Dreams for a Nation
Louise Quayle
Fawcett, 1989, 120 pages

IN HIS LONG and arduous struggle for civil rights, Martin Luther King, Jr., repeatedly put his life and well-being on the line for the cause he believed in. In time he paid the ultimate price for this courageous defense of the truth. Like so many great moral leaders, King had an intense devotion that was essentially religious in nature. The son of a preacher, King, after some hesitation, followed his father and became a minister. Drawing on the African-American religious tradition, King saw the fight against segregation and prejudice as a journey—an exodus—from bondage into freedom. Inspired by the non-violent protest techniques of Gandhi, King led peaceful marches, sit-ins, and boycotts, even though he and his followers were always vulnerable to violence themselves. In his famous 1963 speech at the Lincoln Memorial, King said, "I have a dream my four little children will one day live in a nation where they will not be judged by the color of their skin but by the content of their character." The content of King's character constitutes his greatest legacy.

The Lady of Guadalupe
Tomie de Paola
Holiday House, 1980

IN TOMIE DE PAOLA'S rendering, this book is not merely
a story of Mexico's most famous religious miracle; it is equally
about the humility and simplicity of the Mexican Indians.
When the white men come to Mexico in the sixteenth century,
a young Indian named He-who-speaks-like-an-eagle and his
wife are converted to Christianity by the friars. He changes his
name to Juan Diego. Not long after his wife dies, Juan sets out
for a church service but stops when he hears a strange, un-
earthly music. On the hilltop near him, he sees a white cloud;
as he approaches the cloud the whiteness is refracted into the
colors of the rainbow. Suddenly he beholds a beautiful woman,
standing in a nimbus of radiant light. She tells the trembling
Juan that she is the Mother of God and that he must ask the
bishop to build a church on the hilltop. It is her wish to show
the Mexican Indians how much she loves them. The rest of the
story chronicles Juan's attempts to speak to the bishop, convince him of his vision, and achieve the Lady's wish. Juan is patient but also persistent; the bishop and his court are skeptical.
We see Juan run from the bishop's house to the Lady on the
hilltop and to his sick uncle in the village. Juan's humility and
his capacity to endure patiently are among the virtues of Mexico's Indians. The Lady causes a miraculous image of herself to
appear on Juan's cloak and the bishop is convinced. De Paola's
stylized illustrations perfectly capture the innocence and
beauty of this story.

America's Robert E. Lee
Henry Steele Commager and Lynd Ward
Houghton Mifflin, 1951, 115 pages

THE CIVIL WAR, our greatest national tragedy, ended slavery once and for all. But not even the most biased historian

would argue that the war was a battle between the forces of pure good and pure evil. Both sides demonstrated bravery and compassion, and both produced outstanding leaders. In remembering this traumatic period of our history, we can place Robert E. Lee alongside Abraham Lincoln as a man of equal moral stature. As Commager and Ward emphasize in the title of this book, we should celebrate *America's* Robert E. Lee, for his character is a beacon for all of us. The son of a famous Virginia family, Lee grew up in the shadow of his father, "Light-Horse" Harry Lee, a hero of the Revolutionary War and a governor of Virginia. But Lee's father was a troubled man, and after his early achievements he fell into debt and despair. When his father left for the East Indies to regain his health, young Robert took charge of the family. After a distinguished career at West Point, Robert rose rapidly in the army, fighting in the Mexican War and other minor conflicts. He was so respected as a military leader that on the eve of the Civil War, he was offered the command of the Union armies. Lee not only disliked slavery but had freed all his slaves before the war erupted. But in those days, loyalty to one's home state was far more intense than it is today, and Lee felt honor-bound to fight on behalf of his state. He was the most brilliant general in the Civil War, but his greatness stems not from that only; he was the epitome of the southern gentleman. He could say, with deep honesty, "It is well that war is so terrible, or we should grow too fond of it." Lee's virtues remain an inspiration for all Americans.

Martin Luther
May McNeer and Lynd Ward
Abingdon, 1953, 96 pages

THE SON OF a miner, Martin Luther was destined by his father to become a prosperous lawyer. But something in the young man remained unsatisfied. Though he was an outgoing lad who had often sung in public for his supper, Luther was

also drawn to the religious life. He became a monk and a professor of theology. But there were practices going on within the Catholic Church, such as the selling of indulgences, that disturbed him. He especially wanted every Christian to be able to read the Bible. When he nailed his ninety-five theses to the door of Wittenberg Church, the Protestant Reformation had begun. Luther braved the full institutional and intellectual force of the Catholic Church, but never backed down from his position. With the help of a friendly prince, he was able to remain safe and to form his religious ideas. In his later years, after he had married and helped to establish a new church, he turned to one of his greatest achievements: the translation of the Bible into German. A controversial figure who was not without his weaknesses, Luther remains one of the key figures in the history of Western civilization.

Magellan: First Around the World
Ronald Syme. Illustrated by William Stobbs.
William Morrow, 1953, 71 pages

WHEN FERDINAND MAGELLAN was twelve years old, Christopher Columbus sailed on his fateful voyage to the New World. Though the son of a noble, Magellan wanted to learn how to be a sailor and went aboard an expedition to India as a common deckhand. This experience, ending in his being given command of a ship, enabled him to conceive of his grand ambition: sailing completely around the world. Like Columbus, Magellan had the gifts of persistence and persuasion. With five ships he sailed west to the South American coast. As he sailed south, into increasing cold and dangerous seas, Magellan fought off mutiny attempts and recovered from accidents, finally discovering what is now known as the Strait of Magellan and sailing west to the Philippines. He was killed there while attempting to help a friendly king fight off a rival. His men, however, continued to sail westward, reaching the port of Seville in Spain and telling the world that Magellan had been right.

Our Golda: The Story of Golda Meir
David A. Adler. Illustrated by Donna Ruff.
Viking, 1984, 52 pages

GOLDA MEIR'S LIFE encompasses all of the sufferings and triumphs of the Jewish people in this century. Born in Russia at a time when anti-Jewish persecution there was at its height, Golda and her family knew poverty, discrimination, and fear. Her father left to find work and opportunity in America, and eventually made enough money to send for the rest of his family. In Milwaukee, Golda showed remarkable initiative in starting an organization that held meetings and told people of the plight of the Jews. As a girl, Golda showed her ability as a speaker. Though it pained her, Golda had to leave her family in order to pursue her education and political activities. After her marriage, Golda and her husband moved to Palestine, and she continued her work on behalf of a Jewish state. After the Second World War and the Holocaust, Jews fought for, and achieved, their dream of nationhood when Israel was established. At the age of seventy-one, Golda Meir became prime minister of Israel and governed for five years, including during the 1973 Arab-Israeli War. She worked assiduously for peace, meeting with figures such as Egyptian president Anwar Sadat and Pope Paul VI. Golda Meir, known affectionately in Israel as "Golda Lox," was much loved by her people.

Jesse Owens: Champion Athlete
Rick Rennert
Chelsea, 1992, 80 pages

THERE IS A widespread feeling that sports today are overshadowed by money, fame, and violence. Athletes earn multimillion-dollar salaries; they appear in countless advertisements, television programs, and feature films. Fights on the playing field are more frequent, even affecting the gentlemanly game of baseball; football coaches punch each other on the sidelines on

network television. While it is wrong to make excessive general-
izations, we do believe that it is important to young people to
look to some of the great sports heroes from the past to get a
clearer idea of the nature of sportsmanship. Jesse Owens is just
such a figure. The tenth child of a poor Alabama sharecropper,
Owens pursued excellence in track and field with a single-
minded devotion that caught the world's imagination. The high
point of Owens's career, of course, was the 1936 Olympics,
which were held in the German city of Berlin. Adolf Hitler was
then in power, and he expected his athletes to show the world
the dominance of Germany and the Aryan race. But it was Jesse
Owens who dominated the track and field events, winning four
gold medals, including the 100- and 200-meter dash, and the
long jump. The high point of that competition was the way
Owens and his German competitor Luz Long encouraged each
other during the long jump event. Hitler and his Nazi hench-
men were stunned that a black man had defeated their greatest
athletes. Owens had a very simple philosophy: an athlete must
go "to the limit, past your limit, where victory is always found.
Because it's a victory over yourself."

Mr. Revere and I
Robert Lawson
Little, Brown, 1981 (1953), 152 pages

HOW DOES A writer tell the well-known story of the Midnight Ride of Paul Revere, and the Shot Heard Round the
World, without falling into sentimentality and a host of patriotic clichés? Robert Lawson, a beloved author and illustrator
of children's books, came up with the perfect solution in *Mr.
Revere and I*. The narrator of the story is a horse named
Scheherazade, a proud member of His Majesty's army. Lawson
gives the horse, Sherry, a typically condescending attitude toward the American colonists. But when she arrives in Boston
and undergoes a number of adventures, Sherry is slowly convinced of the validity of the colonists' cause. Saved from the

glue factory by a silversmith named Paul Revere, Sherry becomes an indispensable part of the opening acts of the American Revolution. But Sherry's development is not merely political; she becomes a more humble and generous horse, her pride and haughtiness left behind. Among Lawson's other historical novels told through the eyes of animals are *Ben and Me* (on Benjamin Franklin) and *Captain Kidd's Cat*.

The Story of Junipero Serra, Brave Adventurer
Florence Meiman White
Illustrated by Stephen Marchesi.
Dell, 1987, 86 pages

THE TITLE OF this book is somewhat misleading, since the word "adventurer" suggests a swashbuckling Indiana Jones figure. Nothing could be more different from the humble Franciscan priest named Junipero Serra, whose life was focused on the good of others. In the history of the European settlement of North America, Father Serra's story is one of the most inspiring. A brilliant young theological student, Serra was asked to postpone his desire to become a missionary for nearly twenty years. But in 1749 this Spanish priest finally found his opportunity to go to the New World. After he worked to improve the lot of the Mexican Indians, Serra was chosen to undertake a major task: the establishment of missions along the coast of California. He and his party made the trek from Mexico City, a one-thousand-mile journey over land. In the last fifteen years of his life, he founded nine missions from San Diego to San Francisco. In this work he certainly needed the hardiness and courage of an adventurer. Whenever the tension between Spanish soldiers and the local Indians erupted into violence, Father Serra intervened as a peacemaker. He labored tirelessly to educate the Indians and meet their physical needs. Today many of his missions still stand, a tribute to the peace and unity he strove to bring to the Pacific coast.

A Day of Pleasure
Isaac Bashevis Singer
Farrar, Straus and Giroux, 1986 (1969), 227 pages

ISAAC BASHEVIS SINGER, the Nobel Prize–winning Pol-
ish-born writer, shares his childhood with us in this poignant
memoir of life in the Jewish quarter of Warsaw. Born in 1904,
he was the son of an Orthodox rabbi. Isaac was an insatiably
curious boy, always asking questions and reading books well
beyond his comprehension level. Though his mother and older
brother were somewhat progressive rationalists, Isaac never
lost his respect for his father's religious worldview. His father
would tell stories of goblins, imps, and angels to remind the
children of the reality of the supernatural, and the constant
battle between good and evil. Isaac drank all of these stories in;
they would later be transformed into his own wonderful folktales. Told in short chapters, this memoir is filled with vivid
sketches of the social life of the Polish Jews and of Isaac's own
childhood joys and sorrows. The title is taken from a chapter
about an escapade the young Isaac went on through the city of
Warsaw. This spree, made possible by an amount of money
that was not really his, started out wonderfully but ended in
remorse and contrition. Singer's snapshots of a vanished world
will remain in the memory and in the heart.

Squanto: First Friend to the Pilgrims
Cathy East Dubowski
Illustrated by Steven James Petruccio.
Dell, 1990, 91 pages

THE EUROPEAN MIGRATION to the New World was a
complex historical event and not all of its episodes were happy.
That is why it is worth cherishing moments that do credit to
the Europeans and Native Americans. The story of Squanto
and his relationship to the Pilgrims is one such episode. Born
in the late sixteenth century, Tisquantum (his full name) was a
member of a tribe living on the Massachusetts coast. His first

contact with white men was not happy: he was kidnapped and taken to Spain. Somehow he avoided being sold as a slave and ended up in England. There he worked and learned English. He was able to return to Massachusetts as an interpreter and eventually gained his freedom. Sadly, his tribe had died of a plague, making him the last of his people. When the Pilgrims arrived on the *Mayflower* in 1620, Tisquantum was able to help them survive in the often harsh and unfamiliar land. The Pilgrims, for their part, were true to their intense religious convictions, making peace with the local tribes and even protecting Squanto (as they called him) from a local chief who wanted to kill him. Squanto did not always act wisely or well, but the story of this encounter between two peoples is marked by a commitment to peace and tolerance.

Harriet and the Runaway Book: The Story of Harriet Beecher Stowe
Johanna Johnston
Illustrated by Ronald Himler.
HarperCollins, 1977, 80 pages

HARRIET BEECHER WAS the daughter of one of America's most famous preachers and brilliant in her own right, but in the mid–nineteenth century her options in life were limited. She could either become a wife or a schoolteacher. "If only she'd been a boy," her father said (rather insensitively). This feeling of helplessness was compounded when she considered the problem of slavery. Her father was a leading abolitionist, but she felt there was little she could do. Harriet worked as a schoolteacher and became the wife of Calvin Stowe, but she found another outlet for her talent: writing. While living in Cincinnati, on the border of the slave-holding state of Kentucky, Harriet came face to face with the harsh realities of slavery. One day she had an intense daydream, where she saw a black man being savagely beaten. Though the image frightened her, it was the germ that grew into the novel *Uncle Tom's Cabin*. With its depiction of the inhumanity of slavery, this novel captured the attention of the world. More than any book, speech, or party platform, *Uncle Tom's Cabin* swung public opinion against slavery. President Abraham Lincoln later greeted Harriet Beecher Stowe with the words "So this is the little lady who started this great big war." She had found a way to transcend the limitations placed on her by society and to contribute to a cause that she passionately believed in.

Maria Tallchief
Tobi Tobias. Illustrated by Michael Hampshire.
Crowell, 1970, 32 pages

ONCE UPON A time, we used to encourage children to emulate the lives of heroes and heroines. Nowadays we want them to look up to "superstars." Our contemporary superstars are all fantastically wealthy media icons, but they are not necessarily heroes or heroines. Maria Tallchief was a woman who always kept her fame and success in perspective. Born on a Native American reservation in Oklahoma in 1925, Elizabeth Marie Tallchief came from an important family in the Osage tribe. A lithe, graceful child, she was taught music and ballet and excelled in both. The discovery of oil on the reservation enabled her family to move to California, where she made the difficult decision to concentrate on ballet. Eventually she made it to New York, where she was told she had to change her name to something more elegant. She agreed to become Maria, but she insisted on retaining the name Tallchief; she was proud of her heritage. The great George Balanchine made her a prima ballerina and married her. She performed all over the world in the leading roles, but she was often unhappy: traveling, rehearsing, and performing took all of her life, and left nothing for her private life. When it was clear that Balanchine did not want to have children, the marriage ended. Maria remarried and hung up her toe shoes to become a wife and mother. Her decision was not a rejection of her career, but a desire to fulfill another dimension of herself. Maria Tallchief always kept things in perspective.

Mother Teresa: Sister to the Poor
Patricia Reilly Giff. Illustrated by Ted Lewin.
Puffin, 1987, 58 pages

IN RECENT YEARS, whenever the results of the Most Popular Woman in the World are published, it has not been hard to guess who would top the list. Not a gorgeous movie star, or a female senator, or a businesswoman, or even a queen, but a tiny, wrinkled old woman wrapped in a plain white cotton sari: Mother Teresa of Calcutta. This Catholic nun founded a religious order that now has over one hundred and twenty houses in dozens of countries around the world. Born Agnes Bojaxhiu in Albania in the early years of this century, she grew up in a religious household. As a young woman she heard about the missionaries in India and the terrible poverty and disease in the cities of that nation. She felt called to a life as a nun, but the order she chose, the Loreto Sisters, were not based in Albania, so she had to leave her home and travel to Ireland to be trained. Eventually she made her final vows and got her wish, working in India. But after several years as a teacher, she became restless, wanting to go outside her convent and into the streets and gutters where the poor lay dying. In 1948, she finally received permission to leave her order: she changed into a cheap sari, common to the people of India, and set out to bring love and care to the sick and suffering in Calcutta. She has always insisted that she is doing nothing extraordinary: she is simply living out the teachings and example of Jesus Christ. The very purity of her faith has drawn thousands to her over the years. "Everyone has something to give," she has said; this is a message that both children and adults need to hear.

Jim Thorpe: Olympic Champion
Guernsey Van Riper, Jr. Illustrated by Gray Morrow.
Aladdin, 1986 (1956), 192 pages

THE DAY JIM THORPE was born, the sun shone brightly on the path to his family's cabin. His Native American parents decided that he should be named Wa-tho-huck, or Bright Path. Throughout his illustrious career as an athlete—an Olympian and a football player—Jim Thorpe would run as if a bright path guided his legs. Intermarriage among his ancestors had given him an American name, but Jim grew up on land in Oklahoma given to the Sac and Fox tribes. His father encouraged Jim and his brother Charlie not only to hunt and fish, but also to get an education. Jim was taught to revere the memory of his forebear, the great chief Black Hawk. "When he lost," Jim's father said of Black Hawk, "he lost with honor." Jim would lose very few sporting events in his life, but he lost his brother to illness and had to struggle to complete his education. Later, he had to forfeit his Olympic medals in track and field because he had briefly played professional baseball. In 1950, Thorpe was named the greatest all-around athlete of the half-century. This biography concentrates on Thorpe's youth, and so will be accessible and appealing to young readers.

J. R. R. Tolkien: Master of Fantasy
David Collins. Illustrated by William Heagy.
Lerner, 1992, 102 pages

TWO OF THE greatest writers of fantasy in this century were C. S. Lewis and J. R. R. Tolkien, both dons, or professors, at Oxford University in England. Their lives would not at first glance seem to offer much for a biographer to write about. But these university professors both had difficult childhoods, and their inner lives were rich and exciting. Tolkien's father died when he was very young, and his mother had to take care of Tolkien and his brother. His mother became a Catholic, and her new faith sustained her through hard times. Then, when he was only twelve, Tolkien's mother died, leaving him an orphan. Tolkien excelled in his studies, but he found his greatest delight in sounds and meanings of words, whether ancient Greek or Norse or Welsh. He also loved the epic sagas told in these old languages, and began to dream up his own tales of dragons, goblins, elves, heroic warriors, and enchanting ladies. The result, of course, was *The Hobbit* and *The Lord of the Rings,* the most popular fantasy books of all time. Readers of this biography will find the real-life models for some of these creatures!

George Washington:
The Man Who Would Not Be King
Stephen Krensky
Scholastic, 1991, 116 pages

NO FIGURE IN American history has been so mythologized and exalted as our first president, George Washington. Legends such as the story of his chopping down the cherry tree have made their way into our national consciousness. But aside from patriotic feelings, what is it about Washington that deserves emulation? Author Stephen Krensky has come close in the subtitle to this biography: Washington was "the man who would not be king." As the general who fought and won the American Revolution, Washington had enormous prestige and power. Though the American colonies were glad to be rid of British rule, they so admired Washington that he could have taken power at the war's end. But he refused to do so. He remembered the ancient Roman story of Cincinnatus, the aristocrat who left his farm to save his country, but who returned to his farm after the crisis was over. Washington believed in the republican virtues of honesty and integrity, and in the subordination of personal ambition to the public good. During the war, he had strongly affirmed the civilian control of the military; this is a tradition that became central to American democracy. At a time when corruption at all levels of government is more and more common, George Washington shines even brighter as the model of a public servant.

Benjamin West and His Cat Grimalkin
Marguerite Henry. Illustrated by Wesley Dennis.
Macmillan, 1947, 146 pages

BENJAMIN WEST WAS the first great American painter, even though he spent much of his adult life in England, as court painter to King George III. This biography—a classic by the beloved children's book author Marguerite Henry—concentrates on West's youth in mid-eighteenth-century Pennsylvania. Benjamin's father runs an inn, and Benjamin helps his nine brothers and sisters with the daily chores. His boon companion is a black cat, Grimalkin, rescued from illness. Benjamin discovers a talent for drawing and painting, but the making of images is considered worldly by his stern Quaker father. Benjamin's talent, however, cannot be easily repressed. A dutiful, hardworking boy, he waits with anxiety as the Quaker community discusses his future. They decide in his favor, since the reproduction of the beauties of God's creation cannot be wrong. Benjamin's father, though strict, is a loving man, and he eventually finds practical ways to put his son's talent to work. Always at his side, Grimalkin acts as Benjamin's advocate and helper. Henry's narrative is compulsively readable, full of high comedy and verbal energy.

Older Readers

Invincible Louisa (**N**)
Cornelia Meigs
Little, Brown, 1968 (1933), 195 pages

NO ONE WHO has been introduced to the March family and has come to love the gentle Beth, Amy, Meg, and the irrepressible Jo will fail to be absorbed by this marvelous biography. *Invincible Louisa* is an unforgettable portrait of Louisa Alcott, author of *Little Women* (see page 159) and its sequels, *Little Men* and *Jo's Boys*. In it we learn that the character of Jo is undoubtedly based on Louisa herself. As a girl she was always full of restless energy, determined to help her family through her writing. We also learn that Louisa once considered selling her beautiful hair to help her family in a financial pinch. Like Jo, Louisa was filled with a spirit of independence, but she never allowed her ambition to get in the way of the most important thing in her life—her family. She struggled bravely with poverty and early rejection of her writing, taking jobs as a seamstress and living in a tiny garret in Boston so she could send her meager earnings home. Even when she became a celebrated author at the age of thirty-six, she continued to take care of her aging parents and her widowed sister. Louisa was invincible because her whole life was spent in the service of others. Like Louisa herself, *Little Women* and *Little Men* are shot through with this same spirit of heroic generosity. Perhaps that is why her works have remained some of the best-loved children's books ever written.

Bach
Imogen Holst
Crowell, 1965, 88 pages

AFTER READING ABOUT the life of Johann Sebastian Bach, one wonders how he managed to compose any music at all. Throughout his life, Bach had to fight bureaucrats and petty church leaders in order to have any peace or support. Bach was, by and large, unappreciated in his own time. Yet his music soars above all these trials and tribulations. Born into a family of professional musicians, Bach soon turned out to be a prodigy. Far from developing into a temperamental prima donna, however, Bach turned out to be a devout Lutheran, who wrote at the top of every sheet of his music, "S.D.G." (*Soli Dei Gloria;* Glory to God Alone). He was shattered when his first wife died; his sons all became musicians and composers in their own right, including Carl Philip Emmanuel and Wilhelm Friedeman. Bach was an outstanding teacher, who devised special exercises and compositions that would become the standard training for generations to come. Bach's music, though it is often considered to be highly structured, nonetheless covers an astonishing range of emotions, from the humorous to the sublime. Biographer Holst also provides the reader with brief excerpts from Bach's scores that can be played on the piano or organ.

Carry On, Mr. Bowditch (N)
Jean Lee Latham
Illustrated by John O'Hara Cosgrave II.
Houghton Mifflin, 1983 (1955), 251 pages

THIS NOVELIZED BIOGRAPHY of Nathaniel Bowditch justly won the Newbery Medal. Jean Lee Latham has taken what might seem to be unpromising material—the life of a mathematical genius who invented new methods of nautical navigation—and turned it into a moving, unforgettable narrative. Nathaniel Bowditch's family has come down in the world: America is waging the War of Independence with Britain, and Nathaniel's father, once a ship captain, is struggling to make ends meet as a cooper. Eventually Nat has to give up his dream of a first-class education, and becomes apprenticed to a ship supply company. In those days an apprenticeship involved a contractual commitment of many years. There he proves his mathematical skills and engages in a rigorous study of Latin, Greek, physics, and a host of other subjects. At one point he thinks he might be able to attend Harvard, but it never happens. Finally freed from his years as an apprentice, he gets the chance to actually sail in a ship himself. Nat invents a new method for navigating, the lunar reckoning, and corrects many incorrect figures in the navigation charts of his day. It soon becomes clear that Nat is a natural teacher, and in his voyages he takes many rough, violent sailors and helps them learn to become confident officers. We experience Nat's love for his wife and his sense of desolation at her death. We rejoice when he finally receives recognition from Harvard University, which bestows on him a Master of Arts degree. Nat's patience, hard work, love of learning, and willingness to teach—all of these qualities make him an unlikely but worthy hero.

The Diary of a Young Girl
Anne Frank
Pocket, 1990 (1947), 258 pages

ONE AUGUST DAY in 1944, there came a knock on the door of a cramped room in Amsterdam. The Frank family members looked at one another in terror. It was the moment they had been dreading. For over two years they had successfully eluded the brutal Nazi roundup of all Dutch Jews, but now their luck had finally run out. As they were being taken away, the officer in charge asked Anne Frank's father what was in his briefcase. "Nothing," he replied. "Just papers." The officer opened the case, saw that he had been telling the truth, and tossed it contemptuously to the floor. He little knew that the papers that he had so carelessly discarded contained one of the most moving indictments of Nazi totalitarianism that the world has ever known. For among the papers was a diary that chronicled the last two years of a young girl's life. Part of the miracle of Anne's diary is that, despite the terrible times in which she lived, she was still a typical teenager—she talks about boyfriends, schoolwork, and inevitable disagreements with her family. But she was also extraordinary in one respect—she never gave up hope for a better world, a world that, she knew, could be founded only on personal moral integrity. Just four months before she was captured, her diary reads, "Every day you hear, 'If only it was all over.' My work, my hope, my love, my courage, all these things keep my head above water and keep me from complaining." Three months before her sixteenth birthday, Anne was gassed to death in Belsen. Tragically, her death came just eight weeks before the liberation of Holland. But in her short life Anne had written what was later to be called "the conscience of a generation." If our culture is to avoid the sins of the past, if Anne's message is to go on beyond her generation, it must first take root in the hearts of our young. And that message is essentially one of *hope.*

A Deaf Child Listened: Thomas Gallaudet, Pioneer in American Education
Anne Neimark
William Morrow, 1983, 116 pages

IF A YOUNG minister named Thomas Gallaudet had not met a little girl named Alice Cogswell one autumn day in 1814, it would be hard to imagine what life would be like for deaf people today. A short, sickly man, Gallaudet was a deeply religious man, but he was not cut out for the demands of a church leader. He sensed something was wrong with Alice, and was told that she was deaf and dumb, locked out of a major part of human life. Gallaudet befriended her and began to explore what methods had been developed for teaching the deaf to communicate with others. Despite his frail health, he traveled to England to study these methods, returning to America to found what would eventually be known as the American School for the Deaf. Over the years, Gallaudet would suffer from the internal politics of the American School, but his devotion to helping the deaf made him a beloved figure. Today, Gallaudet College, the only liberal arts institution in the world dedicated to the education of the deaf and the hearing impaired, flourishes in Washington, D. C., a testament to the importance of that meeting in 1814.

The Endless Steppe
Esther Hautzig
Scholastic, 1970, 240 pages

THIS IS ONE of those rare stories of courage and perseverance in the face of almost overwhelming odds more extraordinary still because the heroine is only ten and this is a true story based on the author's own childhood experiences. In 1942, when Russia invades Poland, Esther Rudomin and her family are forced to leave their beautiful and cultured home in Vilnius. They are transported like cattle to Siberia for the "crime" of being Jewish. Here, the terrible struggle for survival brings the family even closer together and forms the basis for deep and lasting friendships. Esther's story, told from the perspective of a young girl, proves that despite man's terrible inhumanity to man, it is the power of faith and the courage of the human spirit that will ultimately prevail.

Hitler
Albert Marrin
Puffin, 1993, 249 pages

ADOLF HITLER AND Joseph Stalin had many things in common; they were both born into poverty, they both had abusive fathers, and, subsequently, they learned to hate at a tragically early age and became two of the most murderous and evil men in the history of the world. Hitler is known today as the most violent racist who ever lived, a man who ordered the extermination of over six million Jews, all in the name of ethnic cleansing. Albert Marrin, with his usual sensitivity to his young audience and masterful grasp of human personality, paints an unforgettable portrait of a man motivated by hatred and the lust for vengeance. Hitler became a Jew hater at an early age. Like all corrupt and, ultimately, weak men, he blamed others for the pathetic failures of his own life and that of his country. It took nothing more than seeing a devout Hasidic Jew standing at a railway station in 1909 for Hitler to decide, there and then, that it was the Jewish race that was to blame for all that had gone wrong in his life. This conviction was to lead him to absolute power, to the creation of the dreaded Gestapo, and to the annihilation of millions of innocent human lives. If there is any moral that we can take away with us on reading such a biography it is this: we must never again allow such atrocities as the death camps to exist, we must never again persecute an innocent people, and, above all, we must never again allow murderous hatred to reign in our hearts. A supremely moral book, *Hitler,* as the *Book Report* recommended, "should be required reading" for all older children.

The Story of My Life
Helen Keller
Scholastic, 1967 (1902), 159 pages

PUBLISHED AT THE turn of the century, this is Helen Keller's autobiography, written when she was only a sophomore in college. Because it was penned in an age that was more literate than ours, this book is not for the casual reader. Its language and pace require more attention than many children are prepared to give to books. But for a motivated reader, there is nothing more poignant than the story, told from the inside, of Helen's emergence from the silence and darkness of the deaf, dumb, and blind. Here is the dramatic story of the wild, animal-like child who is taken in hand by a brilliant teacher, Anne Sullivan. After much frustration comes the magical moment when Miss Sullivan takes Helen to the water pump. While the water plays over Helen's hand, Miss Sullivan spells the letters "w-a-t-e-r" into Helen's other hand. Then comes the moment of recognition in Helen's mind: the word corresponds to, and names, the thing. From this moment, Helen follows the light of learning out of her prison and into the world of literature and friendship. Like all those who have to overcome adversity, Helen Keller helps us to recognize the value of things we take for granted. We follow her education, right up to her first year at Radcliffe College. Helen's determination to delve into the meaning of what it means to be human—through literature, art, and relationships with others—cannot fail to inspire those who read her story.

Lincoln: A Photobiography (N)
Russell Freedman
Clarion, 1987, 150 pages

RUSSELL FREEDMAN deservedly won the Newbery Medal for this lucid, moving biography of Abraham Lincoln. Though Lincoln has achieved nearly mythic status in our history,

Freedman never loses sight of Lincoln's very human struggles—with his early poverty and lack of education, in his
courtship and marriage, and in the tumultuous political events
through which he lived and which he profoundly influenced.
Lincoln's early life is a tale of courage, perseverance, and patience—the story of the self-reliant American, determined to
better himself through hard work and education. Freedman
makes it clear that Lincoln's ideas about slavery developed
over time, that he entered the Civil War more concerned about
the Union than the issue of slavery itself. But in the crucible of
the war, Lincoln's character was refined. His eloquence is un-
matched in our history. He never wavered in his belief that
public actions had to be based on the private virtues of citizens.
At the war's end, in his Second Inaugural Address, he said,
"With malice toward none; with charity for all; with firmness
in the right, as God gives us to see the right, let us strive on to
finish the work we are in; to bind up the nation's wounds; to
care for him who shall have borne the battle, and for his
widow, and his orphan—to do all which may achieve and cherish a just, and a lasting peace, among ourselves, and with all
nations." The photographs in this book—including those that
trace the toll the war had taken on Lincoln's craggy face—are
well selected and help to tell the story. There is an index, a bib-
liography, a sampling of Lincoln's writing, and a list of historic
sites.

The Great Little Madison
Jean Fritz
G. P. Putnam and Sons, 1989, 160 pages

JEAN FRITZ, ONE of our finest authors of children's
books, knows how to write biography; she balances the personal life of her subject with his or her public actions. James
Madison is often overshadowed by other Founding Fathers,
such as George Washington and Thomas Jefferson, but his role
in the creation of the Constitution and in the establishment of

our democratic institutions was immense. In her title Fritz has pointed to the paradox of Madison's life: he was a small man, with a weak voice, and yet he looms large in our national history. As one delegate to the Continental Congress noted, Madison was "no bigger than half a piece of soap." Madison did not set out to become a politician. After receiving a degree from Princeton, he fell into depression and did not know what to do with himself. But he was a brilliant intellectual, reading deeply and widely in political thought and philosophy. This knowledge enabled him to address political issues with a wisdom and ingenuity that startled his peers, and helped him to make himself heard. At the heart of Madison's vision was his moral realism, his perception of human failings and the need for government to protect against greed and fanaticism. He is known, rightly, as the "Father of the Constitution."

Nicholas and Alexandra
Robert Massie
Atheneum, 1985 (1967), 584 pages

ROBERT MASSIE BECAME fascinated with the court of Russia at the turn of the century for a very personal reason—his own son was a hemophiliac like Csarevich Alexis, the little son of Czar Nicholas and Czarina Alexandra—and everywhere the personal touch predominates. We are given much more than bare historical facts; we are allowed a privileged look into the most intimate lives of the members of that ill-fated family. Deeply in love, Nicholas and his bride presided over an opulent court. The only blight on their happiness was their son's serious illness, a debilitating disease for which there was no known cure. Only the hypnotic blue eyes of Rasputin, that strange Siberian mystagogue, could bring Alexis relief from pain. He quickly became an indispensable member of the imperial family and, later, an influential adviser to the czarina. It was he who counseled Alexandra to convince her husband to resist crucial reforms in the government; this act, more than any other, made the Russian Revolution inevitable and signed the royal family's death warrant. Filled with haunting photographs, *Nicholas and Alexandra* makes the individuals of that great but doomed family live again. A masterpiece of the biographer's art, *Nicholas and Alexandra* gives the reader a chance to look at the other side of the story of the famous October uprising.

Saint Philip of the Joyous Heart
Francis X. Connolly
Ignatius, 1993 (1957), 168 pages

WE USE THE PHRASE "plaster saints" when we describe some great man or woman who is taken for granted, who is nothing more than a symbol. Plaster is hard and cold; there is nothing of the warmth of humanity in it. When it comes to those in the history of the Catholic Church who have been called saints, the danger is that these figures often seem to be made of plaster: the heroism of these men and women is somehow seen as being totally beyond the average person's experience. But those who know the saints are vividly aware of their humanity; their struggles are our struggles. Children are reassured and heartened when they discover this truth. This book is part of an outstanding series of saints' lives that read like novels. Philip Neri, though he was never a dissolute young man like Francis of Assisi, nonetheless had his own troubles. Like so many young people, he did not know what to do with his life. It took him years to realize that his vocation was to the priesthood; he felt utterly unworthy of the office. But when he finally was ordained, he became a beloved priest, whose happy spirit drew the inhabitants of Rome to his church. Once, in the confessional, he gave this penance: "You may weep on my heart if you choose. God understands you are sorry. . . . But after you weep you must remember to laugh, too. Laugh because God has forgiven you. . . . I give you a penance. You must stand on the Corso and laugh for one whole minute." Other saints in this series—the Vision Books published by Ignatius Press—include Isaac Jogues, Kateri Tekakwitha, and Edmund Campion.

Stalin: Russia's Man of Steel
Albert Marrin
Puffin, 1993, 244 pages

ARGUABLY ONE OF the most monstrous personalities in history, Joseph Stalin ruled the Soviet empire for over a quarter of a century. How could such a man have come into being? What shaped him and why was he able to successfully tyrannize one of the largest nations on earth for so long? These are the questions that this comprehensive and lucid biography seeks to answer. Born to Georgian peasants in 1879, Joseph Dzhugashvili was an abused child from an early age and grew into a hate-filled and violent youth, changing his name to Stalin—"steel." He spent the rest of his life living up to this inhuman new name. When he joined the Communist Party in the early 1900s he quickly saw that Communism was merely czarist imperialism in disguise; for all its talk of democracy its actual goal was nothing short of absolute dictatorship, and that suited Stalin just fine. He rose rapidly in the ranks to become one of Lenin's right-hand men and played a crucial role in the famous October uprising that toppled the czar in 1917. (See *Nicholas and Alexandra,* also in this section, for the other side of the story.) As a reward, Lenin made him part of his inner governing circle; this was an act that he was to bitterly regret later. Stalin now had his foot on the first rung of absolute power and he mounted the ladder steadily, ruthlessly eliminating anyone who got in his way. He used to say that "a single death is a tragedy; a million deaths is a statistic," and it is estimated that Stalin was personally responsible for the deaths of over thirty million people. Although the biography is a somber and sometimes horrifying story, it is a tribute to the author's skill that he manages always to keep his younger audience in mind without sacrificing the truth. Marrin knows that it is only by a thorough understanding of Stalin's evil personality and the ideology that was to become such a murderous tool in his hands that we can avoid repeating the horrors of the past. He knows, like all great biographers, that history not only teaches us about the past but teaches us what to do, and what not to do, in the future. And the future belongs to the young. This biography is for mature readers.

APPENDIX ONE

Book List at a Glance

Picture Books

Younger Readers

The Black Falcon
Boccaccio. Retold by William Wise. Illustrated by Gillian Barlow.

The Boy Who Held Back the Sea
Lenny Hort. Illustrated by Thomas Locker.

Brave Irene
William Steig

Clancy's Coat
Eve Bunting. Illustrated by Lorinda Bryan Cauley.

The Clown of God
Tomie de Paola

Dogger
Shirley Hughes

Elfwyn's Saga
David Wisniewski

The Emperor and the Kite
Jane Yolen. Illustrated by Ed Young.

Forest of Dreams
Rosemary Wells. Illustrated by Susan Jeffers.

The Gold Coin
Alma Flor Ada

The Griffin and the Minor Canon
Frank Stockton. Illustrated by Maurice Sendak.

The Happy Funeral
Eve Bunting. Illustrated by Vo-Dinh Mai.

Harald and the Giant Knight and *Harald and the Great Stag*
Donald Carrick

The High Rise Glorious Skittle Skat Roarious Sky Pie Angel Food Cake
Nancy Willard. Illustrated by Richard Jesse Watson.

Ida and the Wool Smugglers
Sue Ann Alderson. Illustrated by Ann Blades.

In My Mother's House (**CH**)
Ann Nolan Clark. Illustrated by Velino Herrara.

Just Like Max
Karen Ackerman. Illustrated by George Schmidt.

King Nimrod's Tower
Leon Garfield. Illustrated by Michael Bragg.

The King's Fountain
Lloyd Alexander. Illustrated by Ezra Jack Keats.

The Little Brute Family
Russell Hoban. Illustrated by Lillian Hoban.

The Little House (**C**)
Virginia Lee Burton

The Man Who Kept His Heart in a Bucket
Sonia Levitin. Illustrated by Jerry Pinkney.

Marcella's Guardian Angel
Evaline Ness

Ophelia's Shadow Theatre
Michael Ende. Illustrated by Friedrich Hechelmann.

Owl Moon (**C**)
Jane Yolen. Illustrated by John Schoenherr.

Miss Rumphius
Barbara Cooney

The Runaway Bunny
Margaret Wise Brown. Illustrated by Clement Hurd.

The Story About Ping
Marjorie Flack and Kurt Wiese

The Story of Ferdinand
Munro Leaf

Through Grandpa's Eyes
Patricia MacLachlan. Illustrated by Deborah Kogan Ray.

Thy Friend, Obadiah
Brinton Turkle

Tico and the Golden Wings
Leo Lionni

Tim and Ginger
Edward Ardizzone

The Tunnel
Anthony Browne

Wagon Wheels
Barbara Brenner. Illustrated by Bill Bolognese.

Waiting for Hannah
Marisabina Russo

The Warrior and the Wiseman
David Wisniewski

When I Was Young in the Mountains (**CH**)
Cynthia Rylant. Illustrated by Diane Goode.

Where the Wild Things Are (**C**)
Maurice Sendak

Wilfred Gordon McDonald Partridge
Mem Fox. Illustrated by Julie Vivas.

Yonder
Tony Johnston. Illustrated by Lloyd Bloom.

The Young Artist
Thomas Locker

Fables and Fairy Tales

Younger Readers

Beauty: A Retelling of Beauty & the Beast
Robin McKinley

The Book of Virtues: A Treasury of Great Moral Stories
Edited, with commentary, by William Bennett

Dawn
Molly Bang

Dear Mili
Wilhelm Grimm. Illustrated by Maurice Sendak.

The Emperor's New Clothes
Hans Christian Andersen. Retold by Virginia Lee Burton.

Fables
Aesop. Illustrated by Arthur Rackham.

The Hare and the Tortoise
Caroline Castle. Illustrated by Peter Weevers.

It Could Always Be Worse (**CH**)
Margot Zemach

The King of the Golden River
John Ruskin. Illustrated by Richard Doyle.

The Lion and the Puppy
Leo Tolstoy. Illustrated by Claus Sievert.

The Little Match Girl
Hans Christian Andersen. Illustrated by Rachel Isadora.

The North Wind and the Sun
Jean de La Fontaine. Illustrated by Brian Wildsmith.

The Pied Piper of Hamelin
Retold by Sara and Stephen Corrin. Illustrated by Errol Le Cain.

The Selfish Giant
Oscar Wilde. Illustrated by Lisbeth Zwerger.

The Sleeping Beauty
Mercer Mayer

The Ugly Duckling
Hans Christian Andersen. Retold by Marianna Mayer. Illustrated
by Thomas Locker.

Middle Readers

The Cat Who Went to Heaven (**N**)
Elizabeth Coatsworth. Illustrated by Lynd Ward.

The Cuckoo Clock
Mary Stolz. Illustrated by Pamela Johnson.

Gudgekin the Thistle Girl and Other Tales
John Gardner. Illustrated by Michael Sporn.

The Light Princess
George MacDonald. Illustrated by Maurice Sendak.

The Little Prince
Antoine de Saint-Exupéry

Pinocchio
Carlo Collodi

The Shadowmaker
Ron Hansen. Illustrated by Margot Tomes.

Myths, Legends, and Folktales

Younger Readers

Always Room for One More (**C**)
Sorche Nic Leodhas. Illustrated by Nonny Hogrogian.

Anansi Finds a Fool
Verna Aardema. Illustrated by Bryna Waldman.

Dream Peddlar
Gail E. Haley

John Henry: An American Legend
Ezra Jack Keats

Johnny Appleseed
Reeve Lindbergh. Illustrated by Kathy Jakobsen.

Jump On Over!
Joel Chandler Harris. Illustrated by Barry Moser.

Ma'ii and Cousin Horned Toad
Shonto Begay

The Man Who Loved Books
Jean Fritz. Illustrated by Trina Schart Hyman.

Mufaro's Beautiful Daughter: An African Tale
John Steptoe

The Painter and the Wild Swans
Claude Clément. Illustrated by Frédérick Clément.

St. George and the Dragon (**C**)
Margaret Hodges. Illustrated by Trina Schart Hyman.

St. Jerome and the Lion
Margaret Hodges. Illustrated by Barry Moser.

The Stonecuter
Pam Newton

The Tale of the Mandarin Ducks
Katherine Paterson. Illustrated by Leo and Diane Dillon.

The Unicorn and the Lake
Marianna Mayer. Illustrated by Michael Hague.

Middle Readers

The Adventures of Robin Hood
Roger Lancelyn Green. Illustrated by Arthur Hall.

Canterbury Tales
Geoffrey Chaucer. Retold by Barbara Cohen. Illustrated by Trina Schart Hyman.

The Children's Homer
Padraic Colum. Illustrated by Willy Pogany.

Crow and Weasel
Barry Lopez. Illustrated by Tom Pohrt.

Cupid and Psyche: A Love Story
Edna Barth. Illustrated by Ati Forberg.

D'Aulaires' Book of Greek Myths
Ingri and Edgar Parin D'Aulaire

Dick Whittington and His Cat
Eva Moore. Illustrated by Kurt Werth.

Dragon Slayer: The Story of Beowulf
Rosemary Sutcliff. Illustrated by Charles Keeping.

Heather and Broom: Tales of the Scottish Highlands
Sorche Nic Leodhas

Island of the Mighty: Stories of Old Britain
Haydn Middleton. Illustrated by Anthea Toorchen.

Merlin Dreams
Peter Dickinson. Illustrated by Alan Lee.

The People Could Fly: American Black Folktales
Virginia Hamilton. Illustrated by Leo and Diane Dillon.

Stories for Children
Isaac Bashevis Singer

Tales from Silver Lands (**N**)
Charles Finger. Illustrated by Paul Honoré.

The Truthful Harp
Lloyd Alexander. Illustrated by Evaline Ness.

Sacred Texts

Younger Readers

The Children's Bible

Days of Awe: Stories for Rosh Hashanah and Yom Kippur
Eric A. Kimmel. Illustrated by Erika Weihs.

Ladder of Angels: Stories from the Bible
Madeleine L'Engle. Illustrated by Children of the World.

The Song of the Three Holy Children
Pauline Baynes

Middle Readers

The Book of Adam to Moses
Lore Segal. Illustrated by Leonard Baskin.

In the Beginning: Creation Stories
Virginia Hamilton. Illustrated by Barry Moser.

The Message: The New Testament in Contemporary English
Eugene H. Peterson

Books for Holidays and Holy Days

Younger Readers

Amahl and the Night Visitors
Gian Carlo Menotti. Illustrated by Michèle Lemieux.

A Gift from Saint Francis: The First Crèche.
Joanna Cole. Illustrated by Michèle Lemieux.

Just Enough Is Plenty: A Hannukah Tale
Barbara Diamond Goldin. Illustrated by Seymour Chwast.

The Legend of the Christmas Rose
Selma Lagerlöf. Retold by Ellin Greene. Illustrated by Charles Mikolaycak.

The Other Wise Man
Henry van Dyke. Retold by Pamela Kennedy. Illustrated by Robert Barrett.

Petook: An Easter Story
Caryll Houselander. Illustrated by Tomie de Paola.

The Plymouth Adventure
Leonard Weisgard

The Power of Light: Eight Stories for Hanukkah
Isaac Bashevis Singer. Illustrated by Irene Lieblich.

The Story of the Three Wise Kings
Tomie de Paola

What a Morning! The Christmas Story in Black Spirituals
Edited by John Langstaff. Illustrated by Ashley Bryan.

Yussell's Prayer: A Yom Kippur Story
Barbara Cohen. Illustrated by Michael J. Deraney.

Middle Readers

Angels and Other Strangers
Katherine Paterson

The Bells of Christmas
Virginia Hamilton. Illustrated by Lambert Davis.

The Best Christmas Pageant Ever
Barbara Robinson. Illustrated by Judith Gwyn Brown.

A Christmas Carol
Charles Dickens. Illustrated by Trina Schart Hyman.

The Gift of the Magi
O. Henry. Illustrated by Lisbeth Zwerger.

A Gift for Mama
Esther Hautzig. Illustrated by Donna Diamond.

Historical Fiction

Middle Readers

Adam of the Road (**N**)
Elizabeth Gray. Illustrated by Robert Lawson.

All-of-a-Kind Family
Sydney Taylor. Illustrated by Helen John.

Black Beauty
Anna Sewell. Illustrated by John Speirs.

Blue Willow
Doris Gates. Illustrated by Paul Lantz.

The Borning Room
Paul Fleischman

Caddie Woodlawn (**N**)
Carol Ryrie Brink. Illustrated by Trina Schart Hyman.

The Door in the Wall (**N**)
Marguerite de Angeli

Dragonwings (**NH**)
Laurence Yep

A Gathering of Days (**N**)
Joan W. Blos

Hans Brinker, or The Silver Skates
Mary Mapes Dodge

The House of Sixty Fathers (**NH**)
Meindert Dejong. Illustrated by Maurice Sendak.

I, Juan de Pareja (**N**)
Elizabeth Borton de Treviño

Island of the Blue Dolphins (**N**)
Scott O'Dell. Illustrated by Ted Lewin.

Johnny Tremain (**N**)
Esther Forbes

King of the Wind (**N**)
Marguerite Henry. Illustrated by Wesley Dennis.

The Little House in the Big Woods
Laura Ingalls Wilder. Illustrated by Garth Williams.

Little Women
Louisa Alcott

Number the Stars (**N**)
Lois Lowry

Perilous Pilgrimage
Henry Treece

Prairie Songs
Pam Conrad. Illustrated by Darryl S. Zudeck.

The Red Badge of Courage
Stephen Crane

The Red Pony
John Steinbeck. Illustrated by Wesley Dennis.

Sarah, Plain and Tall (**N**)
Patricia MacLachlan

The Secret Garden
Frances Hodgson Burnett. Illustrated by Shirley Hughes.

Shades of Gray
Carolyn Reeder

The Sign of the Beaver (**NH**)
Elizabeth Speare

The Singing Tree (**NH**)
Kate Seredy

The Slave Dancer (**N**)
Paula Fox

Smith
Leon Garfield

Sounder (**N**)
William H. Armstrong

Treasure Island
Robert Louis Stevenson. Illustrated by N. C. Wyeth.

The True Confessions of Charlotte Doyle (**NH**)
Avi

The Trumpeter of Krakow (**N**)
Eric Kelly

Twenty and Ten
Claire Huchet Bishop. Illustrated by William Pène Du Bois.

Under the Hawthorn Tree
Marita Conlon-McKenna

The Writing on the Hearth
Cynthia Harnett. Illustrated by Gareth Floyd.

Older Readers

The Adventures of Huckleberry Finn
Mark Twain

Billy Budd, Sailor
Herman Melville

The Call of the Wild
Jack London. Illustrated by Martin Gascoigne.

David Copperfield
Charles Dickens

Dr. Jekyll and Mr. Hyde and *The Body Snatchers*
Robert Louis Stevenson. Illustrated by Gerard Gibson.

Emily of New Moon
L. M. Montgomery

Flambards
K. M. Peyton. Illustrated by Victor G. Ambrus.

A Girl of the Limberlost
Gene Stratton Porter

The Grapes of Wrath
John Steinbeck

Great Expectations
Charles Dickens

The Great Gatsby
F. Scott Fitzgerald

Jane Eyre
Charlotte Brontë

Kim
Rudyard Kipling

The Last of the Mohicans
James Fenimore Cooper

A Man for All Seasons
Robert Bolt

The Master of Hestviken
Sigrid Undset

Moby Dick
Herman Melville

My Ántonia
Willa Cather

One Corpse Too Many
Ellis Peters

A Parcel of Patterns
Jill Paton Walsh

The Plague
Albert Camus

The Power and the Glory
Graham Greene

Pride and Prejudice
Jane Austen

The Prisoner of Zenda
Anthony Hope

Robinson Crusoe
Daniel Defoe. Illustrated by N. C. Wyeth.

Roll of Thunder, Hear My Cry (N)
Mildred D. Taylor

Saturnalia
Paul Fleischman

The Scarlet Letter
Nathaniel Hawthorne

The Scarlet Pimpernel
Baroness Emmuska Orczy

Shakespeare's Stories: Comedies
William Shakespeare. Retold by Beverly Birch.
Illustrated by Carol Tarrant.

Silas Marner
George Eliot

Three Famous Short Novels
William Faulkner

Typhoon and Other Tales
Joseph Conrad

The Witch of Blackbird Pond (**N**)
Elizabeth Speare

Contemporary Fiction

Middle Readers

Cracker Jackson
Betsy Byars

Dear Mr. Henshaw (**N**)
Beverly Cleary. Illustrated by Paul O. Zelinsky.

The Diddakoi
Rumer Godden

A Dog on Barkham Street
Mary Stolz. Illustrated by Leonard Shortall.

Maniac Magee (**N**)
Jerry Spinelli

On My Honor (**NH**)
Marion Dane Bauer

Other Bells for Us to Ring
Robert Cormier. Illustrated by Deborah Kogan Ray.

The Saturdays
Elizabeth Enright

The Summer of the Swans (**N**)
Betsy Byars

Thank You, Jackie Robinson
Barbara Cohen. Illustrated by Richard Cuffari.

Older Readers

Bridge to Terabithia (**N**)
Katherine Paterson. Illustrated by Donna Diamond.

The Chocolate War
Robert Cormier

The Chosen
Chaim Potok

Dicey's Song (**N**)
Cynthia Voigt

Hatchet (**NH**)
Gary Paulsen

Jacob Have I Loved (**N**)
Katherine Paterson

Lord of the Flies
William Golding

The Mozart Season
Virginia Euwer Wolff

The Old Man and the Sea
Ernest Hemingway

One Day in the Life of Ivan Denisovitch
Aleksandr Solzhenitsyn

Onion John (**N**)
Joseph Krumgold. Illustrated by Symeon Shimin.

The Planet of Junior Brown
Virginia Hamilton

Scorpions (**NH**)
Walter Dean Myers

A Solitary Blue (**NH**)
Cynthia Voigt

Fantasy and Science Fiction

Middle Readers

At the Back of the North Wind
George MacDonald. Illustrated by Lauren A. Mills.

The Borrowers
Mary Norton

Charlotte's Web
E. B. White. Illustrated by Garth Williams.

The Chronicles of Narnia
C. S. Lewis. Illustrated by Pauline Baynes.

The Curse of the Blue Figurine
John Bellairs

Elisabeth and the Water Troll
Walter Wangerin, Jr. Illustrated by Deborah Healy.

Five Children and It
E. Nesbit

The Gammage Cup (**NH**)
Carol Kendall. Illustrated by Erik Blegvad.

The Golden Key
George MacDonald. Illustrated by Maurice Sendak.

Gulliver's Travels
Jonathan Swift. Illustrated by David Small.

The Hobbit
J. R. R. Tolkien

Hounds of the Morrigan
Pat O'Shea

The Indian in the Cupboard
Lynne Reid Banks

Mrs. Frisby and the Rats of NIMH (**N**)
Robert O'Brien

Phantom Tollbooth
Norton Juster. Illustrated by Jules Feiffer.

The Princess and the Goblin
George MacDonald. Illustrated by Jesse Wilcox Smith.

The Prydain Chronicles (**N**)
Lloyd Alexander

Redwall
Brian Jacques. Illustrated by Gary Chalk.

The Reluctant Dragon
Kenneth Grahame. Illustrated by Ernest H. Shepard.

The Shining Company
Rosemary Sutcliff

Tom's Midnight Garden
Philippa Pearce. Illustrated by Susan Einzig.

Tuck Everlasting
Natalie Babbitt

Westmark
Lloyd Alexander

The Wind in the Willows
Kenneth Grahame. Illustrated by Ernest H. Shepard.

A Wrinkle in Time (**N**)
Madeleine L'Engle

Older Readers

Animal Farm
George Orwell

Antar and the Eagles
William Mayne

The Arthurian Trilogy
Rosemary Sutcliff

The Book of the Dun Cow
Walter Wangerin, Jr.

The Dark Is Rising sequence (**N**)
Susan Cooper. Illustrated by Alan Cober.

The Dream Time
Henry Treece. Illustrated by Charles Keeping.

Frankenstein
Mary Shelley. Illustrated by Charles Keeping.

The Hero and the Crown (**N**)
Robin McKinley

The Lord of the Rings
J. R. R. Tolkien

The Pilgrim's Progress
John Bunyan. Retold by Mary Godolphin. Illustrated by Robert
Lawson.

Something Wicked This Way Comes
Ray Bradbury

The Space Trilogy
C. S. Lewis

Watership Down
Richard Adams

The Wizard of Earthsea tetralogy
Ursula K. Le Guin

Biography

Younger Readers

*Note: In this section, books are listed in alphabetical order
according to subject of biography.*

Barry, the Bravest Saint Bernard
Lynn Hall. Illustrated by Antonio Castro.

Thomas Alva Edison: Great Inventor
David A. Adler. Illustrated by Lyle Miller.

St. Francis: The Poor Man of Assisi
Tomie de Paola

The Boy Who Loved Music
David Lasker. Illustrated by Joe Lasker.

Hello Amigos!
Tricia Brown. Photographs by Fran Ortiz.

Keep the Lights Burning, Abbie
Peter and Connie Roop. Illustrated by Peter E. Hanson.

The Microscope
Maxine Kumin. Illustrated by Arnold Lobel.

Louis Pasteur: Enemy of Disease
Carol Greene

The Story of William Penn
Aliki

Peter the Great
Diane Stanley

Middle Readers

Jim Abbott: All-American Pitcher
Howard Reiser

Clara Barton: Founder of the American Red Cross
Susan Sloate

Louis Braille: The Boy Who Invented Books for the Blind
Margaret Davidson

Rachel Carson: Who Loved the Sea
Jean Lee Latham. Illustrated by Victor Mays.

Columbus
Ingri and Edgar Parin D'Aulaire

Frederick Douglass: Voice of Freedom
Eric Weiner. Illustrated by Steven Parton.

Amelia Earhart: Pioneer of the Sky
John Parlin. Illustrated by Wayne Alfano.

Homesick: My Own Story (**NH**)
Jean Fritz. Illustrated by Margot Tomes.

Martin Luther King, Jr.: Dreams for a Nation
Louise Quayle

The Lady of Guadalupe
Tomie de Paola

America's Robert E. Lee
Henry Steele Commager and Lynd Ward

Martin Luther
May McNeer and Lynd Ward

Magellan: First Around the World
Ronald Syme. Illustrated by William Stobbs.

Our Golda: The Story of Golda Meir
David A. Adler. Illustrated by Donna Ruff.

Jesse Owens: Champion Athlete
Rick Rennert

Mr. Revere and I
Robert Lawson

The Story of Junipero Serra, Brave Adventurer
Florence Meiman White. Illustrated by Stephen Marchesi.

A Day of Pleasure
Isaac Bashevis Singer

Squanto: First Friend to the Pilgrims
Cathy East Dubowski. Illustrated by Steven James Petruccio.

Harriet and the Runaway Book: The Story of Harriet Beecher Stowe
Johanna Johnston. Illustrated by Ronald Himler.

Maria Tallchief
Tobi Tobias. Illustrated by Michael Hampshire.

Mother Teresa: Sister to the Poor
Patricia Reilly Giff. Illustrated by Ted Lewin.

Jim Thorpe: Olympic Champion
Guernsey Van Riper, Jr. Illustrated by Gray Morrow.

J. R. R. Tolkien: Master of Fantasy
David Collins. Illustrated by William Heagy.

George Washington: The Man Who Would Not Be King
Stephen Krensky

Benjamin West and His Cat Grimalkin
Marguerite Henry. Illustrated by Wesley Dennis.

Older Readers

Invincible Louisa (**N**)
Cornelia Meigs

Bach
Imogen Holst

Carry On, Mr. Bowditch (**N**)
Jean Lee Latham. Illustrated by John O'Hara Cosgrave II.

The Diary of a Young Girl
Anne Frank

A Deaf Child Listened: Thomas Gallaudet,
Pioneer in American Education
Anne Neimark

The Endless Steppe
Esther Hautzig

Hitler
Albert Marrin

The Story of My Life
Helen Keller

Lincoln: A Photobiography (**N**)
Russell Freedman

The Great Little Madison
Jean Fritz

Nicholas and Alexandra
Robert Massie

Saint Philip of the Joyous Heart
Francis X. Connolly

Stalin: Russia's Man of Steel
Albert Marrin

APPENDIX TWO

Twenty Great
Children's Videos

If you can't bring yourself to throw away the television set, you can use it to introduce your children to great stories. Here is a short list of outstanding films for the family that are available in VHS. Keep in mind that some titles (e.g., Chariots of Fire, High Noon, A Night to Remember, The Scarlet Pimpernel) may be above the interest level of younger viewers. And almost all of the films listed contain some very intense scenes. Watch these movies with your children. We guarantee you'll enjoy them too. And don't forget to remind them that, as good as the films are, the books on which they're based are even better.

All Mine to Give
(1956) 102m C

A SCOTTISH FAMILY of eight braves the hardships of the Wisconsin frontier. Tough winters, a diphtheria epidemic, and hostile neighbors bring this tight-knit family even closer together. The death of the mother and father leaves the oldest son the task of keeping the family together. Fortunately, not all the neighbors are hostile. Have some handkerchiefs on hand. With Glynis Johns, Cameron Mitchell, Rex Thompson, Patty McCormack, Ernest Truex, Hope Emerson, Alan Hale, Sr., Royal Dano. Directed by Allen Reisner.

Anne of Green Gables
(1985) 197m C

A SUPERB ADAPTATION of L. M. Montgomery's classic about an orphan girl growing up on Prince Edward Island. Anne has a sparkling personality and winning ways—the perfect complement to the dour temperament of the couple that adopts her. The story is notable for its portrayal of individuals who, sometimes grudgingly and sometimes willingly, feel an obligation to work not only on their personalities but also on their characters. Outstanding photography and great acting. (For more on L. M. Montgomery's books, see page 175.) With Megan Follows, Colleen Dewhurst, Richard Farnsworth, Patricia Hamilton, Schuyler Grant, Jonathan Crombie. Directed by Kevin Sullivan.

Captains Courageous
(1937) 115m bw

THIS FILM WON an Oscar and a number of nominations in 1937, and it's easy to see why. It would be hard to top this masterful rendition of Rudyard Kipling's sea adventure, and perhaps that is why no remake has ever been attempted. Harvey Cheyne, a spoiled and selfish brat, takes a tumble off an ocean liner and is hauled out of the sea by Manuel, a Portuguese fisherman who takes upon himself the task of reeducating Harvey. One of the best coming-of-age stories ever filmed. With Spencer Tracy, Lionel Barrymore, Freddie Bartholomew, Mickey Rooney, Melvyn Douglas. Directed by Victor Fleming.

Chariots of Fire
(1981, Brit.) 123m C

WINNER OF FOUR Academy Awards, this film tells the story of two Englishmen who compete in the 1924 Olympics. Harold Abrahams is Jewish and his running is powered in part by his hatred of the prejudices he encounters. Eric Liddell is a Christian who runs for the glory of God and almost forfeits his chance at a medal because he refuses to run on the Sabbath.

The story is simple enough, but the acting, the photography, and the musical score are outstanding. It all sums up to a movie that is both powerful and inspirational. With Ben Cross, Ian Charleson, Nigel Havers, Ian Holm, Sir John Gielgud, Alice Krige, Lindsay Anderson. Directed by Hugh Hudson.

A Christmas Carol
(1951, Brit.) 86m bw AKA *Scrooge*

THIS VERSION, STARRING Alastair Sim, is probably the best film adaptation of the Dickens classic. If he is to avoid the fate of his partner, Jacob Marley, Ebenezer Scrooge must be visited by three spirits. The mean-spirited Scrooge has a change of heart after this revelation and sets about to right the damage he has done. Contains some of the most memorable lines in the English language. Among them: "Bah, humbug!" "A poor excuse for picking a man's pocket every twenty-fifth of December," "Are there no prisons? Are there no workhouses?" "God bless us, every one!" For those who enjoy Dickens set to music, the 1970 musical *Scrooge* is also quite good. Albert Finney plays the lead, and Alec Guinness is Marley's Ghost. (For our entry on this book, see page 147.) With Alastair Sim, Kathleen Harrison, Jack Warner, Michael Hordern, Patrick Macnee. Directed by Brian Desmond-Hurst.

Fiddler on the Roof
(1971) 184m C

TEVYE, A POOR Jewish milkman in a czarist-era Ukrainian village, has three marriageable but dowryless daughters, a lame horse, and plenty of troubles. "On the other hand," as Tevye might say, he has a resilient spirit, a God who seems willing to listen to his worries, and the sustaining traditions of his community. These strengths see Tevye through joys and sorrows, good times and bad. This award-winning musical features a number of captivating songs, including "Sunrise, Sunset," "Tradition," and "If I Were a Rich Man." With Chaim Topol, Norma Crane, Leonard Frey, Molly Picon. Directed by Norman Jewison.

High Noon
(1952) 85m bw

MARSHALL WILL KANE tries unsuccessfully to recruit deputies for a showdown with four professional killers. Abandoned by the townspeople and even by his bride (a committed Quaker), he has to face his enemies alone. A powerful drama about courage and cowardice, pacifism and self-defense, *High Noon* ranks among the best westerns of all time. The action and the tension mount as the clock ticks off the minutes toward noon and the arrival of the train carrying the gunmen. With Gary Cooper, Grace Kelly, Lloyd Bridges, Lon Chaney, Jr., Katy Jurardo, Lee Van Cleef. Directed by Fred Zinneman.

The Hobbit
(1976) 76m C

THERE ARE THOSE who say that stories of this caliber shouldn't be illustrated, because to do so is to impair a youngster's ability to create her own mental images. If you plan to ignore this caution, this animated interpretation of J. R. R. Tolkien's myth world is a fine place to start. Among other things, Ralph Bakshi's "live motion" animation gives a lifelike quality to the action. The story follows the adventures of Bilbo Baggins, a peaceful Hobbit, after he accepts Gandalf the magician's invitation to join a treasure hunting expedition. Bilbo and his companions encounter giant spiders, trolls, and the evil but ingratiating Gollum along the way. Of particular interest are the differing codes by which Hobbits, Dwarves, and Elves live. The Dwarves favor the fighting virtues, the Hobbits prefer more peaceful pursuits, the Elves celebrate artistic excellence. But all three agree when it comes to basic virtues such as justice, loyalty, and friendship. Bakshi later directed the epic *The Lord of the Rings*. (For our entry on *The Hobbit*, see page 221. For *The Lord of the Rings*, see page 237.) Directed by Arthur Rankin, Jr., and Jules Bass. Animation by Ralph Bakshi. Voices: Orson Bean, John Huston, Otto Preminger, Richard Boone.

Hoosiers
(1987) 114m C

A MOVIE ABOUT starting over. The small-town high school basketball team is trying to start over, so is the new coach, so is the alcoholic father of one of the players. This film is also about doing your best and even a little bit better than your best. Great performances by Gene Hackman as the coach and Dennis Hopper as the town alcoholic raise this well above the level of most sports movies. With Gene Hackman, Barbara Hershey, Dennis Hopper, Sheb Wooley, Fern Persons, Chelcie Ross, Robert Swan. Directed by David Anspaugh.

It's a Wonderful Life
(1946) 129m bw

ONE OF THE most popular films ever made, this classic tells the story of George Bailey, a small-town businessman who gives up his own dreams in order to help family, friends, and fellow townspeople. Mounting problems and frustrations bring George to the point of a Christmas Eve suicide, but thanks to the intervention of a guardian angel, George gets a new lease on life and a new vision of the part he has played in the lives of others. *It's a Wonderful Life* belongs to the heart-warming and sentimental genre of films but also manages to transcend that level. The film's joyful scenes work only because of the dark possibilities that have been introduced. Frank Capra's directorial intelligence is in evidence throughout. Several of the scenes approach perfection. With James Stewart, Donna Reed, Lionel Barrymore, Thomas Mitchell, Henry Travers, Beulah Bondi, Gloria Grahame, Ward Bond. Directed by Frank Capra.

Mary Poppins
(1964) 140m C

JULIE ANDREWS IS radiant in her screen debut as the magical nanny who helps a London family to regain intimacy and love. The two children are suffering from neglect because their mother is overly involved in political causes and their father is a wage slave in a stuffy bank. When Mary Poppins arrives, the children no longer feel the need to run away or misbehave; she introduces them to a world of laughter and imagination—and moral responsibility. When the family is brought together again, Mary Poppins moves on. With Julie Andrews, Dick Van Dyke, David Tomlinson, Glynis Johns, Ed Wynn, Arthur Treacher, Hermione Baddeleley. Directed by Robert Stevenson.

The Neverending Story
(1984) 92m C

A SENSITIVE AND introspective ten-year-old named Bastian comes across a magical book. When he begins to read, he finds himself literally drawn into the story. Transported to a strange new realm, Bastian must undergo a series of heroic adventures. He must battle the Nothing, an evil force that threatens to destroy the land of mankind's hopes and dreams. This entrancing film, though it is beautifully photographed and designed, is really an homage to reading—a rare tribute from the screen to the printed page. We also recommend the sequel: *The Neverending Story II*. With Barrett Oliver, Noah Hathaway, Tami Stronach. Directed by Wolfgang Petersen.

Night Crossing
(1981) 106m C

TWO EAST GERMAN families attempt a daring flight to freedom in a homemade hot air balloon. Full of suspense and heart-stopping action, this is also an inspiring account of family members working together toward a common goal. Includes a fine performance by John Hurt in the lead role. With John Hurt, Jane Alexander, Glynnis O'Connor, Doug McKeon, Beau Bridges. Directed by Delbert Mann.

A Night to Remember
(1958, Brit.) 119m bw

THIS IS THE best film version of the *Titanic*'s fatal voyage. Half the film elapses before the liner hits the iceberg and by that time we are completely immersed in the lives of the passengers. Few films can match this one in its level of intensity and in its portraits of duty, honor, courage, and cowardice. *A Night to Remember* is as compelling and cathartic as a Greek tragedy. With Kenneth More, David McCallum, Anthony Bushell, Honor Blackman, Michael Goodlife, George Rose, Laurence Naismith. Directed by Roy Ward Baker.

Old Yeller
(1957) 83m C

AN OUTSTANDING boy-and-his-dog film. Unlike most stories in the genre, however, the boy in this case doesn't want the dog. But the dog eventually wins him over, which makes it all the harder when Old Yeller contracts rabies, and the boy, Travis, is forced to kill him. This is a great family film, which may cause some tears to flow, but they are well-earned tears. A Disney Studios film that brings together a fine cast and a bittersweet plot. With Dorothy McGuire, Fess Parker, Tommy Kirk, Kevin Corcoran, Jeff York, Beverly Washburn, Chuck Connors. Directed by Robert Stevenson.

The Scarlet Pimpernel
(1982, Brit.) 142m C

LORD PERCY BLAKENEY is nothing but a dandy—a shallow, affected man preoccupied with his wardrobe and with petty gossip. Or is he? In fact the foppish role he affects is Blakeney's way of disguising his true identity. He is the legendary and elusive Scarlet Pimpernel who cheats the guillotine of its victims and maddens the French Republicans with his clever escapes. The true test of Blakeney's courage, however, is revealed not in his clashes with the French but in his willingness to suffer his wife's scorn. For reasons too complicated to explain here he can't share his secret with her, and she, as a result, believes she is married to a superficial fool. All is resolved in the end, however, making this not only a great adventure story but also a great romance. (For our entry on the book, see page 191.) With Anthony Andrews, Jane Seymour, Ian McKellan, James Villers, Eleanor David. Directed by Clive Donner.

The Secret of NIMH
(1982) 82m C

THIS ADAPTATION OF the novel *Mrs. Frisby and the Rats of NIMH* (see page 224) is a splendid animated feature. It tells of a widow, Mrs. Frisby, who struggles to save her home, and her children, from destruction. She turns to a group of rats for help. The rats have been subjected to experiments by government scientists and have escaped. Though their intelligence has been augmented, not all of the rats use their knowledge for good. In order to defend her family Mrs. Frisby has to become a heroine; a story such as this reminds us that "ordinary" people are capable of extraordinary things when loved ones are in danger. Directed by Don Bluth. Voices: Dom De Luise, Peter Strauss, and John Carradine.

Sounder
(1972) 105m C

A FAMILY OF black sharecroppers struggles through hard times in rural Louisiana during the Depression. They have to struggle even harder when the father is jailed for stealing a ham, leaving mother and children with the task of getting the crop in. *Sounder* is also the story of the son, David Lee, and his attempt to break out of the sharecropper trap by pursuing an education. Above all it is a story of deep family love and self-sacrifice. Brilliantly acted and directed, *Sounder* is the absorbing drama of a strong family that manages to transcend the harsh circumstances of their existence. (For our entry on this book, see page 167.) With Cicely Tyson, Paul Winfield, Kevin Hooks, Carmen Matthews, Taj Mahal, James Best, Yvonne Jarrell, Eric Hooks. Directed by Martin Ritt.

The Sound of Music
(1965) 174m C

THIS INSPIRING MUSICAL is now thirty years old, which means that a lot of younger people aren't familiar with it. They should be, of course. This story of the Trapp family singers is memorable not only for its songs and lively family romps, but also for its portrayal of character and courage in the face of the Nazi Anschluss. A must see. With Julie Andrews, Christopher Plummer, Eleanor Parker, Richard Haydn, Peggy Wood, Charmian Carr, Heather Menzies, Nicholas Hammond, Duane Chase, Angela Cartwright. Directed by Robert Wise.

Watership Down
(1978) 92m C

RICHARD ADAMS'S EPIC story of a group of rabbits on a dangerous quest for freedom has been wonderfully translated to an animated feature film. Led by the noble Hazel and the mystic Fiver, the rabbits must escape from a tyrannical warren and establish a new way of life. The film opens with a mesmerizing sequence that recounts the rabbits' myth of their origin. Because there are some intense scenes of fighting and menace, this is not a film for small children. Older children will find it unforgettable. (For our entry on the book, see page 240.) Directed by Martin Rosen. Voices: John Hurt, Richard Briers, Ralph Richardson, Denholm Elliott, Joss Ackland, Michael Hordern.

NOTES

Chapter One.
Imagination: The Heart's Best Guide

Page
18 *A 1985 report:* Richard C. Anderson et al., *Becoming a Nation of Readers: The Report of the Commission on Reading* (Champaign-Urbana, Ill: Center for the Study of Reading, 1985), p. 23.

19 *"About ten years ago":* Thomas Lickona, *Educating for Character* (New York: Bantam, 1991), p. 34.

20 *"the central importance of stories":* Paul C. Vitz, "The Uses of Stories in Moral Development: New Psychological Reasons for an Old Education Method," *American Psychologist,* June 1990, p. 711.

20 *A fourth-grade teacher:* From a talk given by Lois Lowry at Boston College, Dec. 1, 1993.

21 *"A story is a way to say something":* Flannery O'Connor, *Mystery and Manners* (New York: Farrar, Straus and Giroux, 1981), p. 86.

21 *According to one study:* cited in Larry Woiwode, "Television: The Cyclops That Eats Books," *Imprimis,* Feb. 1992, p. 1.

21 *"Television," as one critic says:* Ibid., p. 3.

23 *"A good book has a profound kind of morality":* Gladys Hunt, *Honey for a Child's Heart* (Grand Rapids, Mich.: Zondervan Books, 1989), p. 40.

25 *"Am I ever glad":* Ibid., p. 114.

26 *"Secondary students being read to?":* Jim Trelease, *The New Read-Aloud Handbook* (New York: Penguin, 1989), pp. 36–37.

26 *"They [children] may read the story again":* Gladys Hunt, *Honey for a Child's Heart,* p. 52.

27   *"I am almost inclined"*: C. S. Lewis, "On Three Ways of Writing for Children," in Walter Hooper, ed., *C. S. Lewis on Stories* (New York: Harcourt Brace Jovanovich, 1982), p. 33.

Chapter Two.
Example and Empathy

28   *"Do we want our children to know"*: William Bennett, *Our Children and Our Country* (New York: Simon & Schuster, 1989), pp. 82, 83–84.

29   *"Who do I want to be like?"*: Bruno Bettelheim, *The Uses of Enchantment* (New York: Vintage, 1977), p. 10.

32   *"It can't be helped!"*: Leo Tolstoy, *War and Peace,* trans. Louise and Aylmer Maude (New York: Simon & Schuster, 1958), p. 371.

34   *"occupy a moral no-man's land"*: Humphrey Carpenter, *Secret Gardens: The Golden Age of Children's Literature* (Boston: Houghton Mifflin, 1985), p. 4.

34   *"What is your philosophy of writing?"*: Katherine Paterson, "Newbery Medal Acceptance," *The Horn Book Magazine* 57 (1981): 392.

35   *"that extraordinary amalgam"*: C. S. Lewis, "On Three Ways of Writing for Children," p. 36.

36   *"to create an atmosphere"*: W. H. Auden, "Afterword," in George MacDonald's *The Golden Key* (New York: Farrar, Straus and Giroux, 1967), p. 86.

36   *"Suddenly anything other than obedience"*: Gladys Hunt, *Honey for a Child's Heart,* p. 56.

37   *"I never meant to deny"*: Vladimir Nabokov. Cited in "From *Lolita* to *Piss Christ,"* Carol Iannone, *Commentary* 89 (Jan. 1990): 52.

Chapter Three.
Transport: Seeing with Myriad Eyes

39   *"I was* inside *those children"*: Michele Landsberg, *Reading for the Love of It* (New York: Prentice Hall, 1987), p. 3.

40   *"But in reading great literature":* C. S. Lewis, *An Experiment in Criticism* (Cambridge: Cambridge University Press, 1961), pp. 140–41.

40   *Of the twenty best-selling paperback children's books of 1990:* Source: *Publisher's Weekly.* Cited in Tom Engelhardt, "Reading May Be Harmful to Your Kids," *Harper's,* June 1991, p. 59.

40   *"junky" and "trashy" literature:* Mary Leonhardt, *Parents Who Love Reading, Kids Who Don't* (New York: Crown, 1993), pp. 7, 28.

42   *"see books as cures":* Judith Saltman, *The Riverside Anthology of Children's Literature,* 6th ed. (Boston: Houghton Mifflin, 1985), p. 7.

42   *"Some of this determinedly progressive fiction":* Michele Landsberg, *Reading for the Love of It,* p. 240.

43   *"Stacey stared long and hard":* Mildred D. Taylor, *Roll of Thunder, Hear My Cry* (New York: Puffin, 1991), p. 87.

Chapter Four.
Worlds of Meaning

46   *"We turn to fiction":* Robert Penn Warren, quoted in Jim Trelease, *The New Read-Aloud Handbook,* p. 58.

46   *"Human beings require stories":* Neil Postman, "Learning by Story," *The Atlantic,* Dec. 1989, p. 122.

48   *"many adults retain vague memories":* Humphrey Carpenter, *Secret Gardens,* p. 62.

50   *"If stories weren't told":* Isaac Bashevis Singer, *Stories for Children* (New York: Farrar, Straus and Giroux, 1990), p. 173 (from "Naftali the Storyteller and His Horse, Sus").

50   *"The enduring popularity of family stories":* Michele Landsberg, *Reading for the Love of It,* p. 60.

51   *"Endings are as often unhappy as happy":* Jane Yolen, *Touch Magic: Fantasy, Faerie and Folklore in the Literature of Childhood* (New York: Philomel, 1981), p. 64.

52   *"Levin felt more and more":* Leo Tolstoy, *Anna Karenina,* trans. Constance Garnett (Garden City, N.Y.: Nelson Doubleday, 1944), p. 414.

52   *"Everyone brightened":* Leo Tolstoy, *War and Peace,* p. 8.

52 *"genius for the normal"*: Clifton Fadiman, Foreword to *War and Peace,* trans. Louise and Aylmer Maude (New York: Simon & Schuster, 1958), p. xxviii.

53 *"Papa and I walk to our church"*: Tricia Brown, *Hello Amigos!* (New York: Henry Holt, 1982).

54 *"Baby, we have no choice of what color we're born"*: Mildred D. Taylor, *Roll of Thunder, Hear My Cry* (New York: Puffin, 1991), p. 129.

Chapter Five.
Selecting and Sharing Good Books: Some Guidelines

59 *"When I was a child, a relative gave me* Ivanhoe*"*: Beverly Cleary, quoted in Eden Ross Lipson, *The New York Times Parent's Guide to the Best Books for Children* (New York: Times Books, 1988), p. xii.

Index